Robert Drury's Journal and Other Studies

Robert Drury's Journal and Other Studies

ARTHUR W. SECORD

University of Illinois Press, Urbana, 1961

A grant from the Ford Foundation has helped to defray the cost of publishing this work.

PREFACE

When Professor Arthur W. Secord died suddenly on 16 May 1957, he left a number of manuscripts representing years of patient research in many libraries and archives that resulted in solutions to some persistent problems of literary scholarship. The four pieces here printed are drawn from manucripts on which, after Secord's death, little more than editorial work was imperative. Less finished manuscripts calling for additional research have not been included and have been deposited in the University of Illinois Library.

We have chosen to let the papers stand as Professor Secord left them and have not undertaken to impose our own opinions on the materials. Undoubtedly, if Professor Secord had lived to see his own manuscripts through the press, he would have wished to modify, alter, or condense some of his arguments; but under the circumstances we have, we hope wisely, determined to work within the limits of the manuscripts left to us and considered sufficiently finished to warrant publication. It has obviously not been possible to check all quotations and references; but the errors that can be found should not alter the general tendency of the arguments.

We wish to acknowledge the assistance of Professor James R. Sutherland of the University of London, Professor Spiro Peterson of Miami University, and Dr. William H. Bond of Harvard University, all of whom have answered our queries concerning minutiae. We are also grateful to Professor G. Blakemore Evans of the University of Illinois for his help in proofreading the manuscript.

ROBERT W. ROGERS
GEORGE SHERBURN

CONTENTS

Robert Drury's Journal

Mrs., or as we would say, Miss Veal died on 7 September 1705 and appeared next day to her friend Mrs. Bargrave at Canterbury; but she never returned to keep house for her brother William Veal of the Dover customs. A few months later William remedied that misfortune by marrying a young widow and thereby linked Defoe's *True Relation of the Apparition of One Mrs. Veal* to another famous narrative. For the widow, Elizabeth Hughes, was the daughter of Captain William Young of an East India ship, the *Degrave;* and the foundering of the *Degrave* upon the coast of Madagascar plunged Robert Drury into the experiences which form the basis of *Madagascar,* or to use its better-known subtitle, *Robert Drury's Journal.*

This, the last long narrative now attributed to Defoe, appeared in May 1729, almost two years before Defoe's death. It purported to be the autobiography of one who as a boy had survived the wreck of the *Degrave* and the massacre of her people and had lived for many years among the natives of Madagascar. For much of that period he is said to have been a slave of a harsh southern chief named Mevarrow. Later he escaped to the west coast where he received better treatment. In each of these regions he took a native wife. In 1717 a slave trader, Captain William Mackett, rescued him and took him home to England.

Drury's Journal, long read and recommended as the best English book on Madagascar, has fallen into a twilight of neglect. It suffers, not from competition with later and fuller accounts, but, like the *Memoirs of Captain Carleton,* from uncertainty about its credibility. Until recently the article on Madagascar in the *Encyclopaedia Britannica* cited it as an authority.[1] In 1941 the late Professor Donald Stauffer called it one of the best travel books extant.[2] A few years earlier Sir Richard Carnac Temple used it for his history of the *Worcester* affair. But other critics have been increasingly skeptical of Drury's part in writing it and of its value as history.

The original preface remarked that it was in danger of being

---

[1] Sibree used it in the eleventh edition (1910).

[2] *The Art of Biography in Eighteenth-Century England* (Princeton, N.J.), pp. 136, 209–210, 524.

taken for another romance like *Robinson Crusoe*. But it was meant
to pass for an authoritative treatise on Madagascar, a large and
mysterious island then principally known as a rendezvous of pirates.
The French had taken possession and in 1640 settled at a place on
the southeast coast called Fort Dauphin. Trouble with the natives
led to brutal attacks and reprisals. Before long the French retired
and left Fort Dauphin in ruins. Not till after the Napoleonic wars
did they regain effective control of the island, which in 1896 became a French colony. One of their early governors, Étienne de
Flacourt, in his *Histoire de Madagascar* (1658), gave the best account of the island before *Robert Drury's Journal*. In the Low
Countries, Blaeu copied Flacourt's map in the *Grooten Atlas* of
1664–65, and O. Dapper used both his map and his text in a volume
on Africa which John Ogilby put into English dress in 1670.

Hydrographers like John Thornton of the East India Company
were familiar with the Madagascar coast, but they knew little of
the interior. That is why *Drury's Journal* loomed so large in nineteenth-century accounts. It described areas not in Flacourt and gave
a more intimate and supposedly more accurate account of native
life. Its large folded map on heavy paper was more up-to-date than
Blaeu's, or Thornton's, or Moll's.[3] And it had a remarkable English-
Malagasy word list.

Drury's Journal was written in an easy, competent style by one
who knew how to manage a long story. Its authenticity was attested
by title-page references to John Benbow, son of a famous admiral,
and to Captain William Mackett, a well-known East India commander; by a clever preface; and by a statement printed on the
verso of the title page and attributed to Captain Mackett. The
title page, moreover, assured the reader that copies could be had
of the author at Old Tom's Coffee House in Birchin Lane, and a
note at the end of the volume said that at the same place Drury was
every day to be spoken with by the curious and was ready to confirm any details that seemed doubtful. Though some of these features have aroused skepticism, they were intended to allay it. *Drury's
Journal* was offered as a romantic but true adventure story and as
an authoritative treatise like Robert Knox's *Ceylon* (1681), which
in many ways it resembles.

For all the care in the preparation, the book was not widely advertised and was slow in gaining attention. The Directors of the
East India Company seem to have been unaware of it ten months

---

[3] See John Robert Moore, *Defoe's Sources for "Robert Drury's Journal"*
(Bloomington, Ind., 1943), pp. 68–73.

after publication late in May 1729.[4] What is called the second edition (1731) is only the first with a new title page, a certain sign of meager sales. But in 1739 "Timothy Truepenny, Gent.," serialized the book in the *Universal Spy*,[5] and in 1743 it appeared in the true second edition, with a modified text "Corrected from the Original Copy, with Improvements." [6] "The Adventures of Mr Robert Drury during his 15 years in Madagascar. pr. 5s. Robinson" was announced as published in April 1747 but is otherwise unknown.[7]

The 1743 text was reprinted in 1750 and, at Hull, in 1807. In 1831 the *Journal* appeared with the life of Wesley and others in volume V of the thirty-four-volume *Autobiography. A Collection of the Most Instructive and Amusing Lives Ever Published, Written by the Parties Themselves: With . . . Compendious Sequels Carrying on the Course of Events to the Death of Each Writer* (London, 1826–33). The latest English edition is that by Captain Pasfield Oliver, who had lived in Madagascar and was an authority on the island and its people. With an introduction which presented the case for Defoe and its author, Captain Oliver's edition was published in the "Adventure Series" in 1890 and 1897. Since then there has been only the French translation of Oliver's text in volume IV (Paris, 1906) of the monumental *Collection des ouvrages anciens concernant Madagascar* by Alfred and Guillaume Grandidier.[8]

[4] Court Minutes, vol. 53, p. 444. *Drury's Journal* was advertised as "This day published" in *Fog's Weekly Journal* of 24 May and in the *Daily Post* of 4 and 5 June 1729. Its longest advertisement perhaps is that in the *Universal Spectator*, 21 and 28 June 1729, which summarizes the contents under seven headings and in listing the booksellers (W. Meadows, J. Marshall, T. Worrall) specifies that it is sold also "by the Author, at Old Tom's Coffee-House in Birchin Lane" for 6s. One notes the mention of Old Tom's Coffee House.

[5] No. 2093 in the Crane and Kaye *Census;* not to be confused with No. 909, which has a similar title.

[6] *The Pleasant, and Surprising Adventures of Mr. Robert Drury . . . London: Printed, and Sold by W. Meadows . . . T. Astley . . . and B. Milles . . . 1743.* I have not seen the 1750 volume reported by Philip Babcock Gove, *The Imaginary Voyage in Prose Fiction* (New York, 1941), pp. 273–276; but the description of it by Alfred and Guillaume Grandidier, *Collection des ouvrages anciens concernant Madagascar*, IV (Paris, 1906), 2 (notes b and c), and their remark that it is the basis of the Hull printing of 1807 indicate that it is a reprint of the 1743 text. The Grandidiers think that an 1808 reprint mentioned in the article on Drury in *Nouvelle biographie générale* (wrongly identified by the Grandidiers as Michaud's *Biographie universelle*) is a mistake for that of 1807.

[7] *Gentleman's Magazine*, XVII (1747), 204.

[8] The Grandidiers, p. 2n, cite summaries of *Drury's Journal* in over a half-dozen works from 1782 to 1878. They themselves summarize it in their *Histoire . . . de Madagascar*, vol. IV, tome I (Paris, 1908), pp. 498–505. See also Gove, *Imaginary Voyage*, pp. 273–276.

Like the *Four Years' Voyage of Captain Roberts* and the *Memoirs of Captain Carleton, Drury's Journal* came late to the Defoe canon over vigorous opposition. In its first century and a half it was accepted as the authentic product of Drury's own pen. The writer of its original preface says he had had his doubts but was satisfied after investigation. Several others in the mid–eighteenth century testified to their confidence in its authenticity, partly because they believed it corroborated by a journal kept by John Benbow.[9] Early in the nineteenth century the *Gentleman's Magazine* remarked that its authenticity had been confirmed and its data adopted by geographers.[10] It had "all that simplicity and verbiage . . . expected in narratives of the illiterate, but none of the artifices of fiction." In 1810 the *Monthly Review* was equally sure of its truthfulness: readers who knew Madagascar and its people recognized the author's acquaintance with them.[11] It was about this time that Hughes Minet, grandson of Captain William Young of the *Degrave*, whose widow he well remembered, noted that *Robert Drury's Journal* harmonized with family information.[12]

Missionaries and geographers especially admired *Robert Drury's Journal* as a remarkably accurate account of native life. Captain Oliver found that in England Drury's name loomed as large as Flacourt's in France, and that "Good old Samuel Copland, Captain Owen and his Lieutenant Boteler, William Ellis the Apostle and Politician . . . Messrs. Sibree, Richardson, and the missionaries of all sects, have . . . adopted as gospel truth and literal matter of fact Drury's statements . . . and pinned their faith, as to the testimony from an eye-witness . . . [to] the extremely curious and interesting story of the unsophisticated voyager." The Swedish missionaries likewise and "all the best authorities in France . . . every one . . . firmly believes the unsophisticated story of the poor deserted cabin-boy."[13]

Though *Robert Drury's Journal* was occasionally compared to

[9] See Dr. John Campbell, *Lives of the British Admirals*, IV (London, 1744), 281 ff.; *Biographica Britannica*, I (1747), 688–689, and II (1780), 166–167; *Gentleman's Magazine*, XXXIX (1769), 171–172, and LX (1790), 1075, 1189; *Letters by Several Eminent Persons Deceased*, ed. by Rev. John Duncombe, III (London, 2nd ed., 1773), 88–89; *British Biography*, VII (1772), 243–245; *New and Genuine Biographical Dictionary*, V (1798), 158–159.
[10] LXXVIII (1808), 143.
[11] Enlarged ser., LXIII, 110–111.
[12] Hughes Minet's notations were made in copies of *Robert Drury's Journal* placed in the British Museum by Miss Susan Minet of the Huguenot Society of London. See also William Minet, "Daniel Defoe and Kent," *Archaeologia Cantiana*, XXXI (London, 1915), 61–74.
[13] Introduction to *Robert Drury's Journal* (1890), pp. 9–10.

Robinson Crusoe, William Lee in 1869 was the first to discuss seriously whether Defoe might have written it. His decision was that Defoe had not.[14] Since then Oliver and others have presented the evidence for Defoe. More recently Trent and Dottin have found traces of Defoe's hand in its composition. An occasional critic still treats it as autobiography,[15] but the British Museum catalogue has for some years listed it as Defoe's.

Professor John Robert Moore, who has twice treated *Robert Drury's Journal,* regards it as almost wholly fiction by Defoe.[16] He traces the story to

a newspaper item of 1705 telling that a boy had returned to England from Madagascar, where the natives had massacred all his companions who had landed from an abandoned East India ship.

This idea was first modified by substituting for the hero's early escape from the island a long period of captivity among the natives of Madagascar. It was then elaborated into a fictional narrative. . . .[17]

To give an appearance of verisimilitude, Professor Moore continues (pp. 20, 27), Defoe inserted, among other matter, the well-known name of John Benbow, long after Benbow was safely dead and two months after the death of his brother William, "the only one who could have made an effective attack on . . . Drury's reference to John Benbow."

That was the state of the problem when, in 1945, I published two articles in which some slight progress was made in reconnecting Drury with the book which bears his name.[18] My articles made

[14] *Daniel Defoe: His Life and Recently Discovered Writings,* I (London, 1869), 448–449. The manuscript note reported by Captain Oliver, *Madagascar,* II (London, 1886), 266n, to be in the London Library copy of *Robert Drury's Journal* (1743), calls the book a fiction probably by Defoe. The note was written at an undetermined time after 1773, when the second edition of John Hughes's *Letters* (to which it refers) appeared.

[15] See R. W. Frantz, *The English Traveller and the Movement of Ideas 1660–1732* (Lincoln, Neb., 1934), pp. 9, 67, etc.; Stauffer, *Art of Biography in Eighteenth-Century England;* Sir Richard Carnac Temple, *New Light on the Mysterious Tragedy of the "Worcester" 1704–1705* (London, 1930), pp. 12, 266, 324, 329–333.

Professor Sutherland did not discuss *Robert Drury's Journal* in the original printing of his *Defoe* (London, 1937), but in his preface to the 1950 reprint he notes the conflict of opinion between Professor John Robert Moore and me, for which see notes 18 and 19 below.

[16] *Defoe in the Pillory* (Bloomington, Ind., 1939), pp. 104 ff.; *Defoe's Sources for "Robert Drury's Journal."*

[17] *Defoe's Sources for "Robert Drury's Journal,"* p. 8. The "newspaper item" is really from Narcissus Luttrell's *Brief Relation,* 21 April 1705. The newspapers, as we shall see (p. 22), gave a different account.

[18] "Defoe and *Robert Drury's Journal,*" *JEGP,* XLIV, 66–73; "Robert Drury and *Robert Drury's Journal,*" *N&Q,* CLXXXIX, 178–180. The *Journal* also is the subject of a useful dissertation by Miss Eleanor Wyne, unpublished but deposited in the University of Illinois Library. Subsequent research by others shows

clear that though *Robert Drury's Journal* ignored some aspects of the *Degrave's* stay in India, it gave many authentic details of the homeward voyage, such as the grounding in Bengal that caused the *Degrave's* leak, the month's stop at Mauritius where some lascars left by the pirate Bowen were taken aboard, the attempt to reach the Cape of Good Hope, the wreck and massacre in south Madagascar, and details and other features of the Jamaica-to-London voyage of the *Drake,* in which Captain William Mackett was said to have brought Drury home from Madagascar. Professor Moore was not impressed by my arguments;[19] but evidence discovered since then supports my points remarkably well. Even my tentative identification of Drury's family in London and Leicestershire records proves to be almost wholly correct. The only point on which Professor Moore and I seemed to be in agreement was one on which, as will appear later, we were both mistaken: that the brief conclusion of *Robert Drury's Journal,* telling of Drury's return voyage to Madagascar, was an invention in imitation of *Robinson Crusoe.*

There was still no proof, then known, that there was a real Robert Drury, who was more likely than anyone else to have furnished the data for *Robert Drury's Journal.* We did not know for certain that he was on the *Degrave* when she foundered in 1703 or on the *Drake* when she returned in 1717. Nothing but tradition and *Drury's Journal* indicated that he had been on Madagascar at all, or even outside London. And of Captain Drummond's adventures on Madagascar, told most fully in *Drury's Journal,* no other information had come to light since 1705. Drury was a shadowy figure, almost unknown outside the *Journal.* Although some late eighteenth- and nineteenth-century sketches described him as a native of Leicestershire and said that he lived there with a sister after his return from Madagascar, they obviously relied upon a misreading of the conclusion of *Drury's Journal,* which says that his family had moved to Loughborough in Leicestershire and that he went there to visit a sister and other relatives. Accounts giving his death as around 1735 or 1736 cite no evidence and may only be drawing an inference from the allusion to his death in the note at the end of the 1743 edition.[20]

---

its need of revision. In my introduction to Defoe's *Journal of the Plague Year* (New York, 1935), p. xviii, I expressed the current skepticism concerning Drury's part in the book.

[19] See our discussion in *N&Q,* CLXXXVIII (1945), 268 ff., and CLXXXIX (1945), 178 ff.

[20] "The Author (for some Years before his Death) was to be spoken with every Day at Old Tom's Coffee-house in Birchin Lane" (p. 460).

The only information about Drury with any claim to authority was published in a letter of 1769 by William Duncombe, brother-in-law of John Hughes (poet and Spenserian critic), and friend of Samuel Richardson and John Benbow's brother William. Having corrected the account of John Benbow given by Dr. John Campbell in *Biographia Britannica,* I (1747), 688–689, Duncombe stated that Benbow's journal, as far as it went, was in exact agreement with *Drury's Journal* but had, unfortunately, been destroyed in a fire in 1714. Of Drury he added:

> Robin Drury, among those who knew him, (and he was known to many, being a porter at the East India House) had the character of a downright honest man, without any appearance of fraud or imposture. He was known to a friend of mine, (now living) who frequently called upon him at his house in Lincoln's Inn Fields, which was not then inclosed. He tells me, he has often seen him throw a javelin there, and strike a mark at a surprising distance.[21]

While scholars have been posing conjectures, an embarrassing quantity of documentary evidence has been available in parish records and in the voluminous manuscripts of the East India Company, including ship logs or journals, letters, factory reports, and minutes of the meetings of the Court of Directors. But, except for Captain Oliver's letter of inquiry to the India Office Library in 1884, from which he learned nothing about Drury,[22] no student of Drury has previously tried to tap these manuscript sources. Sir Richard Temple, editor of the *Indian Antiquary* and of the papers of Thomas Bowrey, was convinced of the truthfulness of *Drury's Journal;* but, though he had all the resources of the India Office Library at his command, he made no contribution whatever to our knowledge of Drury or his book. This was unfortunate; for he was writing an important study of the related story of the *Worcester,* and had to draw upon *Drury's Journal* to help explain the fate of Captain Robert Drummond and the innocence of Captain Green and his crew, who in Scotland were commonly supposed to have murdered Drummond and pirated his ship.[23]

Instead of searching for primary evidence, critics have speculated upon the validity of the testimony of Dr. John Campbell and William Duncombe in the eighteenth century and of Hughes Minet

---

[21] *Gentleman's Magazine,* XXXIX (1769), 171–172. See also notes by William Duncombe's son, the Rev. John Duncombe, to a letter of 6 September 1759 written by a Rev. Mr. Hirst and published in *Letters by Several Eminent Persons* (1772).

[22] The reply to his letter Captain Oliver printed in the appendix to his edition of *Robert Drury's Journal* (1890), pp. 315–316.

[23] *New Light,* pp. 12, 266, 324–333.

in the early nineteenth. They have wondered whether Defoe might have heard about the *Degrave* through the Veals or whether he had read John Benbow's journal before it was burned in 1714. They have exploited internal evidence: improbabilities, contradictions, impossibilities, and resemblances to Defoe's other narratives. But of Drury they have not learned a single fact.

Captain Oliver did not deny Drury's existence, or even his having been on Madagascar, but called him a deserted cabin boy and pirate, and thought that for some crime or other he might have been in prison between the time of his return and the publication of *Drury's Journal*. Professor Moore has been equally contemptuous of the illiterate and "accommodating" Drury, who had declined from the prosperity of piracy to become a lowly porter in the East India House. Defined in these terms Drury is easily dismissed, and *Drury's Journal* may be explained as a romance fabricated out of lore Defoe had gathered in writing the *History of the Pirates*. But the problem is not so simple as the earlier critics, who ignored Defoe, or the later ones, who ignore Drury, assume. The new evidence includes the ledgers of the *Degrave* with the names of, and other information about, her crew, an abstract of John Benbow's journal made before it was burned, and a statement by a third member of the *Degrave*'s party. For the first time it can be said with certainty that Drury was aboard the *Degrave;* that he witnessed the massacre of her people; that he was almost fourteen years on Madagascar; and that dates and similar details, including the account of Drury's family, are given with remarkable accuracy in *Drury's Journal*. Only Drury could have given much of the material in the book; and it is highly probable that he wrote some kind of an account upon which the book is based.

The most important new evidence is in the records (already mentioned) of the East India Company, preserved in the India Office Library in King Charles Street, Whitehall, London, and in Dutch manuscripts in the archives of the Cape of Good Hope, an abstract of which, apparently unknown to students of Drury, Benbow, and Drummond, was published in 1896.[24] Other significant documents are a statement by Robert Coleson of the *Degrave,* preserved in a Dutch manuscript in the archives at The Hague; the will of Drury's father, John Drury (P.C.C., Fox, 1716, 204, in Somerset House); certain Admiralty and Chancery papers in the Public

---

[24] Hendrik Carol Vos Leibbrandt, *Précis of the Archives of the Cape of Good Hope* (Cape Town, 1896): [I] *Journal, 1699–1732;* [II] *Letters Received, 1695–1708;* [III] *Letters Dispatched, 1696–1708.* These are volumes in a long series.

Record Office in Chancery Lane; the parish records of St. Olave
Jewry, now in the Guildhall Library in Basinghall Street, and of
St. Katherine Cree at that church; and the Court Rolls of the Manor
of Stoke Newington, an indexed transcript of which is in the Stoke
Newington Library.

Poor Jury Lane and Old Jury

The earliest trace we have of the family of Robert Drury, or
Drewry, is in the register of the parish of St. Katherine Cree.[25] The
church is on the north side and near the east end of Leadenhall
Street, in which, until 1862, stood the famous old East India House.
Drury's Journal tells us that Robert was born in Crutched Friars,
a crescent-shaped street now filled with drab warehouses.[26] To the
searcher for Drury records, the mention of Crutched Friars was a
red herring, as technically no part of Crutched Friars was in the
St. Katherine Cree parish, and so the Drurys must have lived in the
northeast extension of Crutched Friars known now as Jewry Street
and then as Poor Jury Lane, or in one of the adjoining courts.[27]

The Drury (or Drewry) entries in the St. Katherine Cree records
begin with 15 April 1685—with the burial entry for John (age un-
specified), son of John Drewry.[28] A second child, Mary, daughter of
John and Mary Drewry, was born 15 February 1685/6 and buried
four days later. Next comes our Robert, who is recorded as "son of

[25] The register is kept in the church. For permission to use it, I wish to thank
the rector, the Rev. Gordon Hall, M.A., and the verger, Miss Furby.

[26] It was once part of Hart Street, until the Brethren of the Holy Cross, or
Crutched Friars, built a convent there, of which nothing remains but the name.
In Drury's time the New Navy Office stood just east of Seething Lane across from
Pepys's church, St. Olave Hart Street.

[27] Crutched Friars proper was divided among the following parishes, none of
which has any mention of Robert Drury's family: St. Katherine Coleman,
St. Olave Hart Street, and Allhallows Barking. I have searched, also, the records
of Allhallows Staining in Mark Lane but not those of St. Peter in the Tower.
For old parish boundaries, see *New Remarks of London* (1732), pp. 5, 74, 124–
125; John Stow, *Survey of London*, I (1720), iii, 52–53. St. Katherine Coleman is
no longer standing. Permission to use its records and those of Allhallows Staining I owe to the kindness of the Rev. A. Powell Miller, Vicar of the combined
parishes and Rector of Allhallows Barking. The records of Allhallows Barking
were made available to me by C. G. Misselbrook, the parish clerk.

[28] Was he the John, son of John and Mary Drury, christened at St. Peter's upon
Cornhill on 23 November 1684 according to the *Publications of the Harleian
Society, Registers*, IV (1879), 11? John Drury, the father, is not on the poll-tax
lists of either Aldgate or Tower ward in the 1680's. For several reasons, my
tentative identification of Robert Drury's father with the John Drury who
married Elizabeth Jurin on 19 February 1684/5 must be given up, but my further
suggestion that the father was the man who married, as his second wife, Elizabeth
Wharton (misprinted Whorton in the published records) 16 December 1703
proves accurate. See my "Defoe and *Robert Drury's Journal*," p. 72.

John Drewry by Mary his wife," born 20 July 1687 and baptized on the same day. *Drury's Journal* gives the date as 24 July, but the register is probably correct, as the next three entries are dated 21 and 22 July. After the baptism of an Elizabeth on 5 August 1688, the St. Katherine Cree register records only Drury burials.

Early in 1690 John Drury moved to Old Jury (Jewry), a short street running from Cateaton (now Gresham) Street to Poultry, and kept the King's Head Inn, which he had acquired from John [James?] King.[29] On 15 April 1690 his name first appears among the signers of the St. Olave Jewry Vestry Minutes; and it continued to appear there for fifteen years, or until 3 December 1705.

Robert Drury, then, came of a well-to-do middle-class family of more than ordinary attachment to the Church of England.[30] His father was a freeman of the city, entitled to wear the white and blue livery of the Worshipful Company of Innholders. At his death in 1716 he owned a half-dozen pieces of property and had money at interest. During his residence in Old Jury he figured prominently in parish and ward affairs. He served two terms as questman (1694–96) and two as churchwarden (1700–1702), and in 1696 he paid the £9 fee to be excused from the ward office of constable. Since churchwardens were responsible for the money assessed for the parish poor, they had to be, as they were described in the tax

[29] Others, like his brother William, might spell the name "Drewry," but John always spelled it "Drury." The Vestry Minutes of St. Olave Jewry (10 September 1690) and the Stoke Newington Court Rolls (2 September 1700) call him an innholder. See also *Lists of the Liveries of the Fifty-six Companies* (London, 1701); *Poll of the Livery-Men* (London, 1710), p. 179, where "John Drewry" is among those who "did not Poll this election." John Drury signed the address of loyalty sent by the Company of Innholders to William III upon discovery of the assassination plot of 1695. How early John Drury became a member of the company we do not know. A list of the company's silver in 1667 has this notation: "one guilt spoon Lost by Mr. Drewry had to make it good." This could, of course, have been John Drury's father or an entirely unrelated person. See *History of the Worshipful Company of Innholders* (London, 1922), pp. 34, 58. Mr. John Bentley, O.B.E., Clerk of the Company of Innholders, informs me that no other list of members in the time of John Drury or his son Robert now exists in the company records.

F. G. Hilton Price, "Signs of Old London," *London Topographical Record*, IV (1907), 92, says that John Drury was keeper of the King's Head in 1698–99. No authority is given for this statement, but it is possibly not *Robert Drury's Journal*.

The poor-tax and poll-tax lists (St. Olave Jewry Vestry Minutes, 1690–1705, in the Guildhall Library, and Coleman Street ward, St. Olave precinct, tax records in the Corporation of London Record Office) indicate that John Drury was at the King's Head for fifteen years (1690–1705). These lists indicate also who preceded and who followed him there.

[30] Robert's half sister Mary married a Loughborough clerk and her eldest son was a clerk in Chester. See "Everard" in the Stoke Newington Court Rolls.

notices, substantial householders. Old Jury was "a very good open Street, graced with good buildings . . . and inhabited by Merchants and Persons of repute." It was plentifully supplied with inns and alehouses, some of them famous for over two centuries.[31] John Drury's house, the King's Head, had twenty windows and in the period around 1700 was taxed for the poor at the rate of 4*d.* a week. Though much inferior to the lordly residence of Sir Robert Clayton nearby (taxed at 1*s.* 6*d.*), the King's Head was not of negligible value.[32]

In 1700 John Drury began investing money in Stoke Newington properties, some of which remained in his family for sixty-four years. One holding was a house in the tenancy of a merchant named Richard Beardsley, and another, according to Drury's will, in the tenancy of a John Taylor. A third was leased to Edward Newen, who tore down an old building and built five new ones in its place. John Drury lived in Stoke Newington from 1701 or 1702 to 1708/9, and in the years 1705–09 and 1714–15 he served as a member of the annual Court Baron of the Stoke Newington Manor, in the records of which he is called "John Drury, gent."[33]

John Drury's wife, called Mary in the St. Katherine Cree records (1686–88, 1703) and Stoke Newington records (1700), is called Elizabeth in those of St. Olave Jewry (1690–92).[34] A second John, son of John Drury and Elizabeth his wife, was born 4 October 1690 and buried exactly a year later at St. Katherine Cree, where his earlier brother John, his sister Mary, and his mother lie. A third John was baptized 3 January 1691/2. No Drury children were reported in the ward poll-tax records, though early in the 1690's Richard Brooks was listed as an apprentice and Elizabeth Plumbly

[31] Stow, *Survey of London,* I, iii, 163.

[32] The Coleman Street ward record of the 1696 tax on windows lists John Drury for twenty windows at 6*d.* each.

[33] John Drury's will, P.C.C., Fox, 1716, 204; transcript of the Court Rolls of the Stoke Newington Manor, pp. 54, 59, 60, 62–63, 65, 67, 76–78, 83, 107. The transcript with a good index is in the Stoke Newington Library. The Stoke Newington parish register (a transcript and an index of which are in the library) has no reference to John Drury or to his family. See my "Defoe in Stoke Newington," *PMLA,* LXVI (1951), 222.

[34] That Mary and Elizabeth were the same person is obvious. (1) *Drury's Journal* says that Robert Drury's mother died after 1701; (2) there are no records of the death of Mary Drury or the remarriage of John Drury between 1688 and 1690; and (3) John Drury's wife is called Mary again in Stoke Newington Court Rolls of 1700 (transcript, p. 54) and in her burial entry at St. Katherine Cree in 1703 (21 September). John Drury's will mentioned his first wife's picture and wedding ring but referred to no other wife except the one then living whom as Elizabeth Wharton he had married in 1703 (St. Mildred Poultry register, marriages, 21 December 1703).

and Anne Street were listed presumably as servants.[35] But the Drury children in order, Robert (1687), Elizabeth (1688), and John (1691/2), and the parents, John and Mary Elizabeth Drury, made up the family until in 1701 Robert, nearing the age of fourteen, went to India on the *Degrave*.

The Mystery of the Degrave

The *Degrave* sailed from the Downs 19 February 1700/1, spent eighteen months in Bengal, and in 1703 totally disappeared on the return voyage. Had she foundered on the moon her fate might have been learned sooner. An interchange of letters with India then took from one to three years. From an unfrequented part of Madagascar the fate of the *Degrave* might never have been known at all. A few of her party, however, survived, and one boy, *mirabile dictu,* escaped to reach Portsmouth on an East India vessel in March 1705, within two years of the disaster. Only three other persons certainly got off Madagascar. A youth named Robert Coleson was rescued by the Dutch and brought to the Cape late in 1705. John Benbow was similarly rescued by the Dutch; he was brought to the Cape early in 1707, from where he was taken home to England by the *Loyal Cooke* before the end of the year. The third was Robert Drury, who did not reach home until September 1717. Some others are said to have joined pirate gangs on Madagascar.

What became of the *Degrave?* That she had foundered had been assumed, but, when news came, truth and rumor were so mixed that the whole story was very slowly—if ever, outside *Robert Drury's Journal*—pieced together. In more recent times the facts have been buried in various places. For example, the exact date of the *Degrave*'s 1701 departure for India seems not to have got into the East India Company records, and in the Dutch abstract of John Benbow's journal it is given incorrectly (20 instead of 19 February). Only by following a clue in *Robert Drury's Journal* did I find independent corroboration of the date given therein. *Robert Drury's Journal* tells us that as they passed through the Downs, Admiral Benbow, "whose son . . . was fourth mate of our ship," lay there with his squadron destined for the West Indies. The newspapers do, indeed, show that Admiral Benbow had arrived four days earlier to take command and that he was aboard the *Winchester.* They also give the names of the ships in the squadron, and I have examined their journals in the Public Record Office. Two of these journals,

---

[35] The list of Londoners of 1695, compiled from tax records, lacks a dozen or so parishes, among them St. Olave Jewry.

both from the same ship, as we shall see, give the date wanted. Some other details are forever lost. But enough remains for a reasonably full account.

This voyage was the *Degrave*'s second to the "Coast and Bay," as the Coromandel Coast and the Bay of Bengal were called to distinguish them from Bombay on the west and Sumatra on the east. She was in the service of the New or English (East India) Company, which in 1698 had risen to plague and, in 1702, to unite with the Old or London Company. As one of the first ships chartered by the New Company in 1699, the *Degrave,* commanded by Captain William Young, had reached India in five months and, more remarkably still, had returned in five months.

The New Company was delighted and was hurrying the *Degrave* out again early in 1701. Her second mate—this will be news to the Veals and Minets and other descendants of Captain Young—was the captain's son Nicholas, not William, as previously supposed.[36] Charles Newton (to die in India), Matthew Pratt, John Benbow (son of an admiral famed in song and story), and William Carleton were first, third, fourth, and fifth mates respectively. The *Degrave*'s ledger lists a few of 123 members. Joseph Chamberlain, mentioned in *Robert Drury's Journal* as having survived drowning on the coast of India, was number 87. Twenty-one boys (numbers 103–123) at the end of the list, described as midshipmen, were really apprentices. Of these number 115 was the Robert Coleson rescued by the Dutch in 1705. Number 113, Nicholas Dove, was later with the pirates Zachary, Pro, and Burgess to figure as "Nick" in the book attributed to Robert Drury, who was number 118.

Among the outbound passengers were John Landon, a chaplain for the Bay; John Hall, a surgeon for the Bay who died promptly upon arrival; Samuel Blunt, a company writer; and ill-fated Samuel de Paz, a Jewish diamond merchant who, with his son Lewis (already on the Coast) and Isaac Abendana, would, it was hoped, secure the diamond trade to the New Company. De Paz had with him a younger son and a servant named John Lepee or Lapee.

Captain Young bade a final farewell to his new estate at Capel-le-ferne near Dover, to his wife (Alice Watson Young, who had over a half-century yet to live), and to his daughter Elizabeth Hughes. Like her mother, she was soon to be a widow—and in 1705 to marry William Veal, Controller General to the Custom House of Dover,

---

[36] There was a William Young on board, but he could hardly have been the captain's son. Otherwise his pay, like that of Nicholas Young, would have gone to his mother, Alice Young. See East India Company, Marine Records, CLIX.

Deal, Sandwich, and Feversham by a life patent granted by the late Queen Mary.[37] On 13 February seventeen of Captain Young's "loving friends" fixed their names to his letter of dispatch. They were the New Company's Court of Directors, among them Sir James Bateman, R. Mead, Streynsham Masters, and Samuel—but for some reason not Gilbert—Heathcote.

They directed him to sail with the first fair wind upon "a Voyage to be made (by the Blessing of God) to & from yᵉ East Indies." He was to take in wine at the Madeiras on the way out and provisions at the Cape or St. Helena or Ascension on the return. Among other things he was to "cause Religious Worship to be observed Solemnly & Devoutly on yᵉ Lords Day," and to use daily a printed form of prayer approved by the Bishop of London and the Archbishop of Canterbury. These were presumably the duties of the *Degrave's* chaplain, John Lodwick.

"Littell wind hase ffogge wether"

Heavy gales delayed sailing until the morning of Wednesday, 19 February. On that day Master William Franklin of H.M.S. *Winchester,* then at anchor in the Downs, entered in his journal, "Littell wind hase ffogge wether," and noted that in the morning several merchantmen had sailed westward and "yᵉ Degrafe to yᵉ E Ingis Capᵗ Young Commdʳ." Admiral John Benbow, who four days earlier had hoisted his flag on board the *Winchester,* doubtless watched the *Degrave's* departure with interest; he was never to see his son John again. Though the latter survived for a few months after his return from Madagascar, the admiral, six months or so before the sinking of the *Degrave,* died (1702) of wounds received fighting the French in the West Indies.[38]

[37] *Political State,* XXXVIII (1729), 496. Here (a death notice) the name is spelled, as doubtless it was often pronounced, "Weel." That may account for its having previously been overlooked. See my "A September Day in Canterbury . . . ," *JEGP,* LIV (1955), 639–650; Minet, "Daniel Defoe and Kent," pp. 61–74. Do we find in the Veal obituary additional evidence of Defoe's hand in the *Political State* immediately after Abel Boyer's death earlier in 1729?

[38] The admiral's biographers are, I think, mistaken in supposing that because he had not got his son a naval appointment, he was at odds with him. His will, made a few months after the *Degrave's* departure (P.C.C., Degg, 1703, 47), treated his three sons with equal favor. He implied that all were under age, though he may have meant only that some of them were. The *Degrave* was an aristocrat among East India ships, and a post of fourth mate on her was not negligible for a youth of twenty or so. Both captain and master of the *Winchester*—and they alone among the officers on the half-dozen warships present— record the sailing of the *Degrave.* Doubtless their admiral had told them of his son's being aboard her. For the journals of the *Winchester,* see P.R.O., Ad 52/120, 6, and Ad 51/4395, 7.

Captain Young continued to outsail Old Company commanders. In the remarkable time of three months and twenty days he reached the Coromandel Coast and on 21 June reached Fort St. George at Madras.[39] As Fort St. George, under the tough ex-mariner Thomas Pitt, grandfather of the Earl of Chatham, belonged to the Old Company, the *Degrave* merely showed her colors and sailed on toward the New Company factory at Masulipatam, where Consul John Pitt, apoplectic cousin of Thomas, was chief.[40] But, blinded by haze and swept by gales and current, Captain Young overshot the port and barely made it into nearby Madapollam on 27 June.

It was at Madapollam that Samuel de Paz drowned. *Robert Drury's Journal* places the event at Madras and, possibly misled by the name of de Paz's servant John Lapee, mistakenly identifies the victim as another London Jew, John Lapie.[41] In his eagerness to join his son Lewis, de Paz disregarded all advice and hurried ashore in the *Degrave*'s barge. A sudden surf swamped the barge and drowned de Paz, his unnamed younger son, "poor Matt. Peirson," young Nathaniel Barnardiston, Mr. Studd (a factor), and ten others.[42]

On 9 July the *Degrave* got back to Masulipatam, and on 31 July sailed past Balasore into one of the mouths of the Ganges called the Hugli River, where John Steel, veteran of sixteen years with the Old Company, met her. Three years earlier an Admiralty court in London had for lack of evidence acquitted him of a charge of piracy, and, in the dearth of good pilots, the New Company had promptly

[39] East India Company, Factory Records, Original Correspondence [hereafter referred to as O.C.], No. 7641: letter of 14 July 1701 from John Pitt and William Tillard in Bengal to Sir William Norris saying the *Degrave* had reached the Coast in three months and twenty days from England. John Benbow (*Précis . . . Letters Dispatched*, pp. 310–313) reported reaching Pondicherry in three months and nineteen days. *Robert Drury's Journal* says that they had stopped a week in the Canaries (instead of the Madeiras as ordered) and reached the Coast in three months and twenty days. Captain Carswell of the *Phenix* (Marine Records, CLIII) recorded in his journal for 21 June that on that day the *Degrave* paused at Fort St. George to show her colors and then went on without anchoring.

[40] Thomas Pitt was known as "Diamond Pitt" because of his interest in large diamonds. The great Pitt diamond he sold in 1717 to the regent of France for £135,000.

[41] A son of this John Lapie, John Christian de la Pie, later went to India as a company agent. The confusing of de Paz and Lapie may have been Defoe's; but Drury himself could hardly have organized or set down reminiscences until fifteen years after the fact. Confusion and inconsistencies are to be expected.

[42] O.C., Nos. 7641, 7643, 7724; Factory Records, Misc., vol. 6, p. 81 (Coast letter of 5 October 1701). See also the account in *Robert Drury's Journal* (1890), pp. 41–42, and the notation "drowned" after several names in the *Degrave*'s ledger (Marine Records, CLIX).

sent him back to India.[43] *Drury's Journal* calls him Drury's cousin and says that he met Drury upon hearing of his arrival. But it fails to tell us that Steel piloted the *Degrave* over the Braces into the New Deep and on the long voyage up the treacherous river to the settlement of Hugli, where she arrived 11 August.[44]

The *Degrave* was expected to start home early in 1702, and for a while, in spite of Old Company skepticism, it seemed that she would. She was reported sixty miles down the river on her way when trouble with the Indians, which had been threatening for some time, broke.[45] Lacking a fort, the New Company's Bengal Council on 27 March ordered the *Degrave,* which had fifty-two guns, back to Hugli to protect the factory, and then kept her there another nine months. Old Company agents in India estimated that it would require the interest on £100,000 to maintain so large a ship, and the New Company Directors in London, when they finally heard about it, hotly denounced Sir Edward Littleton, their Bengal president, for "bringing up the De Grave upon pretence to guard the Factory, and detaining her with all her goods aboard, untill she at last sayld . . . a leaky ship. . . ." At another time they declared with some obviousness that the long detention of ships "in the Country proves often very fatall." [46]

Captain Young, however, was not likely to have canceled his voyage for any but the gravest reasons. The native government, angered by depredations of European pirates and confused by the rivalry of the two English companies, had been less than mollified by the badly managed mission of Ambassador Sir William Norris to the Mogul emperor, Aurangzeb, on which the New Company in 1699–1702 lavished vast sums.[47] Europeans were ordered put under arrest and their property confiscated. At Patna, the order was enforced against both the Dutch and the English. At Bombay, Old Company President Sir John Gayer suffered confinement for several

[43] Court Minutes, vol. 37, pp. 174(b), 250(a), and vol. 37A, 3 November, 6 and 13 December 1698, and 3 January 1698/9; O.C., Nos. 7632, 7724, 7810, 7892, 7957. Col. John Biddulph, *Pirates of the Malabar Coast* (London, 1907), p. 15n, refers to Steel as the uncle (cousin) mentioned by Drury. He goes on to say, echoing Captain Oliver, that much of the time Drury pretends to have been a slave on Madagascar he really spent among the pirates.

[44] See the journal of the *Phenix*, which tells a good deal about the movements of the *Degrave* before and after this point. See also O.C., No. 7632.

[45] P.R.O., C9/466, 9.

[46] Letters to India (Letter Book), vol. 11 (New Company Letters, 1698–1708), p. 470, in letter to the Bay of 10 January 1703/4.

[47] The New Council at the Bay reproved their colleague Sir Nicholas Waite at Surat for saying bluntly that the mines of Mexico could not defray Norris' expenses (O.C., No. 7885).

years and died soon after his release. Fort St. George was threatened by the soldiers and elephants of Daud Khan. The Old Company, the French, and the Dutch (wrote the New Company Council at Bengal) were getting ready for a siege. Captain Young no doubt felt that English lives were at stake.

The Death of Captain Young

The war clouds cleared noticeably in May. In July, treasure placed on the *Degrave* for safety was removed, but she was not allowed to leave until the end of the year. Meanwhile on 9 October Captain Young, who had passed up his best sailing time to defend the factory and who boasted that he could sail home in any season, succumbed to the deadly climate and followed Pilot John Steel and Chief Mate Charles Newton to the grave.[48] Other officers and "at least Forty of the Shipps company" died. The senior surviving officer was the captain's son, Second Mate Nicholas Young, nearing his twenty-sixth birthday. In spite of his youth the Bengal Council placed him in command and doubtless promoted Matthew Pratt and John Benbow, third and fourth mates, to be chief and second mates.[49]

On 25 September the *Degrave*'s cargo had been reported damaged by rain seeping through the decks. Toward the end of October she was leaking badly. A committee of captains from other ships found the leak to be an inch an hour, but they added that "some of us do know she hath been always subject" to leakage since first going to sea. She was, they said, short of powder but otherwise in condition to sail. Her commander was thereupon directed to get ready to proceed down the river. Much of the cargo had been aboard since March. The Council wrote home that it consisted of 130 bales of cloth, 100 tons of saltpeter more than her kentledge (ballast), and 40 or 50 tons of pepper. Though the *Degrave* was unable finally to hold so much, still she was, as the Council said, a full and rich ship, invoiced at nearly 500,000 rupees.[50]

---

[48] Journal of the *Phenix*, 11 October 1702; O.C., No. 8038. The letter, though dated 6 October and begun before Captain Young's death, was not finished till after it.

[49] P.R.O., C9/466, 9. Steel, as *Drury's Journal* says, died not long after the *Degrave*'s arrival. A letter from the New Council in India (O.C., No. 7810, 29 December 1701) calls him perhaps the ablest English pilot at Bengal and his death a very great loss. See also Factory Records, Misc., vol. 6, p. 88; Marine Records, CXX (journal of the *Antelope*), 3 November 1699, 9 February 1699/1700, and later, and CXLVIII (journal of the *Rising Eagle*), 25 April, 19 and 24 December 1701, and 3 January 1701/2; Court Minutes, vol. 37, pp. 174, 250, and vol. 37A, items of 25 October, 6 and 13 December 1698, and 3 January 1698/9.

[50] O.C., Nos. 7632, 7885, 7892.

The Degrave *Damaged*

On 17 November the *Degrave* was declared ready, and the pilot ordered to take charge the next day. By 22 November she had dropped down from Hugli and anchored west of Calcutta.[51] At some time in her passage through the treacherous river she touched bottom, damaged her rudder, and either sprang a new leak or aggravated an old one.[52] The extent of the damage was not known till she was at sea.

Besides the *Degrave's* crew and the "midshipmen" like Robert Drury, several passengers were aboard. Two had been ordered home: James Wilcox, a profligate young company agent at Cazimbuzar, and Susanna Exeter, who had gone out on the *Degrave's* previous voyage and had behaved lewdly. Drury mentions two women. Was Susanna Exeter the one who drowned getting ashore at Madagascar, or the one who had the water rolled out of her lungs and lived to be slain in the massacre? A Mr. Cater who had intended going may have changed his mind. Three other men purchased passage: William Longvill, Edward Bolitha, and Samuel Conyers. Conyers, a prospective pilot, had fallen heir to a fortune and was going home to enjoy it.[53]

The Embarkation

The final days were at hand, and the Council sent Jonathan Winder to dispatch the *Degrave*. A copy of his letter (O.C., No. 8096) reached London by the *Upton Galley* 10 November 1703, nearly ten and a half months later. The original sent on the *Degrave* was, of course, lost at sea. It was dated on board the *Degrave* at anchor off the island of Cocks, Bengal, 23 December 1702. Winder wrote that that day he had given Captain Nicholas Young his dispatches, his sailing orders, and the company packets. He added, "I pray God grant said ship and cargoe a safe arrival." With that benediction the *Degrave* two days later—Christmas day—released her pilot and seemed to vanish in the Indian Ocean.

[51] Journal of the *Phenix*, 22 November 1702.

[52] Her owners said the damage occurred in March when she was ordered back to defend the factory. *Drury's Journal*, which says nothing about the long delay in India, implies that it occurred as they were descending the river on the way home. Neither account is wholly convincing. The owners admitted that they lacked witnesses. Their only chance of remuneration lay in proving the damage due to use of the ship in defense of the company's property rather than to the ordinary hazards of her voyage. An account by the Dutch governor of Mauritius says merely that the *Degrave* touched in the Gulf of Bengal. See P.R.O., C9/466, 9; *Robert Drury's Journal* (1890), p. 43; *N&Q*, ser. 10, XI (1909), 162–163; Albert Pitot, *T'Eylandt Mauritius* (Port Louis, Mauritius, 1905), p. 303n1.

[53] O.C., Nos. 7982, 8110.

Meanwhile important events were occurring at home. Early in March 1702 the *Norris* hurried off to Bengal—where she exploded on 2 August shortly after arrival[54]—with news (in order of importance to the company) of the union of the two companies, the death of William III, the accession of Queen Anne, and the threat of war with France and Spain. Finch Reddall, commander of the eastbound *Samuel and Anna,* heard of William's death on 21 March 1701/2 and hoped "ye Lord will Receive his soule in heaven in Company with Angles & Arkangles. . . ." The New Company sent warnings to the *Degrave* and to their other homebound ships to avoid the French and wait at the Cape for convoys.[55]

Robert Drury's mother died in September 1703, and exactly three months later his father married Elizabeth Wharton. We know nothing of Captain Young's family, except that his daughter became a widow and presently married William Veal, or of John Degrave and other part owners, during the two-year silence that followed the *Degrave's* sailing from Bengal. Captain Cockburn of the *Bengal Merchant,* which left in the wake of the *Degrave,* reported extraordinarily bad weather from Bengal to the Cape. Toward the end of 1703, after nine months at sea, Cockburn reached Ireland, where he wrote (2 October) that the *Degrave* had not been heard from at the Cape or at St. Helena. Early the following year (10 January 1703/4) the New Company Directors reported having no news of the *Degrave* and expecting none; "we have too much reason to fear she is lost." A year after that the United Company noted that all hope had been given up.[56]

Records of the final fate of the *Degrave* are absent from the logs of certain other ships. John Carswell of the *Phenix,* an Old Company commander, followed the *Degrave* from Bengal and reached the Cape in early May. He could not have been far away when in late April the *Degrave* left her course to run to Madagascar. Buried in two journals are traces of the *Degrave's* stop at Mauritius. The *Nathaniel* (29 April and 26 May 1703) salvaged an anchor left by the last ship, "Capt. Young from Bengall very leaky"; and the *Loyal Bliss* (14 May) took aboard five men who, doubtless thinking the *Degrave* too leaky, had run away.[57]

Two of Her Majesty's men-of-war, the *Scarborough* (George Shelvocke, Master) and the *Severn,* stopped at Mauritius the follow-

[54] O.C., No. 8038.
[55] Letters to India, vol. 11, pp. 324, 389–391, 397, 442, 446 (letter of 30 December 1702, in which reference is made to the *Degrave's* commander "for the time being"), 471; Marine Records, CLXXI.
[56] O.C., No. 8200; Letters to India, vol. 11, p. 463, and vol. 12, p. 368.
[57] Marine Records, CLVIII, 136A(1), and CLXIII.

ing October and then searched for pirates on the east and north coasts of Madagascar. They caught two who figure in the *History of the Pirates,* David Williams and John Pro (the latter of whom Drury reported meeting thirteen years later on the northwest coast), but allowed them to escape. These ships could not have known the desperate plight of the scattered survivors of the *Degrave* on the remote south coast.[58]

It was nearly two years after the *Degrave*'s disaster before real news came. On 26 March 1705 a galley named *Raper* and two other East Indiamen arrived at Portsmouth with a survivor from the *Degrave.* What the survivor had to say, however, was reported very briefly and inaccurately in the newspapers and, apparently, not mentioned in the records of the East India Company at all. One reason for the neglect was the war and particularly the siege of Gibraltar and the jubilation over the victory at Blenheim. Another was the fact that the loss of the *Degrave* had been regarded as a certainty for over a year and was at the moment less exciting than a closely related marine drama then unfolding in Edinburgh. The *Worcester* affair, within two years of the Union, marks a high point in English-Scottish friction.

The Hanging of Captain Green

A series of setbacks to the Scottish Darien Company had reached a climax in the confiscation of the *Annandale* in England and the disappearance in the Indian Ocean of the misnamed *Speedy Return,* commanded by Captain Robert Drummond, and of the *Content,* commanded by Captain Alexander Stewart. When in the summer of 1704 the *Worcester,* en route from India to England, anchored in Leith Harbor, Edinburgh, the rumor got about that she had met and "pirated" the *Speedy Return* somewhere in the Orient. The *Worcester* was seized; and her commander, Captain Thomas Green, and the rest of her men were charged with murder and piracy. Feeling was so intense that the defendants had little chance of escaping with their lives and none whatever of a fair trial.[59]

Into this white-hot controversy plunged two members of Drummond's crew with information which in calmer times would have saved the lives of Captain Green and two others and saved Scotland

---

[58] Sloane MS 3674 (entry of 19 November 1703); P.R.O., Ad 51/864, 3–4, Ad 51/887, 4, and Ad 52/280, 7. The last is George Shelvocke's journal. The *Martha,* an East India ship, was at Mauritius in May 1703; but her log (Marine Records, 118B) lapsed upon arrival.

[59] The best and most recent account is Temple's *New Light.*

from a serious stain upon her honor. Israel Phippany and Peter Freeland, having arrived in Portsmouth on the *Raper* with a survivor from the *Degrave,* deposed on 31 March 1705 that the *Speedy Return* had not been harmed or even seen by the *Worcester* and that Captain Drummond was alive on Madagascar.

According to the deposition, for which there was even then adequate corroboration, the *Speedy Return* and the *Content* had been captured by the pirate John Bowen on the east coast of Madagascar while Drummond and Stewart were ashore. The pirates took the *Speedy Return* to India and burned her at Rajapur. They put her crew aboard a Moorish ship renamed *Defiance.* When they stopped at Mauritius at the end of January 1703/4, Phippany and Freeland escaped. A few months later, three homebound English ships reached Mauritius: on 29/18 May the *Raper,* on 26/15 June the *Gloucester,* both from Batavia, and on 23/12 July the *Regard* from Bombay.[60] The *Raper* took on board Phippany and Freeland and, probably, at a later port, the youthful survivor from the *Degrave.* The three ships left Mauritius on 27 August 1704, passed the Cape without stopping, and left St. Helena on 8 December, with a fourth ship, the *Edward and Dudley,* from Batavia. The *Gloucester* foundered near the Bermudas on 22 February 1704/5, but the others, as we have seen, reached Portsmouth 26 March 1705.[61]

"A Little Boy" from the Degrave

On the morning after arrival in Portsmouth, 27 March 1705, the purser of the *Raper* posted up to London, his mind in ferment with news of three disasters: the *Gloucester*'s, the *Speedy Return*'s, and the *Degrave*'s. He seems not to have understood the situation himself, and his hearers certainly did not. In consequence he started an inaccurate report that reached from London to the Cape and India, and from there re-echoed even in the records of the East India Company in London.

[60] *Précis . . . Letters Received,* pp. 353–359. The *Précis* gives these dates only in New Style.

[61] The only journal, and it is barely legible, which has survived from these three ships is that of the *Edward and Dudley* (Marine Records, CXIII); it tells us nothing about the men aboard the *Raper.* The ledger of the *Raper* exists (Marine Records, 765), but it does not list the purser or give other significant information. Captain Thompson of the *Raper* and Captain Brown of the *Gloucester,* who survived his ship, swore that Phippany and Freeland had told their story to them at Mauritius before they knew of Captain Green's arrest, which in fact did not occur until 12 December 1704, after the *Raper* and the other ships had left St. Helena. See Temple, *New Light,* pp. 266–269.

Only two newspapers are known to have carried the purser's report, both briefly and inaccurately.[62] The fuller account, dated London, 28 March, is that in the *Daily Courant*. It reads:

The purser of the Raper Galley came to Town yesterday Morning Post from Portsmouth, with Advice [that the three ships had arrived, convoyed by H.M.S. *Litchfield,* that the *Gloucester* had sunk, and] That the Degrave, belonging to the New Company, coming homewards, was necessitated in great Distress to put for Madagascar; and that the Pyrates of that Island seiz'd her and murther'd all her Crew, a little Boy only excepted.

Nearly a month later Narcissus Luttrell entered a different account in his diary for 21 April 1705:

A boy lately arrived in a gally from the Indies gives account that the Degrave, an East India ship of 800 tun, valued at 100,000*l.*, sprung a leak some time since on the coast of Madagascar, where the men landed, with their effects, and also carryed their guns on shore, but could get no provisions of the inhabitants, who said 'twas not customary to supply strangers till they delivered up their arms; which they had no sooner done, but those barbarous people killed them all but the boy now come over.[63]

The Little Boy

The most incredible part of the whole *Degrave* story is, I think, this of the boy who escaped and within two years got to London. Practically all of the 150 or so of those shipwrecked must have been killed outright. Of the others, only four, all young, are known to have got off Madagascar, and none, other than this boy, in less than three years. But, incredible as it may seem, there obviously was such a boy on the *Raper*.

The *Daily Courant* says that only "a little boy" survived. Luttrell adds the fact that the boy had arrived on a galley from India, which could have been only the *Raper*. Though Luttrell is sometimes inaccurate, as in his 4 April entry about Phippany and Freeland (corrected 24 April), his information about the *Degrave* is fuller and more accurate than that given the newspapers by the purser. Obviously in the twenty-six days between the arrival of the *Raper* and Luttrell's entry, the boy had got up to London to tell his own story, free from interference.[64]

Who was the boy? How came he to escape? And how and where

---

[62] The *Flying Post,* 27–29 March, and the *Daily Courant,* 28 March 1705.

[63] *A Brief Relation of the State Affairs from September 1678 to April 1714,* V (Oxford, 1857), 542–543.

[64] The boy, who thought himself the only survivor, was intelligent enough when allowed to speak for himself. He seems to have talked with the *Degrave's* owners (P.R.O., C9/466, 9). John Benbow thought only those escaped who fled with him, and Drury makes no place for this boy. But no one could have known what happened to all the others in the party.

did he board the *Raper?* He could have been really a *little* boy, either the child of one of the passengers or one of the two young Moors who, as we shall see, were taken on by the *Degrave* at Mauritius. But the news writer who called him "little" had not seen him and was merely reporting an impression he had got from the *Raper's* purser. More likely he was one of the twenty-three "midshipmen" or apprentices, like Drury and Dove, whose ages at the outset in 1701 ranged from ten, possibly, to sixteen or so.[65]

There is no place for the boy in either Drury's or Benbow's accounts. He must, therefore, have escaped unnoticed at the time of the massacre, about which he would not have known had he left earlier. With native help he may have got to St. Augustine Bay or another port where pirates or interlopers from America or Europe miraculously happened to be and from which they carried him away.

But where did the *Raper* find him? She probably left Mauritius without him; but Mauritius or Batavia, whither the Dutch could have carried him, seem possible places. The governor of Mauritius mentioned the *Raper's* taking on the "two pirates" (Phippany and Freeland) and the *Gloucester's* taking some men from warships; but he said nothing about the boy, and over a month later he was still wondering why the *Degrave* had not reached the Cape. He obviously knew nothing, and so Phippany and Freeland probably then knew nothing, of the boy or his story.

Nor was the boy picked up at the Cape. The Dutch there were in the dark about the *Degrave's* fate until about 27 May (N.S.) 1705.[66] And in any case the *Raper* and the two ships then with her did not stop at the Cape. The *Edward and Dudley,* which joined them at St. Helena, did stop there; but her journal, the only one from these ships which has survived, would almost certainly have mentioned the boy had she taken him on. The two stops between St. Helena and Portsmouth were at Ascension (16–20 December) and Fernando de Noronha off the coast of Brazil (31 December–13 January). (This last stop explains how the convoy came to be near the Bermudas when the *Gloucester* sank.) At Fernando de Noronha H.M.S. *Litchfield* (Captain Rupert Billingsley) met them and convoyed them home.[67] The boy, then, must have been taken on at one of these

---

[65] James Burney, brother of Fanny, is said to have gone to sea at ten.

[66] *Précis . . . Letters Received,* pp. 353–359; *Précis . . . Letters Dispatched,* pp. 265–266.

[67] Though the relevant parts of both master's and captain's journals of the *Litchfield* are lost, an abstract of the captain's journal appears in the report of Captain Billingsley upon his arrival at Portsmouth, 26 March 1705 (P.R.O., Ad

stops, possibly at St. Helena, in the interval preceding the *Edward and Dudley's* arrival.

The news released in England in March 1705 seems not to have reached the Cape before mid-May, which is slower than would be expected had it been known at St. Helena the beginning of December. Captain Finch Reddall, homebound from Batavia in the *Samuel and Anna,* wrote from the Cape on 12 May 1705: ". . . here is a flying report that the Degrave sailed from Mauritius very Leaky, and after she had been at sea some time the leak increased upon them and was forc'd to bare away for the first place she could to save their lives which was Madagascar and there the Pyrates hath Seized her and Cargoe, how true this is I can't tell. . . ." [68]

This was doubtless an echo of the *Raper's* report in which the pirating of the *Speedy Return* was confused with the foundering of the *Degrave.* It was not long in reaching India. What was in the "Relation of the Degraves loss at St. Laurence" (old name for Madagascar) sent to London in a letter from Fort St. George in October 1705 we do not know, as the account has not been found. A Bay letter of a month or two later gave the story a new turn by reporting: "Degrave lost at Madagascar the Ship Comp[a]. killed Cap[t]. Young & were afterwards killed by the Natives." [69] A slightly more accurate account from the Bay (5 December 1705) said that the *Degrave* left Mauritius very leaky and had sunk in St. Augustine Bay, where her men were most, if not all, cut off by the natives. This news, it was said, came from the Dutch and was generally believed.[70]

Though the Directors of the New Company had long before given up hope of the *Degrave's* return, they continued to list its cargo among their assets until December 1707. Then, on the eve of final absorption into the United Company, they voted that the article of the cargo "mentioned in the said account to be doubtful" be deleted.[71]

1/1467). It has no reference to the boy; but the ships he was to convoy had been at Fernando de Noronha five days when he arrived, and the abstract is extremely brief.

[68] Marine Records, Misc., vol. 18.

[69] Abstracts of Letters from Coast and Bay, vol. 1, letters of 1 and 10 October and 30 November 1705.

[70] O.C., No. 8407; Factory Records, Misc., vol. 6, p. 235. The latter is an abstract of the former.

[71] Court Minutes, vol. 39A, p. 437. At some time (1707?) a suit in Chancery was begun by the owners of the *Degrave* to collect demurrage from the New Company. It seems here unnecessary to give the details of this suit (see P.R.O. Chancery proceedings, Reynardson, C9/466, 9). From the bills submitted we learn the names of the owners of the *Degrave,* among whom had been "William Young, late Captaine & Master of the . . . DeGrave."

The Archives at the Cape

In spite of their advantageous position the Dutch were slower than the English in learning about the *Degrave*'s disaster. But they knew more about the voyage from India to Mauritius and in time had the best account of her fate outside *Drury's Journal*. Their information, though printed at Cape Town in 1896, has been unknown to students of *Drury's Journal* and related problems like the *Worcester* affair. Pale French reflections of it got into *Notes and Queries* in 1909 (ser. 10, XI, 162–163) and so into my articles of 1945.

Just before the Boer War, Hendrik Carol Vos Leibbrandt, Keeper of the Archives at the Cape of Good Hope, published in English a series of abstracts of the seventeenth- and eighteenth-century Dutch records in the archives, including correspondence with Mauritius, Batavia, and the Netherlands. Leibbrandt, fortunately, did not know about Drury and so did not corrupt his text by reading into it implications from *Drury's Journal*. He mistook "Degrave" or "Degraaf" for a translation and so changed it to "Earl," which he supposed was the English original. That may be one reason his work has not been noticed by students of Drury.[72]

In a letter of 3 April 1703, sent to the Cape by the *Degrave,* Roelof Deodati, the Dutch governor of Mauritius, described the *Degrave*'s arrival from Bengal and explained that he was allowing some Moors and lascars to board her for the Cape.[73] Six months later (9 October) a Cape letter to Batavia accused Captain Young of purposely passing the Cape in order to sell the Moors in the West Indies.[74] Batavia replied (1 February) that Captain Young was too honorable and too well connected to have passed the Cape intentionally. "It is more to be feared that a fatal disaster has befallen him." [75]

On 27 May 1705, nearly two months after the *Raper*'s arrival in England with the boy from the *Degrave,* Cape officials wrote home to the Netherlands their first information, inaccurate and incomplete, about what had become of the *Degrave*. They had been informed that she had been forced by a leak to keep straight for

[72] See note 24 above for the details of Leibbrandt's books. Only once does Leibbrandt use the word "Degrave." Pitot, *T'Eylandt Mauritius*, p. 303, gives the name as "Grove."

[73] Only a duplicate of the letter is, of course, preserved. All dates in Dutch records are New Style. See *Précis . . . Letters Received*, pp. 321, 327.

[74] *Précis . . . Letters Dispatched*, p. 233.

[75] *Précis . . . Letters Dispatched*, p. 328.

St. Augustine Bay, where she was abandoned and her men were taken prisoner by King Samuel, who treated them well but would not release them.[76]

In the summer of the same year (1705) the Cape officials sent the yacht *Ter Aa* on the first of two voyages to Madagascar for slaves. They wrote a series of letters, with the governor's signature and the Dutch Company's seal in red wax, to several native kings. One, to Andrian Defangandits (elsewhere Defandangets) at Maningare, reminded that "Sublimest King" of their trade with his late father, King Semanetu. Another was to the "King of Madagascar, Resoedja" at "Mattatan or Maratange." A third was to the "King of Magelage [Massalege] . . . and Prince of the island of Madagascar," on the northwest coast.

The *Ter Aa* stopped at Maningare and Maratanga on the east coast and returned to the Cape on 9 January 1706 N.S. with well over a hundred slaves and two other men. One was a half-caste Indian from Nagapatnam, Symon Jansen, sailor and drummer on a small English inland boat which had been captured by pirates. The other was Robert Coleson, "formerly of the English ship 'Earl' [*Degrave*] ran on shore at Madagascar because she was so leaky." This news, together with a "statement of what they went through, made before the commissioners," was sent home to the Netherlands by Governor Van Der Stel in a letter of 26 March 1706. The governor, who seems to have been chiefly interested in what Coleson and Jansen could tell him about pirates, added, "this is all that we could get out of them, and the only further information that I could obtain about the pirates." [77]

John Benbow's Journal

The next entry in the Cape records about the *Degrave* is the most important of all, for it tells us a good deal about the contents of John Benbow's journal (burned in 1714) over which critics of Drury have long speculated. This information is in a letter written to the Netherlands from the Cape on 9 February 1707.[78] The *Ter Aa* had gone to Mauritius a second time for slaves, and 9–31 December 1706 had been at Fort Dauphin, where her "officers found the son of the deceased English Admiral Benbow, who was dressed in the

---

[76] *Précis . . . Letters Received*, pp. 321, 327, 353, 359; *Précis . . . Letters Dispatched*, pp. 233, 235–236, 265.

[77] *Précis . . . Letters Dispatched*, pp. 277, 291.

[78] There are accounts of John Benbow and of the *Degrave* in letters of 9 February and 21 April 1707. See *Précis . . . Letters Dispatched*, pp. 310–313, 325.

same way as the natives there, and lived as intimately with them as if he also were a native of the country." The account which followed, apparently abstracted by Benbow from his journal, is summarized below, where the story of the *Degrave's* disaster will be told in the light of it and of Coleson's briefer statement.[79]

The Disaster

The *Degrave's* leak, aggravated by the grounding in Bengal, rapidly worsened when she struck salt water shortly after 25 December 1702, and forced her against orders to stop at Mauritius before mid-February 1702/3. Fortunately the French had not, as had been feared, captured the island. The Dutch governor, Roelof Deodati, did what he could for the *Degrave* in Northwest Harbor, where she attempted to stop her leak and to get much-needed provisions. Twelve Moors, two of them young boys, and thirty banians out of the *Speaker,* which fourteen months earlier the pirate Bowen had lost there, requested permission to go on the *Degrave* to the Cape. Deodati warned them that the leaky vessel rode low in the water and that she had lost six feet of her rudder, but they persisted. The *Degrave* left Mauritius on or about 25 March O.S.[80]

Captain Young soon found the leak worse than before. It was, in fact, so alarming that in latitude 34° or 35° south he was forced to head for the nearest land, which was Madagascar. On 26 April he reached the southern coast at a harborless region called Androy. The ship then had four feet of water in the powder magazine, and, though her mainmast and foremast had been cut away to lighten her, she was ready to sink at any moment. The following day the crew in desperation "set the ship broadside on, on shore." The end came quickly. The great vessel, which had exceeded all records for speed to India and which was bulging with Indian cloth and other

---

[79] See note 96 below.

[80] Pitot (p. 303), who wrongly transcribes "mores" as "noirs," "Nich." as "Michael" Young, and "Degrave" as "Grove," mistakenly assumes that Deodati's letter, sent with the *Degrave* and dated 3 April 1703 N.S., fixes the date of the *Degrave's* departure. It could have left later. Conflicting statements about the *Degrave's* stay at Mauritius are not irreconcilable. *Robert Drury's Journal* (1890), pp. 43–44, without giving dates, says she was two months en route to and a month or so at Mauritius. The Dutch at the Cape report John Benbow as saying she arrived on 3 February and left on the 25th (*Précis . . . Letters Dispatched,* p. 311). The *Précis* does not give the month of departure, though the natural assumption is that February was intended; but if the Dutch by mistake omitted "March" after the 25th, Benbow's Old Style chronology would approximate that of Deodati, who says the *Degrave* arrived in February and was ready to leave on 2 April. *Drury's Journal* tells of putting up tents on land for the sick and of attempts to dry the cargo.

treasures, was in the high surf broken to pieces against boulders; and her cargo, scattered into every inlet and crevice, was pillaged by the natives. Three persons were drowned, but the others, including the crew, the passengers, and the Moors and lascars, making a party of more than 150, got on shore safely. The natives led them to their king, Decrindo (Benbow) or Crindo (Drury), who, though he promised them kindness, seems to have planned to kill them all.[81] In their dilemma they were assisted by two Scottish mariners whom we have already met.

Captain Robert Drummond and Captain Alexander Stewart

Before Captain Green, John Madder, and James Simpson of the *Worcester* were hanged in Leith Harbor, it was already evident that the notorious pirate John Boon or Bowen had pirated the *Speedy Return* and the *Content* and had left their commanders, Captain Drummond and Captain Stewart, ashore on Madagascar. But there has been until now skepticism, which I have shared, of Drury's seemingly improbable story that Drummond and Stewart were in Androy when the *Degrave* foundered and that they had a part in the adventures of her crew.

The *Speedy Return* and the *Content* had sailed from Glasgow in the summer of 1701 and reached the Cape on 4 January 1701/2. Though their declared intention was to touch on the African coast and return, they went on to St. Mary's Island on the east coast of Madagascar for a load of slaves, which they took to Don Mascareen (modern Reunion). At that island on 19 June 1702 they found the *Rooke,* an East India merchantman whose crew was in revolt against their new captain, John Hunnycomb, successor to Captain George Simmons, deceased. A week later a committee of the crew offered command of the *Rooke* to Captain Stewart. Stewart declined the offer, and he and Drummond sailed on to Maratanga on the east coast of Madagascar, where the supercargo (*Coopman*) Thomas Drummond, brother of the captain, sickened and died.[82] In the meantime the pirate John Bowen, who in a drunken spree had lost the *Speaker* on the Black Rock (St. Thomas' Reef) at Mauritius,

[81] This account is based upon the declaration of the *Degrave's* owners (P.R.O., C9/466, 9) and John Benbow's statement given the Dutch at the Cape (*Précis . . . Letters Dispatched,* pp. 310–312).

[82] Dutch letter from the Cape, 21 April 1707; O.C., No. 7988 ff.; Temple, *New Light,* pp. 266–272. The death of Thomas Drummond at Maratanga has not been known to modern historians. Maratanga, Maratan, and Mattatan were the seventeenth- and eighteenth-century English and Dutch names for modern Matatane. Temple confused it with Maningare, a port much farther north, opposite St. Mary's Island.

16 October 1701,[83] came also to Maratanga with a sloop, got from the Dutch on Mauritius, which they had lengthened and converted into a brigantine. The Dutch at the Cape, like those at Mauritius, suspected Drummond and Stewart of intending piracy. Captain Whaley (often called Weoley) of the *Pembroke,* who escaped from Bowen after the events now being related, asserted that Drummond and Stewart, while at Mascarenhas, had offered to help Bowen take the *Rooke* on condition that they "should be laded home with the *Rooke*'s goods at easy rates." [84] But now at Maratanga Bowen pirated their ships instead. Some reports are that they were ashore at the time; others, that they were put ashore with their surgeon Andrew Wilkie and some others who refused to go with the pirates.

We come now to an extraordinary coincidence. When the *Degrave* party got on shore and reached King Decrindo's village, they found in that unlikely place Captains Drummond and Stewart, three men from their vessels (including, presumably, Surgeon Wilkie), and three other whites, called pirates in the Dutch transcript, but described in *Robert Drury's Journal* as two Englishmen (who had escaped from the pirates) and the wife of one of them. These eight had come in a small boat from Maratanga, in an attempt to reach St. Augustine Bay on the west coast, where they hoped to find a ship returning to Europe. Why they landed at Androy Benbow does not say; but, according to *Robert Drury's Journal,* their boat had been driven ashore and destroyed.[85] At any rate, these hardened adventurers were a welcome support to the youthful officers of the *Degrave.*

Royal Hostages

It was soon clear that to escape from King Decrindo was not going to be easy. The plight of the refugees became desperate when an old woman brought them word that Decrindo intended to murder them all on 6 May, and they took measures accordingly. With only a few weapons and with sticks and hand pikes, they managed

[83] Deposition of Thomas Towsey, formerly carpenter on the *Speaker,* O.C., No. 8057. But (*Précis . . . Letters Received,* p. 308) the Dutch governor of Mauritius gave the date of the wreck as 7 January 1702, which would have been 27 December 1701 O.S. See also Temple, *New Light,* p. 136, and his index under "Whaley."

[84] See Temple, *New Light,* p. 271.

[85] Letters from the Cape to the Netherlands, 9 February and 21 April 1707 (*Précis . . . Letters Dispatched,* pp. 311, 325). According to *Robert Drury's Journal* (1890), pp. 48–50, the party escaping from Maratanga consisted of the two Scottish captains, three members of their crew, and four others, who were an unwilling English pirate, another Englishman, his wife, and a Negro.

to enter the royal lodging and seize the king, his wife, and his eldest son. They got also some arms and ammunition, at the cost of one killed and three wounded. Then with the royal hostages they set out over the hot, sandy plain for Fort Dauphin 125 miles or more away on the southeast coast, where a certain Samuel was king. Benbow does not indicate clearly whether the march began before or on 6 May, but three or four desperate days of forced marching and intense thirst are discernible before the catastrophe.

If the whites had adhered to their original scheme, all would probably have reached Fort Dauphin, though whether they would have been much the better for that is a question. At the time, however, it seemed that the native army which followed them might, as it promised, retire if the royal hostages were released. And so a series of concessions brought a plan, begun with intelligence and courage, to a fatal end.

The whites had not got far before 600 or 700 natives threatened them. A bargain was made on the first or second day whereby the king (the queen may already have been freed) was released in exchange for (Drury says six, Benbow ten) guns.[86] The next day the prince was exchanged for three or four natives, presumably men of importance. Both Drury and Benbow indicated that so long as they had royal hostages they were not attacked; but neither explains why the group did not use their advantage to force the natives to bring them food and water. Their intense thirst warped their judgment and deluded them into thinking they were followed only because they still held the prince.

To their dismay, the native threat intensified upon the prince's release, and the army increased to 5,000. That night, which seems to have been the end of the third day, the whites took refuge for a while behind a large tamarind tree, and about nine o'clock, after the natives had withdrawn, they secretly resumed their painful march. The next afternoon they crossed the wide Mandrare River, which separated Decrindo's realm from King Samuel's and beyond which they expected safety. The natives, who had overtaken them again, killed from seventeen to twenty in the crossing. But the main body got over, and on a sand hill, for some hours in the late afternoon, they fought off an attack in which several on each side were killed.[87]

[86] Drury places the king's release on the second day. Benbow does not indicate the passage of time until he comes to the release of the prince, which, like Drury, he says was the day after the release of the king. Drury says that Captain Young released the queen almost at the start; Coleson does not mention the queen.

[87] The Dutch, who seem to have misunderstood Coleson at this point, reported

The Massacre

As day closed the whites were in a hopeless predicament. Though in King Samuel's territory, they were scarcely halfway to Fort Dauphin.[88] Doubtless their number, which with the Moors and banians taken on at Mauritius and the eight with Drummond and Stewart had originally been 140 or so, had shrunk to possibly half that many.[89] They seem to have been out of ammunition; according to *Robert Drury's Journal,* some made bullets out of coins and the middle screws of their guns. Many were ill or wounded, and all were desperate for food and water.

Two hours after the sand-hill battle, according to Benbow, the party agreed to surrender all their arms to the blacks on the assurance that they could proceed unmolested to Fort Dauphin the next day. The group was thereupon invited to dinner by the blacks and some, "driven by hunger went thither unhesitatingly. . . ." Drummond, Stewart, "four of their men," Benbow, and others (Coleson among them) to the number of thirty were skeptical and slipped away toward Fort Dauphin. Those who accepted the offer of hospitality were surrounded and slain immediately (as Benbow implies) or the next morning (as Drury, who was certainly present, is reported as saying).[90]

The conduct of the natives, though brutal, was not wholly irrational. An armed white man was worth many native soldiers, and Decrindo seems to have had high hopes of using the *Degrave* party in war with his neighbors. Their seizure of him and his son and

him as saying that upon reaching a river eighteen feet wide (obviously the Mandrare), the whites gave up their weapons in exchange for a promise of help in crossing the next day; that, suspecting treachery, he, Benbow, and sixteen others went into the water that night and escaped to Fort Dauphin; and that those who remained behind were horribly massacred and "since that time no one has heard of them." But though some of the leaders were ready to desert the others whenever it seemed to their advantage, they did not do so for another day.

[88] Benbow's account implies that this was the end of the third day. The Drury account makes it the fourth day but calls the next day the fourth. Whether "fourth" is a misprint for "fifth" or whether we see here a conflict between Drury's original manuscript and amplifications by Defoe, it is impossible to tell. Drury, of course, was writing at least fifteen years after the fact.

[89] Five had deserted at Mauritius; three were drowned in escaping from the *Degrave;* one was killed and three were wounded in the seizing of the royal hostages; and twenty or so were slain in crossing the Mandrare and several in the sand-hill battle. Doubtless a good many others had perished unnoticed in the flight. Drury is reported as saying that in the sand-hill fight they had not over thirty-six weapons among them and "not many more people fit to fight."

[90] Benbow said that all were slain except those in his party. But the boy from the *Raper* and Drury were exceptions; and *Robert Drury's Journal* mentions several boys who were spared.

their attempt to reach Fort Dauphin, from which King Samuel might have counterattacked, aroused first anger and then fear. When the natives found that nearly half of their captives had escaped, the fate of the others was sealed. The following simple account attributed to Drury may not be wholly accurate, but it is the only one we have which gives any details of the massacre itself.

Drury and three or four other youths were seized and bound. Then the prince, who had seized Drury, stuck "his lance into Captain Younge's throat and afterwards into his sides. He had no sooner killed him, but he went on to another, and the rest of his people immediately followed his example, and soon murdered every man; they then fell to stripping them of their clothes, and even butchering them; for they ripped open several of their bellies." [91] If my estimates are valid, perhaps not more than twenty-five or thirty met this fate. And it may be that their sudden death was preferable to the lingering one which dogged Drummond and nearly all of his comrades.

Hunger, Disappointment, and Piracy

The massacre, as nearly as we can tell, occurred between 8 and 10 May 1703. By the evening of 14 May the Drummond-Benbow party, which had broken into smaller groups in their flight, all arrived at Fort Dauphin. King Samuel, whose romantic fortunes will be described later, befriended them for four months but then refused to feed them longer. From this point their movements are difficult to trace in the two different versions which the Dutch sent home of their interviews with John Benbow [92] and in their interview with Robert Coleson, who, as we have seen, was rescued by the Dutch a year earlier than Benbow.

The first Dutch report on Benbow quotes him as saying that when King Samuel withdrew his hospitality, twelve of them set out for Maratanga, a port farther north. They were eighteen days en route, though whether by land or water is not stated. After a year of fruitless waiting at Maratanga for a chance to escape, during

[91] *Robert Drury's Journal* (1890), pp. 73–74.

[92] *Précis . . . Letters Dispatched,* pp. 310–313 (Cape letter of 9 February 1707 N.S.), 325 (Cape letter of 21 April 1707). When Benbow's rescue is mentioned again in the second of these letters, Leibbrandt inserts a misleading parenthesis which implies that the story was not there retold. But the manuscript of the letter gives a second though briefer account of Benbow's adventures from the time the *Degrave* left England to that of his departure for England from the Cape in January 1707. It has also several paragraphs about the movements of Captain Drummond and Captain Stewart, so far as Benbow knew them. A little more light comes from English sources, notably *Robert Drury's Journal.*

which half of them died, the remaining six returned to Fort Dauphin. They had been back only four months when they heard that the *Ter Aa* had been at Maratanga for slaves soon after their earlier departure. But they stayed on at Fort Dauphin, living on sweet potatoes and other vegetables, which they themselves had to grow, until the *Ter Aa* came again the following year. "With her," the account concludes, "Benbow was brought over hither [to the Cape], not more than one man, who is semple (simple?) having survived of the whole troop, the others having died, been killed or departed with pirates." By this account, Benbow and his comrades would have returned from Maratanga by mid-October 1704. But if they had been back only four months when they heard of the *Ter Aa*'s visit to Maratanga, which occurred in November 1705, a gap of nine months is unexplained.

The second Dutch summary [93] of Benbow's story says that when after four months King Samuel left the refugees to find their own food, some went here and some there, growing their own potatoes and other vegetables. Captain Stewart went pirating with some rovers, in a ship which they had seized as it arrived from Martinique to trade, and Benbow knew nothing further about him. Captain Drummond, with two other whites and four blacks, had set out a second time in a canoe for St. Augustine Bay, to see if there or elsewhere they could find a ship in which to escape to Europe. Drummond refused to take Benbow with him, hoping that if something happened to one of them the other at least might get home with information.[94] We know from East India Company records that Drummond drifted about Madagascar in misery for several years,[95] and *Robert Drury's Journal* (preface) quotes Captain Mackett as saying that he was finally killed there by a Jamaican Negro named Lewes.

Coleson, who was rescued at the end of 1705, had a year less in which to observe than Benbow, and his account is difficult to

[93] See *Précis . . . Letters Dispatched*, p. 325.

[94] In the midst of these details the narrative reverts to an earlier time and recounts the illness and death of Thomas Drummond at Maratanga, the pirating of the *Speedy Return* and the *Content,* and the escape of Captains Drummond and Stewart to the point on south Madagascar where the *Degrave* was to founder. This account of the loss of the *Speedy Return* and the *Content* dovetails with that in the deposition of Phippany and Freeland (members of the *Speedy Return*'s crew, who escaped from the pirates and returned home on the *Raper*), from which are taken the accounts in the *History of the Pirates* (New York, 1926), p. 374, and Temple, *New Light*, pp. 266–268, 322–325.

[95] Misc. Letters Received, vol. 1, no. 192 (Charles Robertson's letter of 7 September 1709).

integrate with Benbow's.[96] Coleson is quoted as saying that when he, with Benbow and others, escaped from King Decrindo's army to Fort Dauphin, he found there a small English ship taking on water. He joined five of the ship's men, who had gone ashore, in a boat. Meanwhile the ship had got under sail, and the men in the boat with Coleson, being left behind, followed the coast northward to Maratanga. Shortly after their arrival at that port, a small ship with a crew of sixteen came directly from France with wine and other merchandise in order to trade with the pirates. Some English pirates, who had been living with the local king, Resoedja, and who had his permission for their act, set upon the ship at night in canoes and took it. The pirates, numbering twenty (including some Frenchmen from the ship's crew), went away in the ship. At Fort Dauphin, Coleson reported, Benbow alone was found, all his companions having died. Benbow was taken aboard, his intention being to reach India and there get passage to England, as it appeared hopeless to get home from Fort Dauphin. Coleson had heard nothing more of the venture at the time of his rescue.

The Dutch were grilling Coleson for information about pirates. He was not likely to admit having been aboard a pirate vessel even if he had been. But, if he had not, how came he to think that Benbow had? One is tempted to identify the small French ship taken by English pirates at Maratanga with the (French?) ship from Martinique which took Captain Stewart pirating, and with the small French ship commanded by one Herault, which, according to the *History of the Pirates* (1926), p. 433, was taken at Maratanga by some members of the *Degrave's* crew, to whom the master had refused passage to Europe. Herault's ship, we are told in the *History of the Pirates,* was taken to Massalege on the northwest coast and deserted by the pirates. The men from the *Degrave* seem to have been preparing this ship for a voyage to India, where they hoped for passage home, when along came the noted Captain White, himself an unwilling pirate. With him they went roving to the Red Sea and captured the *Dorothy*, an English ship commanded by Captain Penruddock coming from Mocha. But, as this foray to the Red Sea occurred in 1706,[97] neither Coleson nor Benbow could then have been aboard, though they might have been aboard until,

[96] The "Relass van Robbert Coulsin" is in the archives at The Hague. It was annexed to a Cape letter of 31 March 1706. *Précis . . . Letters Dispatched,* p. 291, mentions the annexure but tells only of Coleson's rescue.

[97] Abstracts of Letters from Coast and Bay, vol. 1, pp. 126–127, letters of September and November 1707.

in preparing for the Red Sea voyage, the ship touched at a port on the east Madagascar coast.

The Rescue by Captain Mackett

In October 1715 a Captain Thomas White, who had been in the Guinea slave trade, enlarged his plans to include Madagascar.[98] He petitioned the East India Company for a license to send three small ships and a sloop to Delagoa on the southeast coast of Africa and to Madagascar for whale fishing, teeth, and "other commodities"—a euphemism for slaves. The ships were not named, but they were the *Henry* (Captain Harvey), the *Drake* (Captain William Mackett), the *Mercury* (Captain White), and, to serve as a tender to the others, a ketch or sloop also called the *Mercury* (Captain Henry Mackett, brother of William). The owners were well-known London merchants, Captain John Hyde, Francis Sitwell, and Samuel Houblon. The license was granted 7 December 1715, simultaneously with one to William Heynsham for the *Sarah* (Captain Bloome).[99]

We know nothing more of these ships, except what we read in *Drury's Journal* and the *History of the Pirates,* until they were well on their way home from Madagascar. But it seems beyond serious question that William Mackett had been requested by a friend of Robert Drury's father to rescue Robert and that he took him on board the *Drake.*[100] The *Drake* reached St. Helena 28 February 1716/7 and the factory records tell us a good deal about her stay there. A sale bill announced that provided the high surf abated, on Wednesday, 6 March, Mackett would offer four children (seven to twelve years), four boys and girls (twelve to seventeen years), six men, and four women, able-bodied and in good health; and, if these sold well, a like number more. On 11 March he re-

[98] Elsewhere ("Robert Drury and *Robert Drury's Journal*," pp. 178–180) I have discussed the difficulty of identifying this Captain Thomas White with the Captain Thomas White of the *History of the Pirates*. The argument seems to me conclusive. In addition, there is the improbability that so notorious a pirate or ex-pirate should have been trusted by the East India Company. Possibly the account in the *History of the Pirates* is inaccurate.

[99] Court Minutes, vol. 46, pp. 469, 513, 588, 595, 597, 602, 606, 608. The preface to *Drury's Journal* calls William Mackett a principal owner of the first four ships. The terms of the license throw interesting light on the slave trade and refute those who deny that the East India Company participated in Madagascar slaving. The licensees were to deliver to the East India Company at St. Helena nine slaves for each £1,500 value in the cargo carried on the outward voyage, fractional parts to be paid in boys or girls. Otherwise slaves were to be between sixteen and thirty, two-thirds of them males.

[100] See "Thirteen Years on Madagascar," pp. 55–56.

ceived from the factory gunner three barrels of powder, and on his departure (16 March) a bill on the East India Company in London for £869 18s. 8d. to pay for the slaves purchased by the planters.[101] The *Mercury,* sloop, reached St. Helena 5 March on the eve of the sale, and Captain White in the *Mercury* on 28 April.

The *Drake,* according to *Drury's Journal,* arrived at Barbados in the West Indies on 22 April for a week's stay and then went on to Jamaica to deliver the rest of her slaves. The journal of Captain Candler of H.M.S. *Winchelsea,* which mentions nearly all the West India matters presented in *Drury's Journal,* noted that at 11 a.m., 6 May 1717, there came into Port Royal Harbor, Jamaica, "one Capt. Maggett from Maddigascar." [102] Two months later, 5 July, the *Drake,* with twenty-one other merchantmen, three brigantines, and three sloops, sailed for England in a convoy, which the *Winchelsea* was to see safe through the windward passage. Most of them, however, sailed too deep to keep to windward against the strong current, and by 13 July only five of the merchantmen were left. A week later they found two pirate sloops waiting for them in the keys of Crooked Island. One of these sloops made for the *Winchelsea,* but finding her to be a man-of-war stood off and took refuge in shoals behind a "reef where wee could not goe and exchanged some shot with ye Merch^t. Ships [Drury says with the *Drake*] before wee could come up with him againe. . . ." It was then dark, and, though the convoy waited another day, nothing more was seen or heard of the pirates, except that a sloop lading salt informed them that one of the pirates was the notorious Hornigold. On 26 July a merchantman which had fallen behind arrived with word that it and another vessel had been robbed by a pirate.[103]

In the meantime, on 22 July, when weighing to leave Crooked Island, a merchant ship (Drury says it was the *Winchelsea* that ran into the *Drake*) ran the *Winchelsea* "aboard and caried away our flying jibboom spirits yard and . . . broke our best bower anchorstock and yawl in peeces, and wee caried away his foremast and all his larboard bow between wind and watter and disabled one an-

---

[101] St. Helena Records, vol. 6 (1716–20). The paging is unsystematic, but see February–April 1716/7, pp. 33, 35, 41–42, 83. The planters purchased slaves, as they did other commodities, on credit allowed them by the company store, which gave Mackett a bill payable by the company in London. It was received in London 21 August 1717 (Court Minutes, vol. 47, p. 409, where it is called a "Second Bill" from St. Helena).

[102] P.R.O., Ad 52/319.

[103] Additional comment on the fight with the pirate is found in a letter written by Captain Candler (P.R.O., Ad 1/1597), but, like the *Winchester's* journal, it also fails to name the merchant ship that attacked the pirate.

other very much and lay by all night." In the morning, after consultation, they went for repairs to nearby Salt Island.

On 27 July the *Winchelsea* turned back to Jamaica, and the merchantmen made for England. Five of them were reported in the Downs on Sunday, 8 September 1717: the *Tavistock,* the *Althea,* the *Duke of York,* the *Friends Goodwill,* and the *Drake,* which on 13 September reached Gravesend.[104]

Back in the Old Jury Again

Robert Drury, who had left for India as a lad of fourteen, was thirty when he returned to the Old Jury. The King's Head (which survived till within a century), Windmill Court (the fifteenth-century home of Lord Mayor Hugh Clopton), and the spacious residences of wealthy merchants have now given way to commercial buildings, like those in nearby Moorgate Street. Only St. Olave's church, on the west side and toward Gresham Street, stood much as it was in Drury's day, until the blitz of World War II, which demolished nearly all of the Old Jury, blew in its front. But in 1717 Drury found the street hardly changed at all. He doubtless returned through the Poultry, past Grocer's Alley leading to the Bank of England, then in Grocer's Hall, and past St. Mildred's, where, unknown to him, his father had remarried eight months after the *Degrave*'s disaster. Turning to the right into the Old Jury at the south end, he would have found on his left, opposite Dove Court, the school said to have been begun by Thomas à Becket, and just beyond it, at what is now Fredrick Place, the great gates of Fredrick House (then the Excise Office) facing those of Sir Robert Clayton's house on the east side of the street. Farther along and, apparently, close to St. Olave's, where for fifteen years his father had been a faithful vestryman, stood the King's Head with its twenty windows. To the returning traveler it must have seemed that life was continuing in 1717 much as he had left it in 1701.[105]

He quickly found otherwise. That John Drury, his father, had left the King's Head and retired to Loughborough in Leicestershire he knew from a letter his father had written in Loughborough in February 1715/6 and sent to Robert by Captain Mackett. He was now to learn that his mother had died within six months of his shipwreck in Madagascar, and his father a year before his return.

[104] *Weekly Journal; or, British Gazetteer,* 14 September 1717, p. 836 (8 September letter from Deal); Mist's *Weekly Journal,* no. 40, 21 September 1717, p. 241.

[105] Price, "Signs of Old London," pp. 92–93; *N&Q,* VIII (1853), 104; Stow, *Survey of London,* I, iii, 54, 63.

Recently dead also was Samuel Abington of Loughborough who had married Robert's sister Elizabeth in 1709. In partial compensation for these losses, he learned of his stepmother and his thirteen-year-old half sister Mary, both in Loughborough, and possibly of a stepbrother, Thomas Wharton, who would have been nearly sixteen. His brother John, whom he had seen last as a boy of nine, was now a London baker of twenty-five. We know nothing of John after 1721, when he appeared with Robert before the Stoke Newington manorial court to relinquish rights to property left him in his father's will.[106]

The main facts of that will (dated April 1716) seem to have been neighborhood gossip. Robert, provided he returned safe into England, was to have £200, which was at interest with a Loughborough tanner named Edward Bowley, and the reversion of a Stoke Newington house (with yard, garden, long walk, and summerhouse) occupied by a merchant named Richard Beardsley. That the house was to pass only to such heirs of Robert as were lawfully begotten upon an English woman (and so not to any Madagascar half-breeds) was probably not so well known, nor that he was to have his mother's wedding ring, his father's India quill and silver watch, and a good deal more if his brother and sisters died without issue.[107]

William and Margaret Drewry

The King's Head (as *Drury's Journal* tells us) had passed from John Drury to his brother William, who kept it only four years (1705–09). On 9 June 1709 he signed the St. Olave Vestry Minutes in a very shaky hand and, though elected questman on 16 December of that year, died the following February.[108] His widow Margaret continued the King's Head with the help of John Borranskaile, who

---

[106] See St. Katherine Cree parish records for the burial (21 September 1703) of "Mary late wife of John Drewry from Newington." John Drury, who, though then living in Stoke Newington, was still conducting the King's Head and so is described as of St. Olave's, and Elizabeth Wharton—not Whorton, as given in the Index Library's *Calendar of Marriage Licences . . . 1632–1714* (London, 1905), p. 202—of St. Mildred Poultry, were married in St. Mildred's 21 December 1703. Elizabeth seems to have been the widow of Thomas Wharton (buried at St. Mildred's, 2 November 1702). All the Wharton daughters died (1689–97), as apparently had a son Thomas who was born in 1687, since another Thomas was born in January 1701/2. Mary Drury, born to John Drury's second wife, was baptized 1 October 1704. The date of her birth, either 23 or 28 September, is blurred in the St. Olave records.

[107] For John Drury's will, see P.C.C., Fox, 1716, 204. For an account of John Drury's Stoke Newington property, see my "Defoe in Stoke Newington," pp. 211–225.

[108] Buried at St. Olave's, 17 February 1709/10.

had married her by 1712 and who left her a widow again early
in 1716. The scanty evidence of these details dovetails exactly with
the statement in *Drury's Journal* that William Drury's widow had
remarried and become a widow again and that she still kept the
King's Head at Robert's return. In 1718 the King's Head passed to
John Anslow. Whether he had purchased it of Margaret Borranskaile
or married her I refuse to guess.[109]

An Ex-Slave Turns Slaver

Robert Drury had hardly been home a year before he was off again
with Captain Mackett's friend, Captain White, to the scene of
his own enslavement. On 17 October 1717, just a month after his
return and nearly a year before White set out again, Mackett and
White were licensed for a second Madagascar voyage. Nine months
later (16 July 1718) White, who said he had neglected to ask to
take along the *Mercury's* sloop (also called *Mercury*) which he had
used on the previous voyage as a tender, was denied permission to
do so. The reason given was that small vessels had been accused of
bringing East India goods to Jamaica and selling them as from
Madagascar. So the sloop or ketch *Mercury* went for slaves to the
west coast of Africa, where pirates took her, turned her into the
Queen Ann's Revenge, and lost her finally on the coast of Brazil.
This evidence will, I hope, correct my error of 1945 in confusing
the two *Mercurys* and asserting that Drury could not have gone
back to Madagascar in the *Mercury,* since (as the *History of the
Pirates* seemed to say) the pirates had her.[110]

[109] The evidence for John Borranskaile's connection with Margaret Drury and
the King's Head is the assessment lists referred to in a previous note and recorded in the St. Olave Vestry Minutes. In these lists names follow each other
year after year in the same order. When property changed hands, the name of
the new owner replaced that of the old, as in 1690 John Drury's replaces James
[John?] King's and in 1706 William Drewry's replaces John Drury's. The 1710
list, which should give us "Widow Drewry" in William's place, is missing. These
lists from 5 October 1711 through 16 October 1716 have "John Borenscale" in
the Drury spot, though his will had been probated in May 1716 (P.C.C., Fox,
91). All we learn from that will relevant to the Drury problem is that Borranskaile's wife was named Margaret. Curiously enough, her sister-in-law by her
first marriage, Elizabeth Drury, in probating her husband's will six months later
in the same year, is by obvious error miscalled Margaret in one place in both
the original and the copy.
From the evidence mentioned above, John Anslow, who seems to have been
an innholder in the published list of liverymen in 1733, gave place to Caleb
Roffey in 1737; Roffey to James Leadbetter in 1745; and he to Mos. Patmore in
1767. Beyond that the ownership of the King's Head is unknown, though it
was reported still in existence in 1853 (see *N&Q,* VIII, 105).

[110] "Defoe and *Robert Drury's Journal,*" p. 71. For Mackett's and White's licenses,
see Court Minutes, vol. 47, pp. 475, 551, and vol. 48, p. 53.

Drury's Journal tells us that Captain White in the *Mercury* left the Downs on 13 September 1718, touched at the Cape for a ten-day stop on 1 April 1719, and then before going on to Madagascar traded for slaves awhile on the southeast coast of Africa, where he released six natives of "Dillagoe, which he took with him the former voyage." There is external corroboration for all of these details except the date of departure from the Downs. The journal of the East India ship *Mary* (Marine Records, 261B) tells of Captain White's arrival at and departure from the Cape precisely on Drury's dates, and the Court Minutes of 1720 discuss at great length what to do with two Delegoa princes brought to see England by Captain White but sold as slaves by him in Jamaica.[111] On 28 August 1719, according to the journal of the *Addison* (Marine Records, 705A), White arrived at Don Mascareen with slaves from Madagascar. He was still there in St. Paul's Harbor when the *Addison* left on 2 September and must soon after have died there, as *Drury's Journal* says.[112] He was succeeded by Captain George Christall, about whom nothing has previously been reported outside *Drury's Journal*.

For the return, *Drury's Journal* is very brief, saying only that they left Madagascar 7 January 1720, touched at St. Helena and Barbados, sold their slaves and took on tobacco in Virginia, and reached the Downs on 11 September of the same year. But we now know that they stopped at the Cape of Good Hope. They reached the Cape on 4 February and were still there on 19 February. On that day the *Prince Fredrick* (Marine Records, 663B) arrived and reported that the "Markary" from Madagascar with slaves had got in her water and was leaving when she sent a boat to say that there had been "a Pyrate and [the pirate] had fought a Dutch ship and had been seen Divers Times." On 7 March the arrival of the *Mercury* and a Dutch ship at St. Helena was celebrated with eighteen guns. To the East India factory "the Mercury Capt. George Christall (who succeeded Capt. White) from Madagascar" delivered according to contract eleven male and five female slaves, all good and sound. When asked about pirates, Captain Christall, Chief Mate William Bennett, and Second Mate Richard Charnock wrote an account dated 11 March of an engagement reported to them by a Dutch ship at the Cape. With the factory gunner's notation of fifteen guns fired on her departure, the *Mercury* passes apparently from

[111] Court Minutes, vol. 49, pp. 121 (23 September 1720), 170, 206, 217, 231, 352, 477, etc. It is not clear whether the two princes were from White's first voyage or his second.
[112] (1890), p. 308n.

East India Company records.[113] Only *Drury's Journal* announces the visit to Virginia and the arrival at the Downs on 11 September 1720.

Later Life of Robert Drury

Robert Drury was home again from what seems to have been his last voyage; but, as his life from this point on is wrapped in obscurity, we cannot be sure. All his early comrades, the Youngs, John Benbow, and Captain White, were dead.[114] Captain Mackett was to command the *Nightingale* for the East India Company and, after losing her at the Cape in 1722, to command the *Princess of Wales,* in which (1726–28) he made a prosperous voyage to India before his death in the spring of 1729.

Of Drury's family we know only that his sister, Elizabeth Abington, remained a widow a year or so before marrying in 1718 John Lee of Leicester, who seems to have died by 1724. Robert, John, and Mary were (upon Elizabeth's death) to inherit a third each of the Newen property in Stoke Newington, and Robert, after the death of his stepmother, was to have the property occupied by Richard Beardsley. But in 1721 Robert and John appeared before the manorial court of Stoke Newington to authenticate sale of their rights to John Curryer, a London scrivener.

In 1723 Mary Drury married George Everard of Loughborough, Clerk, and in 1726 or early in 1727 Elizabeth Drury, her mother and stepmother of the other children, died in Loughborough.

On 24 May 1729 Drury's account of his experiences and travels on Madagascar was advertised as that day published. It promised the reader that Drury would be daily available at Old Tom's Coffee House in Birchin Lane to answer questions. Whether or not he was, or, if he was, how long he continued to be available, we do not know. Old Tom's had long been a depot for books and periodicals (some Defoe's). William Duncombe, who certainly knew something about Drury and gave us the most authentic information we have previously had, said that Drury was well known (at a time un-

---

[113] St. Helena Records, vol. 6, March 1719/20, p. 73, and April 1720, p. 94.

[114] Upon finding a John Bembowe (sponsored by William Bembowe) who served as factor and writer in Sumatra in the period 1714–19, I thought for a while that John Benbow or Bembow (as he is called in *Drury's Journal*) had outlived reports of his death. But I have myself examined the burial record (22 November 1708) in St. Nicholas (then Deptford) parish church, and there is also among the State Papers of 1711 the petition of Admiral Benbow's widow in which the second son William is referred to as the oldest one surviving. The petition is mentioned in an unidentified printed clipping inserted in the P.R.O. copy of Charnock's *Biographia Navalis*, II (London, 1795), between pp. 240 and 241.

specified) as a porter at the East India House, then in Leadenhall Street; that he lived in a house in Lincoln's Inn Fields (without which clue I should never have found Drury's burial entry); and that in Madagascar he had become expert at throwing the javelin. But the East India Company, whose record of details is surprisingly minute, offers, so far as I can discover, no corroboration of his having been a porter.[115]

The Last Records

On 18 March 1729/30 the Court Minutes of the East India Company (vol. 53, p. 444) record what is the next to the last documentary information we have about Robert Drury. It reads as follows:

Request of Robert Drury being read representing he had lived on the island of Madagascar 15 years, that he has now an offer of returning thither in the Sweeds service but will not engage in it if the Company have any objection thereto, or that they will be pleased to afford him an employ in their service whereby he may be able to get a decent livelihood. Ordered that the said request be referr'd to the Committe of Shipping to examine the allegations thereof, and make report with their opinion thereupon.

The petition went to the Committee on Shipping because Drury suggested employment abroad and because the company was very anxious to keep out foreign competitors. There were stern laws against English seamen engaging in foreign ships. But the Committee on Shipping, the graveyard of many comparable requests, made no recorded report. The fact that Drury submitted such a request to the company suggests that he was employed by it; but among the numerous lists and accounts of elder porters, assistants, and other minor employees in the company's warehouses, Drury's name is not to be found.

Other interesting names appear in the Court Minutes of the 1730's and 1740's: Isaac Minet, whose son married Captain Young's granddaughter; Dr. John Arbuthnot; several Pitts; Jane, widow of Captain Mackett, who married John Champion of Wanstead; the captain's two sons, Robert and William Mackett. On 10 June 1730 the company authorized payment from the estate of Joseph Perrin of £743 14s. 6d. to the Countess of Warwick, executrix of Joseph Addison, Esq. It was doubtless the final bit of the shrunken estate of Gulston Addison, who, having succeeded Thomas Pitt as governor of Fort St. George, died there in 1709. But about Drury and his

---

[115] See also Sir William Foster's *The East India House* (London, 1924), pp. 82–83. This has a 1709 list of United Company employees which includes a housekeeper and two ushers, but no porter. There is, however, a doorkeeper (£40 salary), and a common meaning of "porter" was "doorkeeper."

friends of the *Degrave,* the *Drake,* and the *Mercury,* the company records are silent.

Whatever Drury occupied himself with after the petition of 18 March 1729/30, he had not long to work at it. As we have seen, he had been dead for some time when the second edition of *Drury's Journal* appeared in 1743. Following Duncombe's statement that Drury lived in Lincoln's Inn Fields, I began a systematic search of the records of the parishes of which Lincoln's Inn Fields was then a part. St. Andrew's Holborn and St. Giles-in-the-Fields yielded nothing. St. Dunstan in the East I did not get to because St. Clement Danes records the burial of a Robert Drury, who probably is our Robert Drury, on 15 March 1733/4.[116]

JOHN BENBOW'S STORY

As told at the Cape to the Dutch. Printed by
H. C. V. Leibbrandt in his *Précis of the
Archives of the Cape of Good Hope:
Letters Dispatched, 1696–1708,*
pp. 310–312.

9 February [1707] To the Seventeen at Amsterdam:

Our last to you were dated 27th November, 1706. Ships affairs. The "Ter Aa" brought a number of slaves to the Cape from Madagascar. At Port Dauphin the officers found the son of the deceased English Admiral Benbow, who was dressed in the same way as the natives there, and lived as intimately with them as if he also were a native of the country. At his urgent request and prayer, they took him on board on the 31st December, when they left, and brought him hither. He will most likely leave again with one of the English ships now lying here. He told us that he had left England on the 20th February, 1701, as third officer of the "Earl" (Captain Young). In June, after three months and 19 days' sail, they arrived at Pondicherry, and some time later at Masulipatam, where they had partly to discharge. The rest of the cargo was landed in Bengal. In August they arrived in Bengal, and took in other cargo. On the 25th December, 1703, they left for home. Their captain died and was succeeded by his son, who had been second officer on board. On the 3rd February they arrived at Mauritius, to stop a leak and take in provisions. On the 25th they left again. In latitude 34° or 35° South they found their ship so leaky, that they were obliged to decide to make for Madagascar. On the 26th April they arrived at the southern point of that island, at a place named Tanroy, whose king's name was Decrindo. They then had 4 feet of water in the powder magazine, and as they could not get the vessel dry, it was ready to sink every moment; the main and fore masts having already been cut. They were therefore obliged on the following day to set the ship broadside on, on shore. In a little while it was broken to pieces, and nothing was

---

[116] The Robert Drury who wrote ballad operas (1732–37), though otherwise unknown, seems to have been an attorney's clerk (*Grub-Street Journal*, no. 189, 9 August 1733). In any case he was not the Robert Drury of the *Degrave*.

saved. Three men were drowned, the rest reached the shore, and were brought by the natives to the king, who promised to show them great kindness. They found there eight white men, among them three pirates and two Scotch captains, named Drummond and Stuart, who had called there in the beginning of 1702 with two small ships, one of which was a little brigantine. They pretended that they intended to proceed to the East Coast of Africa, but beyond doubt their destination was Madagascar, to support themselves with piracy. The eight men, having come in a boat from Maratanga, intended to proceed to St. Augustine, but landed there. On the 6th May the blacks intended to kill them all, as they had only two guns and two pistols among them, but being warned by a woman they decided the following day to seize the place where the king was living with his family. In this they succeeded, and captured the king, his wife, and eldest son; having fought with sticks and handspikes, and the few firearms. They lost one dead, and had three wounded. At once taking the prisoners with them they went overland across a plain to Port Dauphin. On the way they were overtaken by the blacks with an army of 600 or 700 men, all armed with guns, who requested, and also threatened, that their king and the other prisoners might be released; promising that if they willingly delivered the king, they would give them 10 guns, which they really gave after the release of the king and queen. They kept the king's son, however, promising to release him at the extreme frontier. This they did the following day, and took four other blacks instead, to show them the way to Port Dauphin. Upon that they were followed by a large black army of 4,000 or 5,000 men, who continually threatened to break their necks. That night together they retreated behind a tamarind tree, which had fallen over, in order to be somewhat protected in case of surprise. They remained there until about 9 o'clock, and then marched down to Port Dauphin, whilst the blacks had disappeared in the forests. The next day they arrived with all their people at the Frontier River, which is pretty wide. About sunset they forded it up to their necks in water, when the blacks killed 17 or 18 of the weakest of their party, who could not proceed as well as the others. The rest did their best to reach the seashore and escape their pursuers, missing the four blacks whom they had with them. That same night the natives again attacked them on a high sandhill, and shot two of their men. They in return likewise killed some blacks. Two hours later they agreed with the blacks that they would surrender all their arms to them, which was done, that they might further remain unmolested by them, and be able to proceed to Port Dauphin. They were thereupon invited to a dinner by the blacks. Some of them, driven by hunger went thither unhesitatingly, but were surrounded and killed. The rest, about 30 persons, among them Drummond and Stuart and four of their men, pursued their way, and separated into parties of four, five, and six men; all arriving at Port Dauphin in the evening of the 14th May. They told their adventures to King Samuel, who promised them all affection and friendship. They remained four months with him, but after that, he would feed them no longer, saying that every one should look for the food which formerly they had obtained from him. Benbow and 11 men then decided to proceed to Maratanga, hoping to be received better there. After 18 days' journey they reached it, and remained a year there. The rest having died, the six survivors, not expecting a vessel there, returned to

Port Dauphin, hoping to find a ship there. After four months' stay, they were told that a ship had arrived at Maratanga, which was the yacht "Ter Aa," in 1705, for the purpose of getting slaves. Having arrived there, they remained where they were, living on sweet potatoes and other vegetables, which they had been obliged to plant themselves, until the "Ter Aa" again arrived. With her Benbow was brought over hither, not more than one man, who is semple (simple?) having survived of the whole troop, the others having died, been killed or departed with pirates.

[The rest of this letter concerns escaped slaves, etc., and has nothing to do with Benbow or Drury or the *Degrave*.]

Thirteen Years on Madagascar

The central and major part of *Robert Drury's Journal* purports to narrate Drury's life on Madagascar between the 1703 massacre and his rescue in 1716–17 and to describe his observations of the people and the natural features of the region. There was at that time no written language among the natives, and this part of the book cannot, except here and there, be authenticated with documentary evidence. Captain Oliver and Professor Moore think that instead of living among the natives Drury was really among the pirates who infested the Madagascar coast and that the narrative at least is fictitious.

In the absence of legitimate trade with Madagascar, pirate vessels offered almost the only hope of escape for shipwrecked persons. A Dutch letter from Mauritius in 1704 said that some of the English seamen with the pirate John Bowen were to be pitied because they could find no chance to get home.[1] Many so-called pirates were just such marooned seamen as the persons from the *Degrave*. In 1709 the British Council of Trade and Plantations considered the report of John Benbow, described as having lived four years among pirates, and of forty-eight relatives of Madagascar pirates, that these pirates only awaited a general pardon to return and live honestly. Some of them were elsewhere described as living in luxury and reigning over petty native kingdoms; most of them, however, were stragglers.[2]

The *History of the Pirates* says two groups of survivors from the *Degrave* joined pirate gangs, one at St. Augustine Bay on the west coast and the other, which captured a French vessel commanded by one Herault at Mattatan (Maratan or Maratanga), on the east.[3] Robert Coleson, one of the twenty-one boys listed with Drury as midshipmen on the *Degrave,* says he was at Maratanga when a

---

[1] Leibbrandt, *Précis . . . Letters Received,* pp. 353–359.

[2] P.R.O., C.O. 323, 6, nos. 79–81; *History of the Pirates* (1926), p. 419; *Robert Drury's Journal* (1890), pp. 297–298. The Council of Trade was alarmed at the prospect of a general peace in Europe. They feared that the pirates, augmented by "generating with the women of the country" and by soldiers and sailors out of employment, might become an even greater menace. Hence the urgency of getting the pirates home.

[3] (1926), pp. 417, 433.

French ship (probably Herault's) was taken. He mentions none of his comrades as present, but probably some were. He added that the pirates stopped at Fort Dauphin and took aboard John Benbow, who hoped to escape to India and from thence to England.[4]

Another of the twenty-one boys, Nicholas Dove, is described in *Robert Drury's Journal* as having escaped from such a native master as Drury's and going in a large canoe from Fort Dauphin to Maratanga.[5] There he joined pirates (the ones who took Herault's ship?) who cruised among the Moors and made their rendezvous, probably at Hopeful Point, north of Maratanga. Being vastly rich, they retired to live in ease and debauchery under a carpenter named Thomas Collins, whom they made their governor.[6] They had not been active as pirates for nine years, and Dove, with Pro, Zachary, and Samuel Burgess (sometimes called "Daniel" Burgess in the

[4] This ship seems to have been the one which in 1706 captured the *Dorothy* (Captain Penruddock) in the Red Sea (Abstracts of Letters from Coast and Bay, vol. 1, pp. 126–127). From Coleson's account the French ship seems to have been taken at Maratanga in 1703. The *History of the Pirates* (1926), pp. 433 ff., says Herault's ship was deserted by the pirates and left with the *Degrave* men at Methelage (Massalege) on the northwest coast. The latter, fitting her up to escape to India and thence to England, joined with the pirate Captain White, also "hankering after home," and made him their commander. They sailed around the south end of Madagascar, touched at "Mascarenes" and at Ambonavoula on the east coast of Madagascar, and then went to the island of Mayotte to the north of Madagascar, to prepare "for the season" to go to the Red Sea. How much time all this maneuvering took is not clear. I think it improbable that Coleson or even Benbow could have made a voyage to the Red Sea and yet have been found alone, Coleson at Maratanga late in 1705 and Benbow at Fort Dauphin late in 1706. Benbow gives a different and fuller account of his behavior.

[5] (1890), p. 298. Dove's story is much like Coleson's of going in a small boat from Fort Dauphin to Maratanga and of pirates seizing the French ship.

[6] An agent of the East India Company in Virginia (Misc. Letters Received, vol. 12, no. 256) wrote 26 November 1721 that there had been a contract between a Bristol ship, *Prince Eugene* (Captain William Stretton), "anno 1718 with one Collins a pyrate of Avery's crew who resided at Fort Dauphin [a general term for the east coast of Madagascar] and who they stiled General Collins that he should licence them to trade with the natives &c. . . ." By 1720 Collins was reported dead. The Virginia agent was trying to show that some pretended slave traders to Madagascar were encroaching on the trade of the East India Company. Both of Drury's friends, Captain Mackett and Captain White (not the pirate), are mentioned in this complaint. Drury tells us that White sold some of his slaves in Virginia in 1720.

"General Collins" was no doubt the Governor Collins of *Robert Drury's Journal* and the Thomas Collins, born in Pembroke, Wales, whom the *History of the Pirates* (1926), pp. 427–428, 521, mentions as active on the east Madagascar coast during the years 1700–1717. S. C. Hill, *Notes on Piracy in Eastern Waters* (Bombay, 1923), p. 145, mistakenly cites *Drury's Journal* as saying Thomas Collins was a carpenter on the *Degrave*. Could the old Nick of Dover, whom Hill (p. 140) reports as a former member of Halsey's crew surviving on St. Mary's Island in 1719, possibly be Nick Dove?

History of the Pirates, "Daniel" being a joking name for a pirate), had moved to Massalege on the northwest coast.

By his own admission Drury, in his last years on Madagascar, met these and other pirates. But there is not the slightest evidence that he was aboard a pirate ship or a member of a pirate gang. Those who think he was have disbelieved many parts of his story which I have already shown to be true. In the absence of evidence to the contrary, the probability is that in the main this central story is true also and that on the whole it records Drury's experiences on Madagascar during the years 1703–16.

From the preface to *Robert Drury's Journal* we know that Drury had help from a "transcriber" and that the story as printed had been, to an undetermined degree, modified by him. The author of the preface (obviously the transcriber) assures us that "in all those places where religion is touched on" he has put "some reflections in the author's mouth," as he "could not pass such remarkable . . . topics without making proper applications, and taking useful instructions from them." And, though he denies altering any facts or adding "any fiction of his own," probably he did expand accounts which he thought too brief and distort others which he misunderstood, like the drowning of Samuel de Paz at Madapollam. In an otherwise truthful account, we are told that the victim was Lapie and the place Madras. But the transcriber would not play down piratical adventures or associations which Drury himself dared to record. The burden of proof, then, is on those who deny Drury a major part in writing the central story or hold it to be fictitious. If Drury leads us into the dark woods of Madagascar and at the end leads us out again, we have good reason to think we have been with him in the meantime. And there is evidence that this is so.

This evidence is of four kinds: (1) documents, including some already presented; (2) opinions of Drury's contemporaries; (3) opinions of missionaries and other authorities on Madagascar; and (4) internal evidence.

Those contemporary documents which corroborate Drury's account of the *Degrave* and of the *Drake* throw light on both ends of the central story. We have seen that the petition of the *Degrave's* owners and still more the statements of Coleson and Benbow to their Dutch rescuers confirm the most questionable detail of Drury's story—the presence of Drummond and Stewart at the place where the *Degrave* foundered and participation in the attempted escape from King Crindo before the massacre. Since Drury's account is fuller and more accurate than Benbow's, speculation about whether the "Drury" information came from Benbow's journal (burned in 1714) is idle. Drury or Defoe could have talked with John Benbow's brother William, who until 1723 was a clerk in the Navy Office and died on the eve of the publication of *Robert Drury's Journal;* but the scant attention given to John Benbow's later career indicates that they did not, and renders plausible Drury's casual remark that he learned of Benbow's rescue from Nick Dove in Madagascar in 1716. Of Coleson's escape Drury seems not to have known at all. Benbow's account and, to a lesser degree, Coleson's more fragmentary one supplement Drury's with such minor contradictions as normally appear in honest records.

Whether Nick Dove had had opportunities to return home prior to 1716, when Mackett rescued Drury, we do not know. Had he dared, he probably could have returned with Mackett as Burgess is said to have intended doing.[7] Nick was the son of a widow dependent upon her brother, a cheesemonger in East Smithfield. But Benbow and Drury had great incentives to keep their records clean and to return home as early as possible. Benbow was son of a famous admiral; and Drury, of a prosperous innkeeper. Both could hope to return to England and hence were less likely than Dove to have turned pirates, though circumstances could have forced them temporarily to board pirate ships.

Most of the survivors from the *Degrave* were stragglers. Except for the boy on the *Raper* in 1705, none of them escaped from Madagascar easily, and few escaped at all. Benbow, who with resolute men like Captain Drummond reached a friendly king at a well-known seaport, was forced to go native and live in abject circumstances until rescued. Like Coleson at Maratanga,[8] Benbow was alone at Fort Dauphin when the Dutch found him. He was dressed like the natives and was living "as intimately with them as if he also were a native." His diet was sweet potatoes and other vegetables which he and his five comrades (then either dead or gone with pirates) had had to plant for themselves. The Dutch described him as "semple."[9] His health was broken, and he died a year after reach-

[7] The *History of the Pirates* (1926), p. 529, adds that Burgess later entered the *Drake's* sister ship commanded by Captain Harvey and that he died (possibly poisoned by a native king) before Harvey was ready to sail.

[8] The Dutch brought to the Cape with Coleson a half-breed from India named Symon Jansen; but they were found at different places—Jansen at Maningare and Coleson at Maratanga some distance farther south. Jansen had escaped from a pirate ship.

[9] "Semple" is Leibbrandt's translation of *zunpel* (see p. 45 above).

ing England. Drummond drifted about Madagascar in a wretched state for a number of years before meeting a violent death.[10]

It is not inconsistent with the experiences of these comrades that Drury should have been kept for several years by a cruel master like Mevarrow. Far from being improbable, it is paralleled by other unfortunates of the time. Robert Knox's long captivity on Ceylon in the previous century is well known. Those who say the Malagasy would not have imprisoned white men could have said the same thing about the Sinhalese.[11] Other whites had found them peaceful and friendly; but Knox, a youth of eighteen or so, his father, and members of his crew were in 1659 captured and kept on Ceylon for a long time. Knox's father and others died there. Knox and a friend escaped only at the end of nineteen years; and one of the party escaped to reach England after nearly a half-century in captivity.

This captivity has been explained as a whim of the Sinhalese king to make a menagerie of Europeans and the disinclination of the latter to make a determined effort to escape. The fact remains that the Sinhalese, in temper much like the Malagasy, made captive a group of white adults and kept them longer than the boy Drury is said to have stayed on Madagascar. In a manuscript, not published till 1911, Knox tells us that he and some of his crew were seized by a Madagascar king and released only after taking two natives as hostages. Professor Moore regards this as evidence that the Drury captivity was fiction, suggested by Knox's account. But this account was not published until 1911, and we have independent testimony to the truth of the Drury capture.

Robert Everard's "Relation of Three Years Suffering" on Madagascar, though less credible than Drury's, proves true wherever it can be checked.[12] Everard was rescued by an Arab vessel in 1690 or 1691 from a life among the natives.[13] A mulatto seaman from an

[10] Misc. Letters Received, vol. 1, no. 192 (letter by Charles Robertson, 7 September 1709). Robertson was interviewing seamen in the Thames about Scottish competition with the English company and turned up information about Samuel Burgess and the *Neptune*. The only known report of Drummond's death is in the preface to *Drury's Journal;* the writer, doubtless Defoe, says he learned it from Drury's rescuer, Captain Mackett.

[11] *Historical Relation of . . . Ceylon*, ed. by James Ryan (Glasgow, 1911), p. xiii.

[12] Though the full title places Everard's suffering on "the coast of Assada [an island] near Madagascar" (Awnsham and John Churchill, *A Collection of Voyages*, VI [London, 1732], 257–282), a careful reading of the text shows that it occurred on Madagascar itself. Everard had nothing to do with phrasing the title.

[13] See records of the *Bawden* (and other ships mentioned in the "Relation") in the India Office Library, and Sloane MS 3672 in the British Museum. Pro-

English vessel was captured and kept prisoner for sixteen years (1700–1716—simultaneously with Drury's stay on Madagascar) at Magadoxa, across from Madagascar on the east coast of Africa. His comrades, like those of Everard and Drury, were slaughtered by the natives. He finally escaped by swimming an alligator-infested river to a Dutch ship. In 1724 he wrote an extended account of his experiences which appeared in the second volume of the *History of the Pirates* in 1728,[14] a year before the publication of *Robert Drury's Journal*.

Finally there is the incontrovertible fact that, whether unusual or not, Drury and the whole *Degrave* party of approximately 150 whites were captured by King Crindo and that they regarded their escape as hopeless without the use of force.

The Romantic Story of King Samuel

The extraordinary coincidence, recorded in *Robert Drury's Journal*, that Captain Drummond's party was with King Crindo when the *Degrave* foundered nearby, turns out, as we have seen, to be fact. Another extraordinary report from Drury's early years on Madagascar, long regarded as fiction, likewise proves to be fact, or at least not to be an invention of Drury or Defoe. It is the story of Tuley-Noro, or King Samuel, of Fort Dauphin, to whose province the *Degrave* party (most of them in vain) attempted to escape.

Drury's sketch of King Samuel begins with a Captain Mesmerrico who "about ninety years ago" killed the native king of Anosy (Fort Dauphin) and carried his son to France. Years later (though Drury implies not recently) a French ship in distress for food and water stopped at Fort Dauphin and made a treaty of friendship with the old queen, mother of the stolen prince. One day, having been entertained aboard the French ship, this queen paused to watch the sailors bathing in the harbor and to wonder at the whiteness of their skin. Seeing one darker than the rest coming ashore to dress, she noted a mole under his left pap and ran to him in excitement.

fessor Moore suggested that Everard's story, printed three years after *Robert Drury's Journal*, may have been read in manuscript by Defoe. My discovery that the report of Magadoxa in the *History of the Pirates* was taken (probably by Defoe) from another manuscript in the possession of Sir Hans Sloane gives Moore's suggestion greater probability. Though Everard's story was not essential to the composition of *Robert Drury's Journal*, it is interesting that several Everards crop up in Drury's circle. A John Everard is paired with Drury in the *Degrave* ledger, and a George Everard of Loughborough, Clerk, married Drury's half sister Mary in 1723.
[14] Pp. 144–216. The illustrated original manuscript is Sloane MS 2992 in the British Museum.

After examining the mole more closely she threw her arms about him and cried out that he was the son who had been carried away. She showed the mole to others and convinced them. This was Samuel, who presently was made king and given a native name. About three or four years before we were cast away, says Drury, a drunken seaman who blurted out that Samuel was an impostor and that the real prince was still in France was promptly shot for his indiscretion and his comrades warned to leave and never return.[15]

Captain Oliver thought King Samuel might have been the Tom Similo, described in 1756 as a son of the pirate Tew and a native princess, who ruled in the northeastern part of the island.[16] The Grandidiers replied that Tom Similo lived too far away and too late. They thought that Drury had here mixed three stories: (1) that of Le Vacher, alias La Case, who married a princess of Ambolo and ruled there as Andrian Pousse; (2) that of Andrian Ramach, whom the Portuguese carried away from Fort Dauphin; (3) that of Essomeric, a prince carried away to France by Captain Gonneville in 1605.

It is probable that Drury's Mesmerrico is an echo of Essomeric and impossible that the mother of a prince stolen ninety years earlier could have been alive when Samuel became king. But the confusion was doubtless in the minds of the natives from whom Drury got the story. For King Samuel was a real person, however unknown he was to Captain Oliver. There is in the Public Record Office in Chancery Lane a document of 31 October 1699 which was signed as "A B^m. Samuel Rx [Rex]" and sealed in red wax with a cross and a lamb like the seal of the Templars.[17] The document is a letter of title to the *Prophet Daniel,* a vessel which Abraham Samuel, King of Fort "Dolphin," had sold to some pirates.

A Dutch record, not published until 1887, tells us with fewer details and some variations Drury's very story of how Samuel came to be king. Captain Jan Coin, who had been sent from the Cape to Madagascar for slaves, wrote (20 November 1699) that at Fort Dauphin two Englishmen, having warned him that King Samuel planned to seize his ship, begged to be carried to Batavia and en route gave an account of the "whole affair." Their story was that Samuel was a half-breed from Martinoco in the West Indies and that he had arrived twenty-two months earlier (i.e., 20 January 1698 N.S.) in the *John and Rebecca,* taken by a Captain Orr from

[15] (1890), p. 105.

[16] (1890), p. 44n.

[17] The document is attached to a letter of Captain Rupert (not Robert, as Hill, *Notes,* p. 127, gives it) Billingsley of H.M.S. *Margate,* 13 May 1700, in Ad 1/1462.

the French in the West Indies and brought to St. Mary's Island, near the east coast of Madagascar. There Orr transferred command to Samuel just before his own death.[18] Captain Samuel brought the ship to Taòlanara (Fort Dauphin) and lost it for want of good anchors.

Drury places the arrival of Samuel much earlier and, as we have seen, describes the ship as in command of a Frenchman en route home from India. And, whereas Drury says the queen discovered the mole which she thought proved Samuel her son, Coin says only that the natives observed him bathing and "noticed certain marks on his body." After he had been made king, Coin concludes, Samuel warred against his predecessor, described as his younger brother Dimarung Dimera. According to Drury there was no such brother. Whether these differences are the embroiderings of Defoe, of Drury, or of the natives, they do not obscure the fact that both accounts are on the whole records of what was being told about King Samuel on southeast Madagascar at the time, and that Drury tells the story much as he heard it there.

Drury's description of King Samuel as a benevolent ruler under whom whites "lived free and entirely at their own disposal" is only partially in harmony with Benbow's. Benbow reported that after four months Samuel forced him and the others from the *Degrave* to find their own food. The difference between the two views is explainable as coming from a distant and an intimate acquaintance with the king. Drury's view is not so much evidence of invention as corroboration of his statement that he never reached Fort Dauphin.

A more puzzling circumstance is the episode in which, according to Drury, King Samuel, accompanied by Benbow, Captains Drummond and Stewart, and the other white man in the party, invaded Androy to punish Crindo for the massacre or at least to rescue Drury. The story goes that the price for Drury was agreed upon (two buccaneer guns) when a misunderstanding prevented the exchange. "Captain Drummond, being glad to see me, called me by name and asked how I did." When Drury's master prevented a reply, the whites thought Drury had not heard and stepped closer. The master, fearing a plot to seize the boy without payment of the ransom, precipitated a fight between the two armies and ended all negotiation.[19]

[18] Hill, *Notes*, pp. 127–128, calls him John Hore and gives a fuller account of his piratical career. Samuel seems to have been his quartermaster. H. C. V. Leibbrandt, *Rambles Through the Archives of the . . . Cape of Good Hope, 1688–1700* (Cape Town, 1887), pp. 161–168.

[19] The episode may be either a fabrication or a campaign colored by Drury so as to seem more concerned with his lot than it actually was. In various details elsewhere also Drury gives himself a somewhat improbably important role.

The Dutch abstract of Benbow's journal does not mention this expedition. We must remember, however, that this abstract, though very detailed about the events prior to Fort Dauphin, gives only the briefest sketch of Benbow's subsequent adventures. Drummond and Stewart, much more important than Drury to Benbow, are not mentioned again after the party reached Fort Dauphin. We are told only that after at least four months Benbow and eleven comrades went northward to Maratanga for a year; that six of these comrades died; and that Benbow and the other five returned to Fort Dauphin, where, as we have seen, the Dutch in December 1706 found only Benbow.

Though the Dutch abstract of Benbow's journal ignores the expedition to rescue Drury, its account of Benbow's movements dovetails chronologically with Drury's account of it. Drury places the expedition about two and a half years after the massacre—that is, about November 1705, when Coleson was being rescued at Maratanga. The Benbow chronology is not altogether clear or consistent. But obviously he and his five remaining companions had returned from Maratanga to Fort Dauphin by the spring or summer of 1705. Benbow seems to have remained there until rescued over a year later. He would then have been on hand to accompany such an expedition as Drury describes.[20]

It is less certain that Drummond and Stewart were then in Fort Dauphin. But since my original skepticism concerning Drury's story of their presence with King Crindo, when the *Degrave* was wrecked upon his coast in 1703, has been resolved by indisputable proof that they were there, I am more willing to accept this more credible story that they were with King Samuel in 1705. This is upon the supposition that they were among the five comrades who returned with Benbow from Maratanga and who, say the Dutch, had "been killed or departed with pirates" before the rescue of Benbow a year or so after the time Drury assigns to the expedition.

On the whole Drury's account of the expedition is convincing. The misunderstanding which prevents his rescue is the kind of thing that often determines the course of events. Defoe may have improved upon the details; but some such incident may have occurred. At least the account reveals too much knowledge of King Samuel and local conditions to have been made out of whole cloth. The Drury

[20] Drury speaks as though all the whites who had escaped to Fort Dauphin were present with King Samuel's army. But he could not have been sure of that, or of the number of the whites who had escaped. Earlier (1890, p. 73) he had given the figure as nine or ten, whereas Benbow said about thirty and Coleson about eighteen.

account describes King Samuel as so ill that he had to be carried and that he died two months later—early in 1706. The Dutch corroborate this last detail. When they rescued Benbow at the end of that year they were received by Dimaressive, whom they described as successor to King Samuel. The implication is that the latter had died in the recent past.

Just as Benbow's journal and Dutch records illumine Drury's early years on Madagascar, other records illumine the later ones. *Drury's Journal* tells us that three years or so before Drury's rescue Captain Wilks in the *Clapham* had been on the west coast and had rescued William Thornbury, another Englishman who had been adrift on Madagascar almost as long as Drury; [21] that Drury's brother accidentally met this Thornbury in a Rotherhithe alehouse and so learned that Robert was still alive; and that thereupon Robert's father arranged, through a Mr. Terry, to have a commander (obviously Captain Mackett) rescue Robert. *Drury's Journal* gives us also a letter purporting to come from John Drury to "Son Robert Drury," to have been written at Loughborough, 27 February 1715/16, and to have been delivered by Captain Mackett later in 1716.

Not all of these statements can be verified. There were a Mr. Terry (or Tirrey) and a Mr. Thornburgh both in the employ of the East India Company in London; and there was a Thornbury living in the 1680's in Crutched Friars.[22] These may or may not have significance for the persons whom *Drury's Journal* mentions. But we know that Drury had a younger brother (John) and that the *Clapham,* with Captain Wilks as commander, arrived at Sumatra 11 August 1714 with slaves from Madagascar, that by 15 November 1714 it was at the Cape of Good Hope (en route home), and that by 23 July 1715 it had reached England.[23] Whether it would have taken Thornbury from Madagascar on the way to Sumatra or on the return we can only guess.

It is improbable but possible that Drury (or Defoe) could have got the details of the *Clapham*'s voyage after the book was in process of being written and that the Thornbury incident could have been invented. But he could not have invented the implications in John Drury's will (P.C.C., Fox, 1716, 204), dated a little over two months later than the letter to "Son Robert Drury" just

---

[21] (1890), pp. 273, 279.

[22] Near which Drury was born. See poll-tax lists of Aldgate ward.

[23] East India Company, Sumatra Records, vol. 7, pp. 126 ff.; Misc. Letters Received, vol. 6, no. 78, and vol. 8, no. 76 (letter of John Addison); *Précis . . . Journal,* pp. 261–263, in which Wilks is miscalled Miles.

mentioned, and, like the letter, composed at Loughborough. It implies what, after Robert's fifteen-year absence, would have been
improbable had there been no recent news of him, that his return
was expected and that children by native wives were feared. Besides answering those who think Robert Drury was the boy mentioned by Luttrell as having returned in 1705 with news of the
Degrave disaster, this letter, with the father's will, strengthens the
Drury story of William Thornbury's having brought news of Robert
to his brother in London.

In 1716 Captain William Mackett in the *Drake,* Captain White in
the *Mercury,* Captain Bloom in the *Sarah,* Captain Harvey in the
Henry, and Captain Henry Mackett in the *Mercury,* sloop (*Drury's
Journal* calls it a ketch), did, as *Drury's Journal* says, go to Madagascar for slaves. Drury implies that all belonged to the same owners.
Four of them, however, were sent out by one group of merchants
(Sitwell, Houblon, and Hyde), and the other, the *Sarah,* by another
group led by William Heynsham. Though Mackett and Bloom
(of the *Sarah*) collaborated in friendly fashion, Drury is probably
more correct when he tells us that Mackett and Bloom finally separated, the latter going to Fort Dauphin and the former remaining
on the northwest coast.[24] But we do not know all the owners of
these ships. Drury says that Mackett was an important owner in
them. He was later a man of considerable wealth, and it is possible
that he owned part of even the *Sarah.*

It seems clear that Drury was with Mackett on the voyage home
to England. And that fact renders even more certain Drury's account
of his parting with his native master and friends—an account which
has all the earmarks of truth without such corroboration. It tells
us that when Drury, having been released by Rer Moume upon receipt of a letter from Captain Mackett, came to the seaside at Yong-
Owl, the steward of the *Drake* took him for a wild man and sent
word to Mackett that "the wild Englishman was come." Like others
after years of separation from their countrymen, he was for several
days at a loss for English words. He stared at Captain Mackett and
Captain Bloom "as if I had never seen a white man clothed before;
and what added to the wildness of my appearance, I was naked
except the lamber, my skin swarthy and full of freckles, my hair
long and felted together, so that I really made a frightful appearance to them. . . ."[25] But the steward cut his hair, ordered him

[24] (1890), p. 295.
[25] (1890), pp. 293–294.

shaved, and "clothed in a neat seaman's habit." The sea and the change of food, he tells us, made him sick for several days.

Drury tells us that at Massalege he met the well-known pirates Burgess, Zachary, and Pro, with whom was "Nick," who turned out to be Nicholas Dove, one of Drury's fellow apprentices on the *Degrave*. Nick, "one of the four boys who were saved with me at the massacre of our ship's company," had, he said, run off to Fort Dauphin and after two years (i.e., *ca.* 1705) had got to Mattatanna Road where he joined a band of pirates. These pirates had been in retirement for the preceding nine years. All this has a high degree of probability. Pro, a Dutchman, had, with a Welshman named David Williams or Wallen, been captured by H.M.S. *Scarborough* on the east coast of Madagascar 19 November 1703 and had escaped at Mohilla on 28 February following.[26] The journals of the captain and the master of the *Scarborough* in the Public Record Office do not mention the capture; but they mention the escape from the sister ship, the *Severn*, on 28 February 1703/4. About the career of Samuel Burgess we have a good deal of documentary evidence, and he, Pro, and Zachary are mentioned in the *History of the Pirates* as at Yong-Owl when Mackett was there in 1716. All this lends support to Drury's account of meeting these men and of his conversation with them.

This examination has established a considerable amount of factual matter in Drury's account of his earlier and closing years on the island, and it reduces the central core of his unchecked career there from thirteen to less than ten years. Let us see next what further light can be shed by Drury's contemporaries. Now that we have other evidence that Captain Mackett did rescue Drury in 1716–17, we may examine the statement attributed to Mackett in *Drury's Journal* and learn something of how it was composed. Mackett is mentioned in the title and is credited with having written a certificate which appears on the verso of the title page and with certain relevant information in the preface. The certificate reads:

This is to Certify, That Robert Drury, Fifteen Years a Slave in Madagascar, now living in London, was redeem'd from thence and brought into England, his Native Country, by Myself. I esteem him an honest, industrious Man, of good Reputation, and do firmly believe that the Account he gives of his Strange and Surprising Adventures is Genuine and Authentick.

Wm. MACKETT

May 7, 1728

[26] See *History of the Pirates*, II (London, 1728), 260, and a journal of the *Scarborough* in the British Museum, Sloane MS 3674.

The author of the preface, certainly not Drury and probably Defoe, tells us that he had serious doubts about the validity of the certificate, but that upon inquiry into Mackett's character and Mackett's opportunity to learn the details of Drury's experiences he was convinced of the truth of the certificate. The preface continues that "the Captain . . . confirmed . . . to me in conversation" Drury's statements about Mackett's property in the *Drake* and other vessels and Drury's identification of Captain Drummond, who (Mackett reports) was slain at Tullea (west Madagascar) by a Jamaican Negro named Lewes. The preface adds that Mackett had "continued his friendship for Drury, even to be his Patron to this day. . . ."

What does all this amount to? How probable is it, and what light has it for us? Professor Moore says it has none at all; the phrase "Strange and Surprising Adventures" in the certificate is right out of the title of *Robinson Crusoe,* and in general the certificate is an imitation of one in Robert Knox's *Ceylon.* Mackett, to continue Moore's argument, had been a slave trader and a partner of pirates; and he was possibly absent in India or dead in 1729, so that Defoe could flourish his name without authority.

But with the authentication of a large part of the story, we can no longer dismiss these prefatory statements as mere literary tricks. Mackett, I discover, did die a few weeks before *Drury's Journal* appeared in 1729; but he was probably alive when it went to press, and he was certainly in London a year earlier on the date given in the certificate and during most of the following year. There is nothing inherently improbable in supposing that he *signed* the certificate (which Defoe may have written for him), or that Defoe talked with him about Drury's story. After all, Mackett had rescued Drury and brought him home. Mackett's oldest son, born after Drury's rescue, was named Robert, a fact which agrees with (though there may be other explanations) the statement in the preface that Mackett had "continued his friendship for Drury, even to be his Patron to this day. . . ."

Who Was Captain Mackett?

Captain William Mackett came from the London parish of St. Katherine Cree, in which Robert Drury was born. Several of Mackett's brothers were, like him, seamen. From 1715 to 1720 he commanded the *Drake,* in the slave trade to Guinea and Madagascar. In 1721 the East India Company placed him in command of a new ship named for one of the company directors, Sir Robert Nightingale. The *Nightingale* on its maiden voyage foundered with the

Addison and the *Chandos* in a storm at the Cape of Good Hope, 7 June 1722; and late in 1726 Mackett was sworn commander of another East India Company vessel, the *Princess of Wales*. He returned from his only Indian voyage in her on 23 March 1727/28. He completed his unloading and on 8 May 1728 turned in his journal.[27] The certificate in *Drury's Journal* is dated a day earlier, 7 May 1728. Could one have picked by chance a time so likely for Mackett to have signed the certificate? Another significant detail is the spelling of the name. The newspapers and the *History of the Pirates* called him Maggott; and in the preface and the text of *Drury's Journal* his name is spelled Macket. Only in the subscription to this certificate is the name given correctly as Wm. Mackett, precisely as he signed it in the receipt book of the *Nightingale*[28] and elsewhere.

Neither Defoe nor Drury would have ventured to use Mackett's name without permission while Mackett was active about London, as he was in 1728–29, collecting money which the East India Company owed him. That he was highly respected is obvious from the company's treatment of him even before he entered its service. If not rich, he was certainly well off.[29] *Drury's Journal* was advertised as published on 24 May, but may have appeared earlier. The title reference to Mackett as late commander of the *Prince[ss] of Wales* may mean only that he no longer commanded her. If it is an allusion to his death, the matter in the title page was written just before publication. Large payments by the company to him and later to his wife for diamonds in his cargo confirm the implication of wealth in his will. In it he mentioned a fortune to be divided among his children and chose three well-known merchants to administer it.[30]

Why should Mackett not certify the truth of a story in which he had played an honorable part? What happened may have been this. Defoe phrased the certificate, and on 7 May 1728, possibly with

[27] Court Minutes, vol. 52, pp. 159, 452, vol. 53, pp. 15, 22, 52, 58, 60, 242, 401, 915–916, and vol. 56, p. 327.

[28] Marine Records, 795A.

[29] Court Minutes, vol. 53, p. 242, records the payment to him on 30 May 1729 of a sum of over £4,000.

[30] They were released in 1748, when Robert Mackett, his mother having remarried and died, secured an order of administration of the undistributed property. A William Mackett, who seems to have been the captain's second son, went to India as a company writer in 1740. See Court Minutes, vol. 58, p. 560, and vol. 59, p. 226. One of the executors was John Hyde, part owner of the *Drake* and her sister ships, a fact which strengthens statements in *Drury's Journal* that Mackett owned a considerable part in them. Mackett was an aristocrat of the merchant service, and the authors and publishers of *Drury's Journal* were well aware of it.

the help of Drury (who is said by a writer in the *Gentleman's Magazine* in 1769 to have been a porter in the East India House), hunted up Mackett at the docks or at the East India House in Leadenhall Street. On such an occasion Defoe could have held the conversation which is summarized in the preface.

Dr. Campbell and Hughes Minet

Other eighteenth-century witnesses can now have their testimony examined with less suspicion than formerly. Hughes Minet, great-grandson of the *Degrave*'s commander, Captain William Young, obviously knew what he was saying in his manuscript notes in copies of *Drury's Journal*. Dr. John Campbell was not so careless in his methods as has been charged. And William Duncombe shines in the armor of truth. Paul Carlton, Benbow's brother-in-law, seems to deserve the strictures upon his snobbery and dishonesty; but he was probably the only one of those who saw Benbow after his return from Madagascar, though Duncombe knew Benbow's brother William and had a friend who knew Drury.

Dr. Campbell's *Lives of the British Admirals* (1744) made the earliest-known comments on *Drury's Journal*. His life of Admiral Benbow was followed by a sketch of the admiral's eldest son. Having mentioned the foundering of the *Degrave*, the massacre, and the escape of young Benbow to Fort Dauphin, mostly from *Drury's Journal*, he added an account, verified by several (not just Carlton) who had heard it from Benbow's own mouth, of Benbow's harsh life among the natives and his rescue by a Dutch captain. Campbell may be wrong about the Dutch captain's having known Benbow's father, the admiral, and certainly was wrong in saying that Benbow lived many years afterward in England and wrote an elaborate geographical treatise on Madagascar, which unfortunately had been lost.[31] *Drury's Journal*, Campbell says, "so far as it relates to Mr. Benbow, is very exact, as I have been informed by this Gentleman's Relations."

William Duncombe, brother-in-law of the poet-critic and essayist John Hughes, had been a clerk in the Navy Office with John Benbow's brother William. In a letter published just after his death in 1769, Duncombe corrected Campbell's report of an elaborate treatise on Madagascar by John Benbow. In a remarkably accurate report of a fifty-six-year-old event, Duncombe said that William Benbow had read his deceased brother's book to him in 1713 and that to the

[31] Campbell repeated much of this in *Biographia Britannica*, I (1747), 688–689, and II (1780), 166–167.

best of his recollection it was only a seaman's journal.[32] The book had been burned in a fire the next year; but the loss, he says, is the less to be regretted because Robert Drury, one of the boys who escaped the massacre and lived many years on Madagascar, wrote a particular account which, so far as Benbow's journal went, tallied exactly with it.

Similar corroboration comes from the family of the *Degrave's* commander, Captain William Young. Alice Watson Young, his wife, lived until 1750. Their daughter Elizabeth, as we have seen, was the widow (with a young daughter, Alice Hughes) who married William Veel (or Veal) in 1705. What Elizabeth and her mother thought about the history of the *Degrave* in *Drury's Journal* and the death of Elizabeth's father in India and of her brother, Nicholas Young, on Madagascar, we know through Elizabeth's oldest grandchild, Hughes Minet, who, though not born until 1731, tells us that he well remembers his great-grandmother (Captain Young's wife); that she died in his father's home; that he had often read *Drury's Journal* and talked with his grandmother Elizabeth about it; and that as far as the family knew the historical events behind it, the book was scrupulously accurate.[33]

You may, if you like, smile at the credulity of Dr. Campbell, Duncombe, and Elizabeth Veal and her grandson. But we must remember that these people were much closer to the events related in *Drury's Journal*, with opportunities for judging which we can never have, and that they found nothing in it to doubt. And since they, and William Duncombe especially, have been proved accurate in nearly every detail on which we have any evidence at all, we must regard the whole story as substantially true. Their several strands of testimony hang together, and with other supporting strands make an almost unbreakable rope of fact.

Other things being equal, the opinion of those who have been on Madagascar must be more convincing than that of those who have merely read about it. And when, to quote Captain Oliver, who disagreed, we find that "Good old Samuel Copland, Captain Owen and his Lieutenant Boteler, William Ellis the Apostle and Politician, Dr. Mullens, Messrs. Sibree, Richardson, and the missionaries of all sects, have indeed generally, if not altogether, adopted as gospel truth and literal matter of fact Drury's statements as to the manners

---

[32] *Gentleman's Magazine*, XXXIX (1769), 171–172.

[33] See Minet, "Daniel Defoe and Kent," pp. 61–74. Hughes Minet's notes, in a copy of an 1807 edition of *Drury's Journal*, with some correspondence of the late Mr. William Minet, have been placed in the British Museum by Mr. Minet's daughter, Miss Susan Minet.

and customs of the Sakalava tribes, and pinned their faith, as to
the testimony from an eye-witness, on the incidents and adventures"
of Drury,[34] we must admit that their opinion carries more weight
than ours, unless we have positive evidence to the contrary. These
missionaries had no question whatever about the accuracy of *Drury's
Journal*. They were surprised and delighted again and again to find
there depicted aspects of speech and behavior which only one who
had lived long among the natives could have known. Captain
Oliver, who had compiled an elaborate bibliography of works on
Madagascar, found that *Drury's Journal* held in England "the
same honourable position that the great standard work of De
Flacourt" held among French authors on Madagascar, and that not
a single work on Madagascar has been published since which does
not quote, one way or another, largely from Drury's observations.[35]
Oliver argued vigorously against acceptance of *Drury's Journal* as
factual; but he went on to say that British writers were not unique
in their acceptance of it. The "Swedish missionaries . . . and all
the best authorities in France, notably MM. Noel and Barbié du
Bocage, Captains Guillain and De Langle . . . and, above all, the
supreme modern authority on . . . Madagascar, M. A. Grandidier
. . . every one of them firmly believes the unsophisticated story of
the poor deserted cabin-boy, Robin." [36]

William Ellis, Foreign Secretary of the London Missionary Society, had not been to Madagascar when he published his history of
the island in 1838. But he did not change his opinion of *Drury's
Journal* after having been there several times later and having lived
there for over four years in the 1860's. T. Sibree, author of the
article on Madagascar in all but the most recent editions of the
Encyclopaedia Britannica, and J. Richardson were both missionaries
on the island. Richardson published in the *Antananarivo Annual*
(1875) a comment on Drury's English-Malagasy word list, which
Captain Oliver printed in his 1890 edition of *Drury's Journal*.[37]
Richardson, who later compiled the *New Malagasy-English Dictionary* (Antananarivo, 1885), asserted that nothing had given him
so much pleasure as Drury's word list. "Many of the words," he
added, "are there just as the Betsileo would speak them to this day."

When we pass from missionaries to scientists, we get even stronger
affirmations of the Drury story. Here I shall discuss only the

---

[34] *Robert Drury's Journal* (1890), p. 9.
[35] (1890), pp. 9–10.
[36] (1890), pp. 9–10.
[37] Pp. 316–318.

Grandidiers, Alfred and Guillaume, who with collaborators have produced nearly half a hundred massive volumes on Madagascar. These are chiefly in two collections. The first, planned in thirty-nine enormous volumes but incomplete, is entitled *Histoire naturelle, physique, et politique de Madagascar* (Paris, 1875–1928).[38] The second, entitled *Collection des ouvrages anciens concernant Madagascar* (Paris, 1903–20), is in nine volumes. Drury and his book are mentioned many times in both works; but it is in the second that he looms large. *Drury's Journal*, translated into French from Captain Oliver's text, and annotations upon it fill volume IV (1906).

The Grandidiers are positive that *Drury's Journal* is on the whole faithfully related matter of fact written by Drury but that here and there it is marred by inventions of the editor. All who have written on Madagascar, they tell us, agree that it gives wholly new and important information on the south and west parts of Madagascar.[39] As to themselves, who had traveled among the Antandroy, the Mahafaly, and the Sakalavas, "nous ne pouvons que reconnaître la véracité de beaucoup de ses descriptions." Émile Blanchard, William Lee, and Captain Oliver had doubted its claim to historicity; but it seems certain that only a man who had lived the life of the natives for a long time would be able to give the *véridique* and new *renseignements* one finds on every page of Drury's book. The Grandidiers have observed many details of the manners of the people of the south, of which only Drury had previously spoken, and a multitude of words given exactly by him for the first time. They were convinced that Drury had not *rédigé* his narrative, which they found at some points fantastic and apocryphal, and that his social position was less somber than the book paints it. The editor has, they say, imagined the views on politics, the comparison of Malagasy morals with European, the elevated sentiments credited to certain of the natives, and certain inaccurate geographical details.

Some of these discrepancies are incontrovertible and damaging errors. The account of Drury's escape from Androy to St. Augustine Bay introduced nonexistent topographical features, something like Defoe's account of Captain Singleton in crossing Central America.[40] Some are simple mistakes of the sort that travelers are constantly making. Others may only seem discrepancies. Blanchard, the first to

[38] *Histoire . . . de Madagascar*, vol. IV, tome I, pp. 498–505, summarizes *Drury's Journal*, and gives an account of King Samuel on p. 472.

[39] *Collection*, IV, 3 (note 1), and *passim*.

[40] *Collection*, IV, 266.

express doubt of the Drury story, scoffed at the idea of a white man being kept in slavery by Madagascar natives.[41] The Grandidiers think that a native chief, out of pride or in self-defense, might have kept Drury from escaping, but doubt that Drury was really a slave. Another point much doubted is Drury's account of slaves and wives licking the feet of their masters. Drury says that he had licked his master's feet so long that involuntarily he stooped to lick the feet of his deliverer Captain Mackett.

Captain Oliver, whose firsthand knowledge of Madagascar was considerable, thought the practice of licking feet very rare, if it existed at all; but he quoted a passage from the Rev. George Peake of the London Missionary Society which gives two instances of the custom and implies that they seem to indicate a general practice.[42] For, as Peake points out, the native word for submission, *milelalapadia,* means to lick the sole of the foot. The Grandidiers are equally positive that the custom was an ancient one to mark absolute submission to a superior.

Most of the discrepancies and errors which the Grandidiers point out do not seriously weaken the case for Drury's observations as the source of the story.[43] Though the fox does not exist upon the island, the Grandidiers admit (208:261) that Drury meant a dangerous feline, the *fossa.* They deny (260:332) Drury's statement that there are, or were, monkeys, baboons, or *virjees* (the Grandidiers use the word *varika*); but they give several volumes of their *Histoire* to lemurs or *maques.* They deny *pommes de terre* but allow *patates* (sweet potatoes or yams), which Drury calls *ovy* (yams) and differentiates from potatoes. Drury found crayfish on the south Madagascar coast, where the Grandidiers say (207:255) there are none; and he described the ubiquitous *tuluho* (246:312), "like a pheasant but smaller," as very rare.

Drury (165:196) mistook Zaffentumppoey for a king instead of a royal family. He describes (179:217) circumcision as performed at one or two years, whereas, say the Grandidiers, it is in the seventh or eighth year or later. His description of the ceremony itself, more full than elsewhere, though some significant details were in Flacourt,

[41] *Revue des deux mondes,* C (July 1872), 69 ff. Cited by the Grandidiers, *Collection,* IV, 4n.

[42] *Robert Drury's Journal* (1890), pp. 26–27n.

[43] In the following paragraphs references are given in abbreviated parenthetical form. A single-page reference is to the Grandidier's *Collection,* vol. IV. Two-page references separated by a colon indicate, respectively, parallel references to *Drury's Journal* as edited by Oliver (1890) and the French translation of the Grandidiers (with annotations of value).

Ogilby, and Cauche, the Grandidiers tacitly accept as accurate. They say, however, that he is inaccurate in his description of the northwest coast around Massalege (311:409) and the use of tents by the Sakalava army (258:328).

More serious are the discrepancies found in the Drury accounts of the manners and temper of the natives. It is, say the Grandidiers, improbable that a native chief would have surrendered to Drury the profitable privilege of killing cattle (132:15), and absolutely untrue (128:355) that the natives do not regard their kings as ruling by divine right. They think Drury pictures the natives too harshly in accounts of castration (93:95, softened to "mutilation" by Oliver and the Grandidiers, who follow him) and too kindly in accounts of Drury's sleeping innocently with his chief's women in war camp, of their kindness to neighbors (172, 275:208, 355), of their sympathy and tears (281:364, "Des malgaches qui ont des larmes aux yeux, ce n'est pas commun"). They reject as European the sentiments of Drury's second native wife (292:381) and the women of Rer Moume's family upon Drury's departure. And the whole incident (286–289: 371–376) of the burial treatment of Drury by Rer Moume's father at Moherbo is, they say, "de tout point invraisemblable."

The most telling errors the Grandidiers find are those of interpretation, picturing the Malagasy as noble savages, superior in feeling and practices (justice, kindness, chastity) to Europeans. They describe them as adornments added by the "transcriber," whom I have regarded as Defoe. The prefatory admission that the "transcriber" has inserted his views on the religion of the Malagasy strengthens that assumption. But, after all, these form a small part of the book, which is so full of detailed, firsthand observation that Professor Moore, who has been most skeptical of Drury's hand in them, suggests the work revealed to Europeans a whole new storehouse of accurate information about the island and its peoples. This new information, the Grandidiers remark, deals with geography, races and tribes, customs and manners, religions and superstitions, diseases, and language.

The topography of the southern coast of Madagascar where the *Degrave* foundered is still far from well known. As far as it goes, Drury's description of the region is accurate. The cliffs, the reef, and the rocky bank the Grandidiers find (46:57) just as Drury says. The Mandrare, which Drury calls Manderra, still separates the provinces of Anosy and Androy. Drury, though he confuses the name of the people (Antandroy) with the name of the province (Androy), is the first European to give the name at all (82:78). He is likewise the first to mention the west-coast town of Moherbo (Mahabo). He calls it the principal residence of the king of the region. Today, say the Grandidiers (261:333), it is the capital of the province Ménabé Sud. Other rivers which Drury locates and names are the Feraingher (Fiherenana—256:326), the Murnumbo (Manombo—256:327), the Mernee (Mania—265:340), the Munnongaro (Mananara—267:342), and the Munnonbaugher (Manamboka—295:386).[44]

The Mahafaly, the Antanosy, and some other tribes had already been identified. But Drury, as we have seen, was the first to name the Antandroy of the south coast. His is also the first-known printed account of the Saccalauvors (Sakalavas—234:294), a warlike western tribe; the people of Amboerlambo (Ambaa-Lambo—277:357) in the central highlands, usually called the Hovas; and the Virzimbers (Vazimbas—266:340–341), an aboriginal tribe along the Mernee.[45] M. Alfred Grandidier asserted in 1888 that Drury had given the only authoritative account of the Vazimbas he had been able to find.

Drury mentions a Sakalava chief sleeping with his head on the lap of his wife, and the Grandidiers comment that the Sakalava chiefs still sleep so and have their wives scratch their heads (288:375). This statement in Drury is incidental to his story of his treatment at Moherbo which the Grandidiers scoff at. But their skepticism is directed less at the incident than at the sympathy of the king's wives, whom Drury credits with saving his life. The Grandidiers, as we have seen, credit Drury's account of the custom of licking the feet of superiors. Other customs upon which they find that Drury throws light are the eating of meat with the skin on it (289:29, 377), the native method of kindling fire (80:76), the smoking of opium (200–201:244), the use of conch shells as trumpets (77:71), and the native manner of fighting (114–115:125).

Less original are Drury's accounts of religious ceremonies and worship, which had been partially described by earlier writers. But he gives a full explanation of the *owley* (*oly* or *oaly*—85:83), a talisman or charm; the *umossee* (*omasy*—99:104), conjurors working with charms; and native deities (173:209), especially Deaan Antemoor (Antimoro) or Northern Lord; and the ceremony of circumcision (179:217).

---

[44] The "cockneyizing" of personal and place names by Drury is obviously a natural attempt to give words *as he heard them*. These spellings are real evidence that the author of the Drury *Journal* had been in Madagascar and learned (after a fashion) the language. It is improbable that these spellings are Defoe's.

[45] See Alfred Grandidier, "Note sur les Vazimba de Madagascar," *Memoires publiés par la Société Philomathique* (Paris, 1888), pp. 155–161.

On Drury's language the Grandidiers say that the word *par-rapingo* (meaning fetters—95:98) is Soahili and not used in southern Madagascar but in the northwest or among pirates. They find that in Zaffentumppoey Drury confuses a royal family name with that of a chief but that the chief has a real name (Zafitompo—165:196). His *anbatty* (*ambatry*) and *anchoroko* (*tsoroka*) (225:280) are plants mentioned by Flacourt under other names. A phrase, *Robin, mehove a toee* (*Robin, mihavia eto*—262:335), they find unusual but clear for "Robin, come here." The word *maurominter* (*maromainty*—102, 268:107, 345) is of unknown origin but common all over the island. Drury's word *chemerango* (*tsimirango*—271:349), used in the west for the mark on the king's cattle, is still in use.

Even Captain Oliver, who thought that considerable information in *Drury's Journal* came from Flacourt and other earlier writers, admitted that some details must have come from Drury's acquaintance with people of the interior when they brought cattle to sell on the coast. And Professor Moore finds firsthand observation throughout. Defoe must, he says, have seen manuscripts not available to us or have talked with sailors, merchants, and, most of all, ex-pirates who had an intimate knowledge of the island, some of whom were better informed than a 1942 reporter for the *National Geographic Magazine*.[46] Moore says justly that Defoe's knowledge of Madagascar increased rapidly in the decade between the appearance of *Robinson Crusoe* and *Drury's Journal* and that he could not have got all of his new information from books, for he had authentic linguistic and other lore not then in print. "If," Moore continues, "Defoe had mastered all the books about Madagascar then in existence, he would still have lacked some of the details of Drury's map, many of the words of Drury's vocabulary, and the coherent and intimate picture of Madagascar life in which he stands head and shoulders above any of his predecessors and nearly all his successors."[47]

If printed books are an inadequate explanation for Moore of Defoe's new information, no less are the journals of seamen. Defoe's informants were Londoners and close associates of pirates. By a curious bit of reasoning Moore decides that Drury's claim to be the informant is ruled out because only the pirates knew the interior of Madagascar; and so Drury was either a pirate or he did not know the central area.[48] The decision is unanimous, except for the nineteenth-century views of Blanchard and Oliver, that *Drury's Journal*

---

[46] *Defoe's Sources for "Robert Drury's Journal,"* pp. 8, 9, 14–15.
[47] *Defoe's Sources for "Robert Drury's Journal,"* p. 19.
[48] *Defoe's Sources for "Robert Drury's Journal,"* p. 67.

is saturated with firsthand observation. The missionaries and the scientists, who accept it as Drury's, and Professor Moore, who does not, all agree that it was based upon information not then in print.

This is necessarily a brief sketch. It has said nothing of Drury's long account of native dress, funerals, married life, wars, vegetation, and animal life, in some of which he had been anticipated by earlier writers. I once agreed with Captain Oliver that much of the matter had been taken from Flacourt and his imitators (Dapper in Holland and Ogilby in England) and other early travelers. But with the later knowledge that Drury had actually been on the island for at least thirteen years, we have no reason to suppose he is borrowing matter from others unless we have something more than agreement and resemblance. It is not unusual for travelers to supplement and verify their own recollections of remote places by turning to accounts of others, from which, besides corroboration, they may find enjoyment and guidance in shaping their own memoirs.

The Grandidiers say that it is not truthful of Drury to assert he had not read the French histories of the island; but they mistakenly thought he had taken his map and some parts of the King Samuel story from Flacourt. A number of details may have been (as I think they were) taken from Flacourt or Ogilby; and yet the case for Drury's having been the chief source of information is not weakened. Even when he is speaking of matters previously discussed in print, he is usually more copious and more exact. An illustration cited by the Grandidiers is Drury's account of the smoking of opium or *jermaughler* (*jamala*) as he calls it.[49] Another cited by Moore is his account of the *tondruk* (*tenrec*).

Dr. Rost of the India Office Library in 1885 expressed to Oliver the opinion that "the names of the people, places, etc., given throughout Robert Drury's narrative and in his vocabulary, represent with very few exceptions, true and genuine Malagasy words, which could neither have been forged nor taken from the few vocabularies (French, Dutch, and German) previously published." [50] Of Drury's word list I have little to say. Such word lists in manuscript must have been common among traders and seamen. One is reported in the *Travels of Peter Mundy* [51] and one by another English trader, Thomas Bowrey, an acquaintance of Defoe. After a comparison of Drury's list with that in Flacourt's *Histoire de*

---

[49] *Collection*, IV, 244; *Robert Drury's Journal* (1890), pp. 200–201.
[50] (1890), pp. 316–317.
[51] (*Hakluyt Society Publications*, ser. 2, vol. XLVI), vol. III, pt. 2 (1919) pp. 398 ff.

Madagascar (1661) I think more highly of it than does Professor Moore, and only less highly of it than did the Rev. J. Richardson and the Grandidiers.[52]

Richardson explains cockneyisms by supposing Drury's list was written down from oral answers to questions.[53] Unfortunately his theory is negated by the fact that the cockneyisms are not limited to the Malagasy words. They appear also in such English words as "buffuler" (buffalo), "musketeers" (mosquitos), and "years" (given correctly in the text as yaws). Richardson is wrong again in supposing that Drury's word for chief, *deaan*, is a misunderstanding of the name Andrian; it is only an anglicizing of *dian* which is used by Flacourt and others. But the vocabulary, interesting as it is, is not presented as the work of Drury; it is appended, like the map in the fore part, as a useful supplement to the text but with specification of its source. On the whole it is a workaday tool from which Richardson and Oliver, who took his version from Richardson's in the *Antananarivo Annual* for 1875, have deleted several useful but indelicate words. It may have been a copy of a vocabulary used on Madagascar by traders and seamen, who, as logs and journals of eighteenth-century ships indicate, introduced cockneyisms into such word as "starne" for stern and "St. Hellings" for St. Helen's and otherwise spelled words as they pronounced them. It could be a good and accurate list without being evidence for or against Drury as the author of the narrative proper. Drury was himself a cockney. The relative lack of cockneyisms in the text may have been due to the transcriber (Defoe?) who revised the text or narrative.

More significant of Drury's contributions to the book is the use of native words in the narrative. Professor Moore was unable to find in the vocabulary the native word translated in the text as "child"; but it is in the vocabulary under "baby," misprinted as "body (of child)?" by Oliver. I have above cited some phrases which the Grandidiers find unusual but unidiomatic. They recognize easily,

---

[52] See Moore, *Defoe's Sources for "Robert Drury's Journal,"* pp. 74–78, and my review of the *Sources* in *JEGP*, XLIV (1945), 66–73. The Grandidiers waste time explaining Drury's "bandy" = *sekearf*. Unable to find an exact Malagasy equivalent handily, they point out that the word for tortoise (which has bandy legs!) is *sakafo*. But "bandy" is merely a misprint by Oliver for the 1729 word "brandy"; and that *sekearf* (or its uncockneyized form) is the correct Malagasy equivalent of "brandy" is obvious from *wooersekarfe* = "drunk." *Sekearf* may be only a cockney attempt at *siky* = "alcohol" and *afo* = "fire," a Malagasy equivalent of "firewater." The Malagasy word given here for alcohol is from Paul Bourdaise. Drury does not have it; and his word for "fire" (*offu*) is misprinted *ossu* in the first edition.

[53] *Antananarivo Annual* (1875). See *Robert Drury's Journal* (1890), pp. 316–318.

under cockney distortion, the names of many rivers and places. Most significant of all seem to me (as to Dr. Rost) the names of persons who had been Drury's neighbors and associates. There is a very large number of such names, and, though some of them sound only a shade less grotesque than those in *Gulliver's Travels,* the Grandidiers fit them all into the Malagasy pattern. The natives had no written language, and Europeans often made strange work of spelling by ear. Drury's Deaan Woozington is as unconvincing as any; but the Grandidiers equate it with Kosintany. Drury's Deaan Crindo is simpler. John Benbow and others called him Decrindo and prove that Drury had not invented him or his name, any more than King Samuel or Fort Dauphin.

There are five groups of native chiefs and their families among whom Drury claims to have lived. It was this long and complex series of persons and the way in which *Drury's Journal* handles them which seemed to me, before I had discovered the facts about Drury's career, the most convincing evidence of the truth of the central story of Drury's life among the natives. These family groups are as follows.

1. Deaan Crindo in Androy in south Madagascar; his sons, Mundumbo, Frukey, Trodaughe, and Chahary; his grandson, Mevarrow; and his nephews, Deaans Murnanzack, Mussecorrow, and Afferer, and Rer Mimebalambo.

2. Deaan Woozington, King of Merfaughla (Mahafaly) in the southwest; his sons, Chermermaundy, Metorolahatch, and Rer Fungenzer; and his nephews, Rer Chula and Ry-Opheck.

3. Rer Vovvern, King of Feraingher near St. Augustine Bay; his sons, Deaan Mernaugha and Rer Mundrosser; and his nephews, Deaan Trongha and Rer Befaugher.

4. Trimmonongarevo (an error of some sort, since *arivo* is a suffix added after death), King of the Sakalavas in the northwest; his son, Rer Moume; his grandsons, Rer Chula, Rer Chemumghoher, and Rer Vove; and his nephews, Rer Mynebolambo and Deaan Toakoffu, later king of Munnongaro or Massalege.

5. Deaans Tuley-Noro (King Samuel) and Morroughsevea, kings of Fort Dauphin, on the southeast coast.

Besides these there are over sixty other persons (wives, children, neighbors, and servants) mentioned by name as parts of the five groups. (Drury names neither of his two wives nor does he mention any children by them.) Rer and Ry are obviously cockneyized forms of Ra. The Grandidiers correct Drury's names or give more precise forms. For Mevarrow they read Mehavariano or Mivarotsa; for Crindo, Kirindra; for Frukey, Firokey or Pirokey; for Tuley-Noro,

Tolinoro; for Rer Chulu-Mossu-Andro, Rasolomasoandro; and the like.

The remarkable thing is that Drury handles these intricate genealogical matters with precision. There are many accurate and few, if any, inaccurate references to members of the earlier groups after the story has moved past them. The spelling may vary slightly, like Mynebolambo and Mimebolambo, but the persons named are all presented consistently—a remarkable fact in the light of Defoe's notorious carelessness in such details. This complicated genealogical pattern could not have been invented by Defoe or even by Drury; it must deal with real people in the areas assigned to them, and it is almost incontrovertible proof that Drury lived long in the regions in which the *Journal* says he lived. It is the more probable because several members of these native families are independently named by John Benbow and others.

With the discovery of the truthfulness of the framework of *Drury's Journal* and of Drury's contribution to it, we can no longer suppose that all this remarkable revelation of Madagascar, which even skeptics see in the central story, is borrowed from Flacourt and his imitators or from conversation with unnamed seamen and pirates. Drury was on the *Degrave,* and he gave an accurate account of its misfortunes. He was also on Madagascar for something like thirteen years, and part of that time he was with the natives in Androy in south Madagascar, no matter how soon he escaped after the massacre. No one can name a pirate or ex-pirate in London in the 1720's whose experience on south Madagascar was comparable to Drury's. He had been there, he had information, he gave information (which no one else could have given) on other parts of the narrative. Until we have proof to the contrary, we must conclude with little less than certainty that he is the principal source of the information in the central story and description of life among the Madagascar natives. This conclusion agrees with the preface and with the assumption that Defoe was the "transcriber" who put Drury's manuscript into "a more agreeable Method."

The Origins of Defoe's
Memoirs of a Cavalier

A Statement of Problems

When in 1720 Defoe published the *Memoirs of a Cavalier*,[1] he gave England something which, though not completely unknown, had not previously existed in an advanced stage—a historical novel, a fiction with a historical background. In the preceding years he had fabricated the *Memoirs of John, Duke of Melfort* (1714), the *Minutes of the Negotiations of Monsr. Mesnager* (1717), and the *Memoirs of Major A. Ramkins* (1719), and he had sketched the careers of Charles XII of Sweden (1715; 2nd ed., 1720), of the Duke of Shrewsbury, and of Dr. Daniel Williams, the eminent dissenting divine. But those in this last group are not fiction, and those in the former are set in the immediate past, and their plots are amorphous and their political purpose too obvious. Possibly the Mesnager story did something to save Lord Oxford from Whig vengeance in 1717, but Abel Boyer pounced upon it promptly as a forgery by Defoe.

The two kinds of writing just distinguished—more or less factual history and biography on the one hand and on the other works which appeared factual but were really inventions for political ends—are as written by Defoe not easy to separate. The *Memoirs of Charles XII* is presented as the work of a Scottish gentleman in the Swedish service, and the *Journal of the Plague Year*, widely regarded as giving a truthful account of the plague, is set forth as the observations and experiences of a saddler, who seems to have been a creation of Defoe's imagination. Both propaganda and history appear in the *Memoirs of a Cavalier* and in *Colonel Jacque*, but it is obvious that Defoe was moving from fictitious propaganda to fiction in which propaganda is incidental to the narrative.[2]

---

[1] All references to the text of the *Memoirs* in this study will be to the edition of George A. Aitken in *Romances and Narratives of Daniel Defoe*, vol. V (London, 1895). The same plates are used in the Everyman's Library edition (1908).

[2] H. G. Wright, "Some English Writers and Charles XII," *Studia Neophilologica*, XV (1942–43), 105–131.

Long before this Defoe had learned the trick of impersonating others—with unexpected success in the *Shortest Way*—and he had written pamphlets like the *Secret History of the October Club* "by a Member" (1711), *A Seasonable Warning . . . Being a Letter from an Englishman at the Court of Hanover* (1712), *A Friendly Epistle . . . from One of the People Called Quakers* (1715), and several others in the Quaker vein. Here and elsewhere he had practiced the art of concealing his own views and presenting those of others. In the Snape-Hoadly (Bangorian) pamphlets, of which he wrote nearly a dozen in the years 1717–19, he took first one side, then another, and finally a middle position, that of the pacifier who regrets the hot tempers aroused and advises toleration and charity.

Though Defoe began his career as a novelist with marine adventure instead of military and political tales, the difference between *Robinson Crusoe* and the *Memoirs of a Cavalier* is not so great as it may at first seem. Crusoe and the Cavalier belong to different worlds socially and intellectually, but their stories have much in common. Both are about young men who set out to see the world, and they are almost exclusively about adventures that do not involve the fair sex.

The long title of the Cavalier's story, as printed in 1720, indicates its masculine aspects: *Memoirs of a Cavalier: or a Military Journal of the Wars in Germany, and the Wars in England; from the Year 1632, to the Year 1648. Written Threescore Years Ago by an English Gentleman, Who Served First in the Army of Gustavus Adolphus, the Glorious King of Sweden, till His Death; and After That, in the Royal Army of King Charles the First, from the Beginning of the Rebellion, to the End of That War.* The Cavalier, second son of a Shropshire gentleman, attended Oxford for three years before setting out in the spring of 1630 to travel on the Continent. He encounters thieves on the road to Paris, and in Paris kills a man in a fight. He and his companion, an Oxford friend called Captain Fielding, go to Lyons and then on to aid the French in the brief campaign against Savoy. They travel for a while in Italy and Austria before joining the army of Gustavus Adolphus, who with France was helping the German Protestants against the Emperor. The account of this conflict, or of the Cavalier's role in it, completes the first part of the book.

The second and longer part is an account of the Civil War in England (1642–48). The Cavalier had returned home to find England overhung with the storm clouds of Charles I's troubles with Parliament. Eager to further the Royalist plans against the opposition, he served continuously from the skirmishes in the north in 1639 and 1640 until Fairfax captured the broken remnants of the royal army and brought the war to an end.

Defoe took the greatest pains to make the story convincing. The title page tells us that it was all taken from a manuscript written sixty years earlier by the Cavalier himself. The preface has an elaborate account of the manuscript's history. It was, we are told, found over twenty years before publication (i.e., before 1700) among the papers of one of William III's Secretaries of State. A further clue to its origin was this memorandum initialed "I. K.": "I found this manuscript among my father's writings, and I understand that he got them as plunder, at, or after, the fight at Worcester, where he served as Major of ———'s regiment of horse on the side of the Parliament." This seems to put the writing earlier than August 1651, and to end further inquiry. The preface calls attention to its inimitable style, to its having particulars not found elsewhere, and to its corrections of other historians. The writer of the preface hoped that publication would bring to light the remainder of the obviously unfinished manuscript.

The ruse, if it was one, has been successful. The *Memoirs of a Cavalier* has been more generally considered as history than any other of Defoe's major narratives [3] with the possible exception of the *Journal of the Plague Year*. P. Dottin believes (as William Lee and Thomas Wright did) that it had a manuscript source. But though the *Memoirs* highlights two famous wars of the seventeenth century, it lacks the dramatic quality of *Robinson Crusoe, Moll Flanders,* and, to cite a closer parallel, the *Journal of the Plague Year*. Except for a Venetian courtesan and the Queen Mother of France, it introduced no women, and as a picture of war it naturally pales beside twentieth-century fiction. The very reasons for its eighteenth-century reputation, its stories of the Thirty Years' War and of the Civil War, make it less interesting to twentieth-century readers, to whom those events seem remote and relatively unimportant. It is, however, more lively than histories frequently are, and is at its best in minor episodes like the escape over Black-

[3] W. Lobban, in *N&Q*, ser. 4, XI (1873), 193, says Walter Harte used the Leeds edition of the *Memoirs* as a source in his *History of Gustavus Adolphus* (1759). It is listed as an authority only in the third edition, published by J. J. Stockdale after Harte's death. Harte's use of the *Memoirs* seems doubtful, but Stockdale evidently thought well of it. Harte, like Defoe, did use the *Swedish Intelligencer* as a source. Two historians of Leicestershire, John Nichols and James Francis Hollings, quote from the *Memoirs,* but in his life of Gustavus Adolphus (1838) Hollings seems not to have drawn from Defoe.

stone Edge from the disaster at Marston Moor. The book is reported to have been admired by the Earl of Chatham,[4] who thought it the best account of the Civil War. Some nineteenth-century historians drew upon it as an authority. It is remarkable that it was printed seven times within three-quarters of a century.

It was some years after the first edition (London, 1720) that the work was reprinted near the middle of the century (the precise date is unknown) by James Lister at Leeds. The third and fourth editions were brought out in Edinburgh in 1759 and 1766, and the fifth at Newark in 1782. In this last edition appears an editorial preface by E. Staveley, who is otherwise unknown. It imitates Defoe's preface by saying that the story is newly published from a manuscript that "came into my hands many years since." Not until 1784 was the *Memoirs* reprinted in London, by Francis Noble, who brought out an edition in three small volumes. The final eighteenth-century printing was that of Edward Jeffrey and F. Faulder (London, 1792).[5] Dottin describes it as very exact,[6] but it has many of the variations which crept into earlier texts, including (pp. 117–122) a long character of James I "from a master's hand."

In the Leeds edition Lister mentioned skeptics who called the book a romance, but he himself thought it the nearest to truth of any romance he had read.[7] Several later eighteenth-century editions emphasize the original subtitle, and call the book a history of the wars of Germany and England. The Jeffrey-Faulder title page of 1792 calls the Cavalier "the Honourable Col. Andrew Newport."

The Noble edition of 1784 has especial interest in its mention of Daniel Defoe in connection with the *Memoirs*—the earliest such

---

[4] *Retrospective Review*, III (1821), 377–78; Aitken, introduction to the *Memoirs*, p. xviii.

[5] (2) *Memoirs of a Cavalier: or a Military Journal of the Wars in Germany and the Wars in England. . . .* Leeds: Printed by James Lister [n.d.]. (3) *A Military History of Germany; and of England. . . .* Printed for A. Donaldson [Edinburgh, 1759]. (4) *A Military History of Germany and of England. . . .* Edinburgh, 1766. (5) *The History of the Civil Wars in Germany. . . . Also, Genuine Memoirs of the Wars of England, in the Unhappy Reign of Charles the First. . . .* Newark: Printed by James Tomlinson. For the Publisher, in 1782. (6) *Memoirs, Travels, and Adventures of a Cavalier. A New Edition, Being the Second. In Three Volumes. . . . First Published from the Original Manuscript, by the Late Mr. Daniel Defoe, Author of the Adventures of Robinson Crusoe, and Many Other Books of Entertainment.* London: Printed for Francis Noble in Holborn. 1784. (7) *Memoirs of the Honourable Col. Andrew Newport. . . .* London, 1792.

[6] *Defoe et ses romans* (Oxford, 1924), p. 581.

[7] To his edition Lister adds three pages of "The Publisher of this Second Edition to the Reader," in which he raises the question of authorship of the *Memoirs*. Andrew Newport, he concludes, is supposed to be "our author."

mention now known. Very likely for commercial reasons the title page of this edition stresses the historical authenticity of the *Memoirs* by reporting it as "First published from the original manuscript, by the late Mr. Daniel Defoe." The preface ends with the name Daniel Defoe (p. viii), and appends an advertising postscript which mentions him as "editor." Whether Defoe is considered publisher, editor, or author by Noble is not altogether clear. George Chalmers, Defoe's first biographer,[8] does not mention the book in his first account (1786), but he does mention it in 1790. Sir Walter Scott, printing the work in his 1810 edition of Defoe's novels, describes it as on the border line between history and romance. Though it has appeared in all the major collections of Defoe's novels since Scott's,[9] it was still throughout the nineteenth century widely regarded as history. Military men in particular were reluctant to admit Defoe's hand in it. A writer in *Notes and Queries* in 1873 protested vigorously against calling it a fiction, citing especially the episode of the passage of the Lech as a brilliant military exploit that Defoe was incapable of inventing.[10]

Even some Defoe scholars have doubted if the work could be Defoe's. William Lee granted Defoe some part in it, but believed that there must have been a manuscript source.[11] Thomas Wright similarly held that Defoe worked from a manuscript source,[12] and cited what he described as a manuscript relating to Gustavus Adolphus, mentioned in Defoe's *Scots Nation and Union Vindicated* (1714). From the preface and title of the *Memoirs* Wright concluded that Defoe freely revised the manuscript just referred to, which had come down to him from the seventeenth century.

In 1895 Aitken stated in his introduction to the *Memoirs* (p. xii) the view most commonly held now. He pointed out that Andrew Newport was born too late to participate in the campaigns of Gustavus Adolphus and that he took little part in the Civil War. Aitken added that the *Memoirs* are full of historical errors and that

---

[8] If we except the account in the so-called "Cibber" *Lives of the Poets,* IV (London, 1753), 313. See Chalmers, *The Life of Daniel Defoe* (*The Works of the English Poets,* vol. III [London, 1821]), pp. 354 ff.

[9] Tegg, 1840; Hazlitt, 1840; Bohn, 1854; Aitken, 1895; Maynadier, 1903; Blackwell, 1927.

[10] Ser. 4, XI, 509.

[11] *Daniel Defoe: His Life and Recently Discovered Writings,* I (London, 1869), 332 ff.

[12] *The Life of Daniel Defoe* (London, 1931), p. 271. The British Museum copy of the 1782 edition has manuscript notes interchanged by S. F. Creswell of St. John's College, Cambridge, and W. Kelly of Leicestershire in 1857–58. They discuss its authorship and its use by Hollings and Nichols in their histories of Leicester. They think E. Staveley, who signs a preface, is a myth.

for the Civil War it contains little not to be found in Clarendon and other historians, and that in one sentence at least it echoes the very words of Whitelocke. William P. Trent described Defoe's claim of a manuscript source as a device in harmony with those in his other novels.[13] Dottin,[14] however, agrees with Wright that we should not deny Defoe's claim to a manuscript source for the Continental adventures. To that contention I shall return later. In 1935 I remarked,[15] and shall presently show, that Defoe had no manuscript narrative and that for the Civil War at least he wrote with several histories before him. Dr. John Campbell Major has, so far as he has gone, confirmed my statement.[16]

Was There an Actual Cavalier?

We may well first dispose of this preliminary problem. Does an actual person stand behind the Cavalier as Selkirk has been thought to stand behind Crusoe? Lister thought the Cavalier-author might be the second son of Sir Richard Newport, and, in place of Defoe's blank, inserted in the text the name of High Ercall, the Shropshire home of the Newports, as the home of the Cavalier. This insertion started a tradition which lasted until 1895, when Aitken discredited it. It confused Dottin as late as 1924. Aitken pointed out that Andrew Newport was not born until 1623, and so would have been too young to have attended Gustavus Adolphus—would in fact have been under ten years of age. Aitken found that Newport did not participate in the Civil War. It is not true, as Dottin supposed (p. 555), that Defoe courted identification of his Cavalier with Newport by naming High Ercall as the Cavalier's home. The original text did not mention the name of his home; it merely said he lived in Shropshire about six miles from a town which it later implies is Shrewsbury. Dottin is misled by later editions which, following the Leeds edition of James Lister, identified the Cavalier with Newport, and inserted the name High Ercall. Not all later eighteenth-century editions consistently followed Lister, but Sir Walter Scott's edition did, and so did all the other nineteenth-century editors before Aitken.

One may nevertheless still surmise that Defoe had Andrew Newport vaguely in mind when he wrote the story. He had obviously read Clarendon's account of the recruiting of the Royalist

---

[13] *Defoe and How to Know Him* (Indianapolis, Ind., 1916), p. 213.

[14] *Defoe et ses romans*, pp. 559, 570.

[15] Introduction to Defoe's *Journal of the Plague Year* (New York, 1935).

[16] In his *Role of Personal Memoirs in English Biography and Novel* (Philadelphia, 1935), pp. 134 ff.

army in Shropshire and especially about Shrewsbury, and noted the unnamed country gentleman with two promising sons who was ready to give the King a large sum in exchange for a barony. Defoe may not have known that the gentleman was (later) Lord Newport and that his younger son was Andrew; but when he describes his Cavalier as the son of a gentleman living near Shrewsbury, who was educated at Christ Church,[17] as Andrew was, it is difficult not to believe that for some unknown reason he did have that person in mind—impossible as the man's dates are for the Cavalier. On the other hand, Defoe in his *Tour* does not mention High Ercall or the Newports when describing the country about Shrewsbury, and he rather strangely—for him—fails to see the Newport traits as occasion for a compliment to his old patron, Robert Harley, Earl of Oxford. Oxford's grandfather had married, as a second wife, Mary, sister of Andrew Newport; and Oxford, though descended from his grandfather's third wife, might loosely be called a grandnephew of Andrew and of his older brother, Francis, Earl of Bradford (1619–1708).[18]

Whatever he may have got from a reminiscence of Andrew Newport, who had been dead almost twenty years when the *Memoirs* was printed, Defoe obtained even more from a passage in Clarendon —possibly the most interesting passage among the many that Defoe glanced at in writing his story. It seems to have suggested to Defoe the general account of his hero's birth and family:

There was a gentleman of a very good extraction, and of the best estate of any gentleman of that country, who lived within four or five miles of Shrewsbury, and was looked upon as a very prudent man, and had a very powerful influence upon that people, and was of undoubted affections and loyalty to the king, and to the government both in Church and State; his eldest son was a young gentleman of great expectation. . . . This gentleman intimated . . . that if his father might be made a baron, he did believe he might be prevailed with, to present his Majesty with a good sum of money. It was proposed to the king . . . the merit and ability of the person, and the fair expectation from his posterity, *he having two sons both very hopeful*, prevailed with his Majesty . . . and in a

---

[17] The Cavalier (p. 2) tells us: "So my father entered me of ———— College in Oxford"; but he continues: "During my stay at Oxford, though I passed through the proper exercises of the house, yet my chief reading was upon history and geography." The "house" may be Christ Church; but some editions, giving no reasons, have filled Defoe's blank with Wadham.

[18] Herman Hart, in *TLS*, 26 August 1926, reports on a first edition of the *Memoirs* that contains a manuscript note ascribing the work to "Mr. John Bellaris, a younger . . . son of Lord Faulconberg." Another note in another hand remarks, "Others say the author was son of Bradford Earl of Newport."

few days . . . the gentleman was made a baron; who presented the sum of six thousand pounds to his Majesty.[19]

Though Clarendon mentions no name, we know from Echard and others that the gentleman thus created Lord Newport was Richard Newport, and that his second son was Andrew. It was long thought that this Andrew Newport was actually the Cavalier, as I have already indicated. Indeed, Dottin, misled by the interpolation of the name of the Newport seat, High Ercall, into late eighteenth- and nineteenth-century editions of the *Memoirs,* thinks that Defoe courted identification of the Cavalier with Newport. Defoe, however, may have got a suggestion from the passage in Clarendon just quoted, though possibly he did not know the name of the Shrewsbury gentleman on whom he fathered his Cavalier.

The *Memoirs of a Cavalier,* a narrative of military adventure, has thus been a difficult puzzle for those who have believed that it is history, the story of an actual soldier. Ever since it appeared in 1720 with its prefatory claim of a manuscript source, its nature has been questionable. That some problems might be solved by careful comparison of the book with possible sources (some of which Sir Walter Scott indicated a century and a half ago) seems to have occurred to no one.

Defoe's Methods in His Borrowings

A careful study of the sources, however, reveals some surprising things. The first is that the book is almost entirely fabricated from published works. The early career of the Cavalier in the French attack on Savoy (1630) uses ten or so pages of Le Clerc's *Life of Cardinal Richlieu,* translated into English by Tom Brown, and published in two volumes in 1695. Similarities, often identities, in selection of events, in arrangement, in critical comment on men and policies, and in sentence structure and diction, make this certain. The part treating the Cavalier's adventures under Gustavus Adolphus in Germany has long been known to be indebted to the *Swedish Intelligencer* (1632–35), a newspaper probably written by William Watts and issued by Bourne and Butter. What has not been previously known is that the *Swedish Intelligencer* may be the *only* source, and that Defoe selected his matter from it or else invented fictitious adventures from suggestions in it. Aitken and Dottin have unnecessarily suggested other books which Defoe might have used.

In dealing with the English Civil War Defoe proceeded more cautiously. The story of a war well known to some of his readers

---

[19] *History of the Rebellion,* II (Oxford, 1703), 28. The italics are mine.

could not have been safely compiled from a single work. Nor did
Defoe need to limit himself to one. The astonishing thing, however,
is that (except for occasional matter like the Montrose affair) he
relies entirely upon three famous accounts, two of which he mentions in his book. "In a word [says he in the preface], this work is
a confutation of many errors in all the writers upon the subject of
our wars . . . even in that extraordinary history written by the
Earl of Clarendon. . . ." Ludlow's *Memoirs* (1698–99) he cites in a
note in corroboration of a passage in his text. Whitelocke's *Memorials,* a kind of day-by-day record of events during the war,
Defoe used most of all, but he does not mention it.

The question of sources brings up problems. What Defoe seems
to have been trying to do in all his long narratives was to write
fictionized history that would attract readers by seeming to record
actual adventures. He went to much trouble to make these narratives resemble authentic records. A considerable part of his verisimilitude arises from his having taken from his sources not only
their ideas and experiences but also something of their very words.
If Dampier and Ludlow wrote from actual observation, Defoe, who
had already an eye for telling detail, knew how to adapt their
style and materials without seeming to do so, without seeming
to take his matter at second hand. He followed nature, but nature methodized in Whitelocke, Clarendon, Dampier, and other
"Homers."

Defoe took his materials in the large from other writers, usually
writers of what passed for truthful records. His own invention consisted chiefly of fictitious details embroidered about incidents briefly
recorded in his sources. He read in Whitelocke [20] that Essex's men
surprised the troops of Sir Nicholas Crisp and Colonel Spencer at
Cirencester, and captured a good number of them. Defoe expanded
Whitelocke's paragraph into a vivid page and a half that includes
a dramatic report of the means by which some of the Royalist party
escaped out of the town and finally got away to Oxford. A careful
historian, upon discovering that Sir Nicholas Crisp was not in
Cirencester that night (neither Defoe nor his source, Whitelocke,
knew that Sir Nicholas had been called to court-martial the day
before) might shake his head at Defoe's apparently ready method
of playing upon the credulity of his readers. The student of the
novel, however, will find the incident instructive. Details are
fabricated, though they do not contradict Whitelocke's terse account. Defoe's aim was to vivify the facts.

[20] *Memorials of the English Affairs* (London, 1682), p. 69.

The Tradition of the Military Memoir

Biography, sometimes fictionized, is evidently one of the principal streams from which the *Cavalier* has derived. Though there have been studies of biography as a type,[21] little of importance has been done on the relationship of biography to fiction. Relationships have been pointed out with regard to the lives of criminals and fictitious stories, and in this limited field the *Lives of the Highwaymen* (1713), attributed on the title page to "Captain Smith," is perhaps the most important work of fiction between 1700 and *Robinson Crusoe* (1719). But the influence of "criminal" biography upon Defoe is not reflected significantly until three years after *Crusoe* and two after the *Memoirs of a Cavalier*.

If we look for the biographical current which led to the *Cavalier*, we find highly important works among the biographies of soldiers. That of Philip de Commines, translated by T. Dannett (1596), Defoe had read, and he referred to it later in *Colonel Jacque*. Like the Cavalier's story, this is an account of military and political events purporting to be by a participiant. One can hardly assert that Commines does more than furnish a model; and another better model, which is nearer Defoe's time and treats some events that Defoe also used, is Du Fossé's *Memoirs of the Sieur de Pontis* (1676). This interesting work has, so far as I am aware, not received any attention from historians of the English novel, and even in France it has not received much attention. According to the story attributed to him, Pontis was a native of Provence who served in the armies of Henri IV, Louis XIII, and Louis XIV. He was a model soldier, brave, modest, and honorable. His story was translated in 1694 by Charles Cotton, the translator of Montaigne and author of *Scarronides*.

Whether these *Memoirs* should be regarded as history or as fiction is difficult to say. Readers of our time will certainly suspect the work is not by Pontis, and may share Voltaire's doubts that there ever was a Sieur de Pontis. His existence, however, is attested apparently beyond question.[22] In his years of retirement at Port Royal, he is said to have related his adventures to admiring neighbors, from whom, after his death, Du Fossé compiled an account. Whether its exaggerations were due to the vanity of an old man, to the imagination of his hearers, or to Du Fossé himself, we cannot tell. The best

---

[21] Waldo H. Dunn, *English Biography* (1907); Donald Stauffer, *English Biography Before 1700* (1930); Stauffer, *The Art of Biography in Eighteenth-Century England* (1941).

[22] *Biographie universelle,* nouvelle ed., XXXIV (n.d.), 82–83.

opinion seems to be that the *Memoirs* should be considered as historical fiction. In that case it would be just what some writers once thought the *Memoirs of a Cavalier* to be—a fictionized account of a real hero.

We do not know for certain that Defoe had read Pontis, but there is some reason to think he had. The similarity of events is perhaps suggestive. Both Pontis and the Cavalier, we are told, participate in Richelieu's campaign against Savoy in 1630, both tell of the taking of Pignerol, both tell of the march of Montmorency to the relief of Casale, both travel via Paris, Grenoble, and the Piedmont into Italy. In 1635 both are in Holland when the Prince of Orange's army captures a fort called Shenkenschanz.

But the clearest evidence that Defoe knew and used the *Memoirs* of Pontis is the resemblance of two of its adventures to those in the *Memoirs of a Cavalier*. The most important of these is a Parisian encounter. Just before setting out in 1629 with the King's army in the expedition against Savoy, Pontis, commander of a company of Swiss guards, carrying a message from the Louvre to his captain at night, was set upon by one lying in wait and nearly run through. Pontis counterattacked and would have slain his assailant had the latter not apologized and explained that Pontis had been mistaken for another. The Cavalier has a similar experience in the following year, when he too was setting out for Savoy to join the King's army. Walking one day before the Louvre to see the Swiss guards, our Cavalier receives word that his captain (supposedly his friend Captain Fielding) needs him. He follows the messenger in haste and comes to a dimly lighted place, where two men are fighting a third. The Cavalier, failing to recognize that these are all strangers, joins the fight, receives a wound, then turns upon his assailant and thrusts him through. These incidents are not identical, but there is sufficient likeness to suggest indebtedness on the part of the later story. In each the men are en route to fight with the French against Savoy; the men start from the Louvre to seek their captains; both are interested in the Swiss guards, and both are attacked by mistake, and, in the heat of the action, respond by counterattacking and slaying (or nearly slaying) their opponents.

Another significant incident is that in which Pontis on the field of battle turns the cowardice of a comrade to advantage. When it was reported that "such a one runs," Pontis replied: "No, no, he does not run, he is going to the post I have assigned him. And then I have sent a gentleman after him . . . to tell him how I had vindicated his honor and desire him by all means that he would come back to his post immediately, and tell me publicly that he had dispatched the business I had committed to his charge." The device restored the soldiers from their fright and made them eager to advance. So at Berwick-on-Tweed in 1639 the Cavalier points out to Holland the fear that has gripped the English troops. Holland thereupon sends a small party ahead. They go and presently return to say they have captured the river crossing from twenty of the enemy's horse. The ruse restores the waning courage of the troops and makes them ready for an attack.

The two works have much in common in tone and treatment of matter. The Cavalier and Pontis modestly tell of their brave deeds. Louis XIII treats Pontis with an easy familiarity like that shown the Cavalier by Gustavus Adolphus and Charles I. Both stories are chiefly made up of military adventure interspersed with anecdotes.

Another French writer, Gatien de Courtilz, Sieur de Sandras (1644–1712), is a sort of French Defoe: he has received too little attention from students of the English novel.[23] Even in France he seems to be known chiefly as the man who first told the story of d'Artagnan, and prepared the way for the famous story by Dumas. His importance as a model for Defoe and Scott as well as for Dumas and all others who have essayed the historical novel is sure to be recognized by future historians and critics.

An occasional reader may know of Sandras' *Mémoires de M. d'Artagnan* (Paris, 1700), but few indeed know of his other works, like the *Mémoires de J.B. de la Fontaine* and the *Mémoires de M. le C. de R.* Voltaire censures Sandras for his unreliability as a historian; but though some of his heroes are historical characters, Sandras is obviously a romancer. We do not know who translated into English his *Mémoires de M. le C. de R.*, his *Mémoires de la Fontaine*, and his *Colbert*. That Defoe knew these works or some of them is almost certain, and, though I cannot point with certainty to any one borrowed detail, there is much that he could have used. The *Mémoires de M. le C. de R.* (1687) is, like the *Memoirs of a Cavalier*, an account of military adventure in the time of Richelieu. It even has some reflections of the English Civil War, for Richelieu sent Rochefort to England to spy upon the conflict. And the *Mémoires de la Fontaine* (1698) tells of pro-Stuart conspiracies in London in the time of Cromwell.

Sandras' stories are less sober than the *Memoirs of a Cavalier* and on the whole are more like *Colonel Jacque* and the *Fortunate*

---

[23] The chief study of him is that of Benjamin Woodbridge, *Gatien de Courtilz* . . . (1925).

Mistress. Sandras, as Professor Woodbridge points out, had a cynicism which allies him with the picaresque writers. Reared under the influence of the Fronde (a party hostile to the King) and trained in the harsh school of the army, Sandras could not, like Pontis, accept the political and social order without question. With him military adventures are less prominent than in the Cavalier's story: they are only one of many kinds which the hero experiences—with women, footpads, politicians, priests.

We must not forget that Sandras occupies a place in the history of the French novel much like that of Defoe in the history of the English novel. Both produced numerous fictitious works purporting to be genuine memoirs of historical persons; their subject matter is much alike and sometimes identical; Sandras preceded Defoe, and several of his important works had been translated into English at the time when Defoe was much interested in French affairs and French literature.

From the fictionized memoirs we may well pass to more specific indebtednesses of the Cavalier to more or less soundly historical documents.

With the French in Savoy

For the opening episodes in the *Memoirs of a Cavalier,* preceding the Cavalier's entry into the Swedish service, no source has hitherto been suggested, except that Trent and Dottin suppose them to be based on Defoe's own experiences in his Continental travels. If one grants that Defoe took such journeys, I think this a not improbable assumption. Many of the events related about highwaymen or street robbers indicate Defoe's interest in criminals, courtesans, dueling, and sight-seeing, and are not to be looked for in histories. But as soon as the Cavalier touches the campaigns between France and Savoy, Defoe consulted a volume of history. Obviously he knew much about Richelieu, for he possessed a volume of his letters and makes frequent mention of him in other works. He could have read of Richelieu's career in Howell's *Lustra Ludovici* (1646), in J. D[avies'] *History of Richelieu* (1657), and in many other well-known works. But he probably limited himself to Jean Le Clerc's *Life of the Famous Cardinal-Duke de Richlieu* published in London in 1695. This was a translation by Tom Brown from the French text published at Cologne in 1694. Defoe follows Brown's title spelling of the Cardinal's name, "Richlieu."

Defoe begins using this work at that point where the Cavalier and his companion, Captain Fielding, en route to Italy, arrive in Paris;

and he continues to use it until they depart for Italy—approximately twenty pages in all. The Cavalier's whole account of the affairs in France—Richelieu's predominance in church, state, and army, the war against Savoy, the taking of Pignerol, the siege of Casale, and the truce—agrees in general and in detail with that in the *Life of Richlieu*. Significantly, every important detail in Defoe's narrative, except for actions ascribed to the Cavalier himself (actions which students of Defoe will suspect as being in part at least fictitious) is to be found in *Richlieu,* and not infrequently the likeness between the two accounts is so great as to prove borrowing. One notes that the only time Defoe refers to Richelieu by name instead of simply as "the cardinal" he follows Brown in misspelling the name.

One can point to the very sentence in which Defoe first makes use of *Richlieu:* "Cardinal Richelieu, who was not only a supreme minister in the Church, but Prime Minister in the State, was now made also General of the King's Forces, with a title never known in France before nor since, *viz.,* Lieutenant-General *au place du Roi,* in the king's stead, or, as some have since translated it, representing the person of the king." [24] The 1695 translation of Le Clerc's *Life of Richlieu* relates at length the Cardinal's supremacy in church and state, tells of his appointment to command the army, and states that "the army being ready . . . the King caused Letters-patent to be passed to the Cardinal in which . . . he gave him the title of Lieutenant General, *representing the person of the King* which was never before given to any whatever." [25]

The Cavalier next relates that Richelieu led the army against the Duke of Savoy, wrested Pignerol from him, and annexed "it to the crown of France." He mentions the quarrel between the Queen Mother and the Cardinal, and describes the sad state of the French Protestants who had lost Rochelle chiefly because the English and Dutch had assisted the besiegers.[26] *Richlieu* describes in detail the taking of Rochelle, and mentions precisely as the Cavalier does

[24] *Memoirs,* p. 9. "Richelieu" appears as "Richlieu" in the first edition.
[25] *Richlieu,* I, 330.
[26] *Richlieu,* I, 143–144, 229, 337 ff.; *Memoirs,* pp. 9–11. The charge made by the Protestant gentlemen who traveled with the Cavalier between Orleans and Lyons, that the English and Dutch had ruined their fellow Protestants of Rochelle, is an echo from the *Life of Richlieu,* which remarks that it was much wondered at "that the States-General, who were of the same religion as the Rochellers . . . should send a squadron to the King to reduce it." It may be added that Ludlow, in the opening pages of his *Memoirs,* a work used by Defoe in later parts of the *Memoirs of a Cavalier,* vigorously asserts that the English fleet was the chief cause of the loss of Rochelle to the Catholics.

that the English furnished seven ships, and that the Cardinal, having seized Pignerol, refused to part with it.[27] His quarrel with the Queen Mother also receives frequent mention.

The Cavalier found that Paris was deserted, as "the cardinal, with all the military part of the court, was in the field, so *the king, to be near him, was gone with the queen and all the court,* just before I reached Paris, *to reside at Lyons.*"[28] When the Cavalier "came to Lyons the king was gone from thence to Grenoble to meet the cardinal, but the queens were both at Lyons"; and on the day the Cavalier arrived at Grenoble, he learned that "the king and the cardinal . . . went out to view a body of 6000 Swiss foot, which the cardinal had wheedled the cantons to grant to the king" and "after the review the cardinal was absent some days, having been to wait on the queen-mother at Lyons, where, as it was discoursed, they were at least *seemingly* reconciled."[29]

All this matter Defoe found ready for him in a single page of *Richlieu:* "The king, that he might be near to his armies, came with the queen and all the court to Lyons the 4th of May. . . ." There he was informed that the Cardinal, "who had been sent into Switzerland to raise six thousand men there, had returned, having executed his commission. . . . The 14th of May was appointed for the rendezvous of the army" near Grenoble. "The 10th of the same month the king parted from Lyons to go to Grenoble, whither the cardinal was come the day before. The king arrived the 12th, and the cardinal . . . went to Lyons to salute the queens. . . . It is believed he would not have made this journey, but only to endeavor a perfect reconciliation with the queen-mother. . . . The cardinal . . . *seemed* absolutely reconciled with the queen-mother. . . ."[30]

In the matter of dates the two accounts are not wholly in agreement. As the Cavalier left Dover on 22 April (O.S.) or 3 May (N.S.) and reached Paris within a few days, he must have arrived, as is said, just after the King and his court departed for Lyons, according to the chronology in *Richlieu.* But after three weeks in Paris (with a possible ten days more for recovering from a wound received in a mysterious encounter—unless they are included in the three weeks) and another week or two in Orleans, he must have arrived at Lyons and Grenoble too late for the rendezvous of the army on 14 May.

[27] *Richlieu,* I, 339: "Thus France obtained a passage from Dauphiné into Piedmont which she would never since part with, and by means of which she hath ever since held the Duke of Savoy in dependence." Cf. *Memoirs,* pp. 9–10
[28] *Memoirs,* p. 10. The italics are mine.
[29] *Memoirs,* pp. 14, 15. The italics are mine.
[30] *Richlieu,* I, 341. The italics are mine.

But this difficulty is only additional proof that the *Memoirs* is fictitious and that Defoe is again slipshod in matters of chronology.

Before departing from Lyons for Grenoble, the Cavalier and his friend (whom he forgets half the time) experience some rough treatment which ever after gave the Cavalier an aversion to popular tumults: it was later one of the reasons for his espousing the King's cause in the Civil War. It seems that "the troops were ill-paid, the magazines empty, the people mutinous" because of heavy taxes and the pinching of their trade by the war.[31] On a Sunday night the Cavalier was awakened by a tumult. He found the "street as full of mob as it could hold, some armed" and organized, others in disorder. He gives a brisk description of the whole affair and the shrewdness with which the Queen Mother quieted it.[32] Casting a glance ahead, the Cavalier laments that Charles I had not a like skill in quieting popular clamors.

Here we have an illustration of Defoe's assertion in the preface that many accounts in the Cavalier's story "are not to be found even in the best histories of those times," and that it is "embellished with particulars, which are nowhere else to be found." The riot is described with all of the circumstantiality of a passage in *Robinson Crusoe*, but it is not wholly an invention. The suggestion for it is plainly from *Richlieu:* "The new impositions which had been laid on the people for carrying on the wars rendered them discontented; there had been some seditions in Burgundy, and also a commotion at Lyons, although the queens were present, the people refusing to pay the new taxes. . . . The garrisons of Pignerol and the troops in Piedmont suffered infinitely for want of victuals." [33]

From reporting the *seeming* reconciliation of the Cardinal with the Queen Mother, both the *Memoirs* and *Richlieu* proceed to relate that the Cardinal and the King soon reduced all Savoy except Montmelian.[34] It is significant that whereas *Richlieu* gives the French army as 18,000 foot and 2,000 horse, the Cavalier says it was "not above 22,000 men." One who is familiar with Defoe's use of sources will recognize this as his usual procedure. Writing a "memoir" and not a history, he does not pretend to absolute accuracy. As we shall see elsewhere, he frequently alters slightly the figures he finds, and thus more securely conceals his indebtedness to a source.

[31] *Memoirs*, p. 14.
[32] *Memoirs*, p. 15. Dottin, *Defoe et ses romans*, p. 575, asks why the populace cries *du bain le roi* instead of *du pain le roi*. What Defoe actually wrote is *du paix*. *Paix* may be a misprint for *pain*.
[33] *Richlieu*, I, 342.
[34] *Memoirs*, p. 19; *Richlieu*, I, 342, 355.

From Grenoble the Cavalier "went to Pignerol, which was then little more than a single fortification on the hill near the town called St. Bride's. . . . They had begun a new line below the hill, and some works were marked out on the side of the town next the fort; but the cardinal afterwards drew the plan . . . by which it was made one of the strongest fortresses in Europe." The Cavalier comments: "I mention this because of the prodigious works since added to it."

It is pretended, then, that here are details which only an eye-witness could relate. But the *Life of Richlieu* describes the construction of "a fort on the mountain of St. Bridget" near the castle and also the construction of some lines before the castle, and asserts that the Cardinal, who knew the importance of the place, "took care to fortify it regularly," and that although "he had prevalent reasons to return to France . . . yet would not leave Pignerol before he had put it in a state of defense." [35]

Likewise the *Life of Richlieu* furnished the materials for the Cavalier's account of the attempt of the Duke of Nevers and the French to hold Mantua against the Germans and the Italians, who besieged both Mantua and Casale. In *Richlieu* Defoe read that on 23 May Spinola, the governor of Milan, began the siege of Casale, which "by the bravery of Thoiras who was always in the place" remained in the hands of the Duke of Mantua. The Cavalier says that while he was at Pignerol the siege of Casale was begun, and he remarks two paragraphs later that the French held it for the Duke of Mantua, and "had a strong French garrison under Thoiras, a brave and experienced commander." [36]

At this time the Cavalier and his friend Captain Fielding follow the French army with passes to come and go where they please. They take part in maneuvers of the troops under the Duke of Montmorency and the Maréchal d'Effiat, who had been ordered, "with 10,000 foot and 2000 horse, to march and join the Maréchals de la Force and Schomberg." During this movement occur several encounters with the troops of Savoy, in which the Cavalier, never before under fire, behaves unheroically and runs away the first time and takes refuge in a wood on the second occasion. With the account of these skirmishes Defoe spins out to five pages what *Richlieu* suggests in a paragraph:

The army of the Maréchals de la Force and Schomberg . . . required of necessity to be reinforced with a new body of an army, and the conduct

[35] *Richlieu*, I, 338.
[36] *Memoirs*, pp. 20 ff.; *Richlieu*, I, 326 ff.

thereof was given to the Duke of Montmorency and the Marquis d'Effiat. It was composed of ten thousand foot and a thousand horse, and to join the other army they were to hazard a battle against the troops of Savoy. . . .[37] The French being to pass a defile, the Savoyards staid till all were passed but the rear guard, which they charged and put them presently into confusion; but the two French generals having caused some of their troops to turn back, they defeated the Savoyards, and laid near two thousand men on the ground. A few days after they took the city of Saluces by composition, which made the Duke of Savoy much perplexed. Being come . . . with design to repair the loss by a new combat, because he was superior in horse,[38] he received the news of the taking of Mantua, which as much rejoiced him as it afflicted the French.[39]

The sentence in which it is related that the Savoyards attacked the French as they passed through a defile becomes several pages in the *Memoirs* with many details not in *Richlieu*. A great many of the details are obviously invented, and though Defoe may have possibly found others in a fuller history, it is more probable that he fabricated them all. They resemble Robinson Crusoe's reports of skirmishes in Siberia and passages in *Ramkins, Colonel Jacque,* and later portions of the *Memoirs* itself. The Cavalier concludes with the remark that "the French had really a great blow here," and that he "cannot, without smiling, read some of the histories and memoirs of this action, which they are not ashamed to call a victory."

After this encounter, says the Cavalier, "we marched on to Saluzzo" (Saluces in *Richlieu*), which, as we have seen, surrendered upon articles. This is precisely as related in *Richlieu*, as is likewise the Cavalier's account of the death of the Duke of Savoy. The latter had drawn up his army to threaten the French before Saluzzo when the news came of the taking of Mantua by the Imperial army. "We heard it first," says the Cavalier,[40] "from the Duke of Savoy's cannon, which he fired by way of rejoicing, and which seemed to make him amends for the loss of Saluzzo." Shortly thereafter occurred "the death of the Duke of Savoy, Charles Emanuel, who died, as some say, agitated with the extremes of joy and grief." It should be noted that the *Life of Richlieu* uses a similar phrase: "his grief and joy finished his life," and that here and nowhere else both accounts give the Duke's name, Charles Emanuel.

[37] The Cavalier (p. 24) says, "We always said in our camp that the orders were to fight the Duke of Savoy wherever we met him."
[38] The Cavalier (p. 21) remarks, "The Savoyards were stronger in horse by three or four thousand."
[39] *Richlieu*, I, 345, adds that "in this juncture wherein Charles Emanuel had more reason to be sorry than to rejoice, his grief and joy finished his life." Cf. *Memoirs*, pp. 20 ff.
[40] P. 24.

The Cavalier then says that hearing of the Duke's death, the French generals considered "whether they should march to the relief of Casale," but decided to remain in the Piedmont where "they took several small places from the Duke of Savoy, making advantage of *the consternation the duke's subjects were in on the death of their Prince,* and spread themselves from the seaside to the banks of the Po." The *Life of Richlieu* gives these details [41] and relates also that the "French generals . . . deliberated whether they should go to Casale *whilst the courage of the Savoyards was abated by the death of their Prince.*" Upon their decision to remain in the Piedmont they took Villa Franca, Pontcolier, and Carignan, driving the Savoyards over the Po.

At precisely this point in the middle of the paragraph each account introduces the subject of the plague, which, says *Richlieu,* "began to kill many people." [42] The Cavalier, more alarmed at the risk of disease than of battle, left the army immediately to go to Genoa, but "was arrested at Villa Franca [43] by a slow lingering fever which . . . turned . . . at last to the plague." Though Defoe was presently to demonstrate his familiarity with all phases of the plague in his *Journal of the Plague Year,* here he certainly depends upon the passage in *Richlieu* which recounts the experience of Louis XIII with the plague. Like the French King, the Cavalier had escaped from the plague-stricken area before succumbing. In both cases the disease takes the form of a great swelling on account of which the physicians despair: they "gave me over, as past all remedy," says the Cavalier; "gave him up for lost without retrieve," says the *Life of Richlieu.* The swelling finally breaks and drains, after which both King and Cavalier recover.

The Cavalier proceeds to discuss the truce between the belligerents, for, says he, being an onlooker he saw farther into the situation than those actually concerned. He points out the several reasons why France, Savoy, and Spain agreed to the truce: France to save Casale from the hands of Spain; Savoy to keep the French from wintering in the Piedmont; and Spain because Spinola, unable to take Casale, wanted to come off with honor. They were all mistaken, adds the Cavalier, for Spinola's army was too weak to take Casale; the plague-stricken French dared not remain in the Piedmont; and, weak as Spinola's army was, Casale would shortly have been starved into surrender. He describes the condition of the armies at the con-

[41] I, 345. The italics are mine.
[42] The Cavalier (p. 25) uses the phrase, "destroyed abundance of people."
[43] One of the places mentioned in *Richlieu.*

clusion of the truce, and closes with an account of Spinola's death
caused by grief at the failure to take Casale and at the Spanish
government's treatment of him.

These shrewd observations, had they been original with Defoe
or the Cavalier, would testify to skill in statesmanship; but as the
Life of Richlieu had furnished them ready to Defoe's hands, they
merely show skill in adapting a passage from history to the purposes
of fiction. *Richlieu* discusses in detail precisely those reasons which
according to the Cavalier led each party to make the truce,[44] comments on the fact that the truce "seemed strange to those who knew
not the condition of both parties," explains the desperate case of
the army in Casale and the equally weakened condition of Spinola's
army before it, describes at great length the marching out of the
various armies, and tells of the succoring of Casale and of the death
of Spinola, elaborating the causes of his grief.

At this point the Cavalier, recovered from the plague, takes leave
of the French and their affairs and passes the winter in Milan. But
Defoe was not yet finished with the *Life of Richlieu:* he uses one
more paragraph. "Here it was," says the Cavalier, "I first heard the
name of Gustavus Adolphus, the king of Sweden, who now began
his war with the Emperor." He goes on to relate that while "the
king of France was at Lyons, the league with Sweden was made, in
which the French contributed 1,200,000 crowns in money, and
600,000 per annum" toward defraying the expenses of Gustavus
Adolphus.

Except for the matter of 1,200,000 crowns and a slight variation
in the amount to be paid annually,[45] this relation is in agreement
with *Richlieu,* which reports that it "was this year that Gustavus
Adolphus passed into Pomerania, and the king having sent . . . to
propose a league between the two crowns. . . . It is true that it cost
France five hundred thousand crowns yearly." [46]

It is evident that Le Clerc gave Defoe the foundation for his
account of the Cavalier's adventures with the French army and
some suggestions for later enterprises with Gustavus Adolphus.
Could one say that here Defoe, as in *Robinson Crusoe* and *Singleton,* worked only from event to event, without seeing the whole
structure of his book from the outset? The part of Le Clerc's book
that Defoe principally made use of is compact; it amounts to a half-
dozen pages.[47] Defoe's *Memoirs* and Le Clerc's *Richlieu* are in com-

[44] I, 346 ff.
[45] The *Swedish Intelligencer,* I, 75 ff., gives somewhat different figures here.
[46] *Richlieu,* I, 344.
[47] I, 341–347.

plete agreement: only a few minor details in the *Memoirs* are not in *Richlieu;* the order and arrangement of the one have a close resemblance to those of the other, and the similarity of phrasing, often identical, proves beyond doubt that this is Defoe's source. To see how different the *Memoirs* is from other histories of the same period one has only to consult Michel Le Vassor's *Histoire*.[48] Although Le Vassor is far more complete, his arrangement of material is very different from Defoe's. He omits some details which appear both in the *Memoirs* and in *Richlieu;* and his diction has no resemblance to Defoe's.

With the Swedes in Germany

That Defoe in his account of the Cavalier's career under Gustavus Adolphus made use of the *Swedish Intelligencer* has been known—or at least suspected—since 1810, when Sir Walter Scott cited passages from it in his edition of the *Memoirs.* Aitken suggested also Robert Monro's *Expedition with the Worthy Scots Regiment (Called Mackeyes)* (1637), and recently Dottin adds *Le Soldat suédois* (1633), attributed to F. Spanheim, John Fowler's *History of the Troubles of Suethland and Poland* (1656), and Samuel Puffendorf's *Complete History of Sweden* (1702). Aitken's opinion was that Defoe seems to have read his sources with care, but "without troubling to refer to them when he was writing, to ensure perfect accuracy; and with the narrative with which he had thus filled his mind he interwove an imaginary account of a Cavalier, in order to give unity to the whole." [49] Dottin, on the other hand, remarks that certain passages "semblent avoir été copiés presque intégralement" from the *Swedish Intelligencer*.[50] No one, however, has determined to what extent Defoe relied upon these works, if indeed he used them at all, or what he did with the material he may have taken from them.

A careful examination of these works must convince anyone that the *Swedish Intelligencer* is probably the only source of that portion of the *Memoirs* that deals with the Cavalier's adventures under Gustavus Adolphus—that is to say, until Gustavus' death at the battle of Lützen in 1632. It is true that Defoe may have been acquainted with other works. The 1706 edition of Puffendorf was in his library, and Monro's *Expedition* is precisely the sort of book which, except for its copious passages of moralizing, Defoe enjoyed;

---

[48] *Histoire du règne de Louis XIII* (Amsterdam, 1700–1711), VI, 258 ff.
[49] *Memoirs,* pp. xvi–xvii.
[50] *Defoe et ses romans,* p. 560.

and the moralizing, being labeled, can easily be skipped. Perhaps Defoe liked moralizing even in the works of others. Less likely was he to have known *Le Soldat suédois,* which seems to have had no English translation. Like the *Commentarii* of Burgus (*De bello Suecico,* 1641), which Dottin thinks Defoe possessed,[51] it closes with the battle of Lützen, and it is only beyond that point that Defoe needed a new source, since the *Swedish Intelligencer* really came to a close there. Fowler's work, dealing entirely with relations between Sweden and Poland, except for a brief memoir of Sir George Douglas, who for a short time served under Gustavus Adolphus as lieutenant colonel to Sir James Ramsey, contains nothing Defoe has used in the *Memoirs of a Cavalier.* What we are to seek is not accounts like *Le Soldat suédois* and Burgus' *Commentarii,* which merely duplicate the ground covered by the *Swedish Intelligencer,* but works which continue the story to a later point. What we need especially is a source for the battle of Nördlingen (1634) and an account of the progress of the Swedish forces after the Cavalier had returned to England. Except for these details the Cavalier's account of Swedish affairs also ends with Lützen in 1632. The account of Nördlingen Defoe took from Puffendorf's *Complete History of Sweden* (London, 1702), p. 486, either directly or perhaps indirectly through David Jones's *Compleat History of Europe . . . from . . . 1600,* II (London, 1705), 127 ff., which has extracted the account of Nördlingen from Puffendorf.

When Gustavus Adolphus swept through Germany in 1630–32 and revived the drooping head of Protestant Europe, his career naturally was followed with enthusiasm by all who feared the ascendancy of the Emperor and his Roman Catholic supporters. Though Charles I's government took no part in the war, there is no question of the sentiments of the English people, as the long list of English and Scottish gentlemen who joined the Protestant forces shows. The *Swedish Intelligencer* has various mentions of British volunteers;[52] Monro's *Expedition* has a long list of Scots who fought in the Protestant cause on the Continent; and Defoe's *Scots Nation and Union Vindicated* has a four-page list (pp. 25–28) of Scots of the rank of colonel or higher who were distinguished in the Swedish service.

[51] It was recommended to Colonel Jacque by his Virginia tutor.

[52] Among the names in the *Intelligencer* occurs that of Captain Fielding, who may be supposed to be the Cavalier's companion (see note 107 below). The *Intelligencer* consists of four parts, published in 1632–33 and thereafter. All passages here quoted from it, though modernized in spelling and typography, follow the texts of a copy in the Harvard Library, the title page of which advertises it as "Now for the third time, revised, corrected, and augmented."

Lack of space prevented giving a similar list of men who fought along with the French in the same cause.

Reflecting this enthusiasm were the many published accounts of the Swedish progress. Pamphleteers explained the causes of the invasions and related the principal actions. Historians from all parts of Europe celebrated the gallantry of Gustavus Adolphus. News-letters, beginning to develop into newspapers, described the Swedish King's campaigns, meanwhile cautioning readers against the errors in rival accounts. Among such journals the most important for us is the *Swedish Intelligencer,* printed for Nathaniel Butter and Nicholas Bourne and written by William Watts. This periodical was the basis of the portion of the *Memoirs* that deals with the wars in Germany. No other source seems to have the similarity in arrange-ment of material, the agreement in detail, and the complete har-mony of matter emphasized frequently by verbal likenesses and duplication.

Although the Cavalier did not join the Swedish army until shortly before the battle of Leipzig, late in 1631, he is made to give a gen-eral account of the military conditions in Germany which led to the Swedish invasion and of events which occurred before the battle of Leipzig. His introduction of Gustavus and his campaigns was due, it has been suggested, to Le Clerc's *Life of Richlieu.* But full treatment of events in Germany does not begin until the Cavalier, in Vienna, on 10 April 1631, finds the progress of the Swedish arms the principal subject of conversation.

From the *Swedish Intelligencer* came the Cavalier's summary of events prior to his joining Gustavus Adolphus' army. He begins by remarking that there

had been a long bloody war in the empire of Germany for twelve years, between the emperor, the Duke of Bavaria, the King of Spain, and the Popish princes and electors on the one side, and the Protestant princes on the other; and both sides having been exhausted by the war, and even the Catholics themselves beginning to dislike the growing power of the house of Austria, 'twas thought all parties were willing to make peace.[53]

This is precisely the point with which the correspondent of the *Swedish Intelligencer* (after an apology for his tardiness in writing) begins his account:

Now after twelve years of most bloody wars, and almost utter desolation brought upon a goodly country, very probable surely it was that a peace would be desired on all hands. . . . Yea the Catholics themselves, having had often trial of the insolencies of the Imperial soldiers, and of the

---

[53] *Memoirs,* p. 33.

chargeableness of the war, began now also mightily to distaste the covetous-
ness of their own partner, the Duke of Bavaria.[54]

In these two statements, in spite of divergences, there seem to be
undeniable likenesses. Defoe's citing the house of Austria rather than
the Duke of Bavaria may be a change intentionally made to dis-
guise borrowing. It does not conflict with historical fact.

The Cavalier next describes the plight of the Dukes of Mecklen-
burg, who solicit the King of Sweden to assist them against the
Emperor, and the reasons which led the King of Sweden to take up
their quarrel; namely, that the Emperor had assisted the Poles
against the Swedes. This is all related in the *Intelligencer*.[55] Both
accounts, furthermore, describe the landing of Gustavus before
Stralsund, the capture of Stralsund, Stettin, and other Baltic towns,
the Diet of Ratisbon with the Emperor's astute management of it,
the uncertainty of the Protestant program, and the Protestant hesi-
tancy in making a league with Gustavus, the causes which forced
them to it, and the steps which led to the Protestant Diet of Leipzig.[56]

This diet, which the Cavalier says "was held at Leipzic, February 8, 1630," has a whole section of nearly twenty pages devoted
to it in the *Intelligencer*. This section is headed "The Protestant's
Diet of Leipsich, beginning February 8, 1630 . . . with what followed upon it, until their joining with the King of Sweden." The
Cavalier gives only the conclusions, which with some alteration of
the phraseology he lists under ten heads, as the *Intelligencer* does.[57]

The Cavalier's remark that the Emperor, "exceedingly startled at
the Conclusions, issued out a proclamation . . . against them . . .
and commanded Tilly . . . to fall on the Duke of Saxony" echoes
the statement in the *Intelligencer* that the "conclusions . . . did not
slightly displease the Emperor and startle the Catholic Leaguers."
The *Intelligencer* continues with a full account of the Emperor's re-
actions, who "out-thunders . . . his Imperial ban" (called in the
margin a proclamation; Defoe uses both terms), and of the advance
of Tilly against Saxony.[58]

[54] *Intelligencer*, I, 2.

[55] I, 42-43.

[56] *Memoirs*, pp. 39-40; *Intelligencer*, I, 20 ff. There is some discrepancy between
the Cavalier's statement that the Swedish army before Stralsund was less than
3,000 and that of the *Intelligencer*, which says 12,000 men and 3,000 horse.

[57] *Memoirs*, pp. 39-40; *Intelligencer*, I, 20 ff.

[58] *Memoirs*, p. 40; *Intelligencer*, I, 28 ff. The Cavalier's long account of Seigen-
sius, the Lutheran minister, whose shrewdness aided the Duke of Saxony in
getting the Emperor's consent to call the Diet of Leipzig, is not from the
Intelligencer. Whether it is an invention of Defoe's or a borrowing from another

At this point both works relate that the King of Sweden "had already conquered Mecklenberg and parts of Pomerania" and was advancing to Brandenburg.[59] The hesitation of the Duke of Brandenburg to join the Swedish forces is discussed in two places in each book. In the *Intelligencer* this duplication results from the writer's device of handling each thread of the story separately.

Brandenburg had given up the town of Spandau to the king . . . when on a sudden . . . Brandenburg . . . demands to have his town of Spandau restored to him again. Gustavus Adolphus . . . delivered him his town of Spandau, but immediately turns about, and with his whole army besieges him in his capital city of Berlin.

This brought the duke to know his error, and by the interpositions of the ladies . . . the matter was accommodated. . . .[60]

The King having . . . obtained the town of Spandaw . . . the Elector [Brandenburg] demands his town again. The proposition very much displeased the King . . . yet . . . he delivers it, June 8. The next day he sends word into Berlin (the town where the Elector held his court) of a visit he meant to give it . . . he straightly beleaguers Berlin. . . . Out sends the Elector to treat. . . . When the men could not agree, the women draw down the King to milder resolutions.[61]

But the Cavalier has not yet reached Germany; he is in Vienna where he finds that the Imperialists talked slightingly of Gustavus as "one that they might let go on and tire himself in Mecklenberg and thereabout, till they could find leisure to deal with him." This is another echo of the *Intelligencer*, which asserts that one of the great advantages of the King was to be "too much slighted by the Emperor who . . . did . . . not time enough employ any of his great captains against him," and who, when the Swedish forces were "already advanced into Pomerland," wrote to the Duke of Saxony that he was so well provided for them that he was confident of being able to scatter them. The Cavalier concludes that " 'tis never safe to despise an enemy"; and the *Intelligencer* says that a "despised enemy we have by experience seen to have made foul work." [62]

The Cavalier, now resolved to see the Swedish army, sets out, but finding it impossible to pass the frontiers of Silesia, he turns to an-

source is unknown. At any rate it is not the kind of detail a real Cavalier would give us. It is not pretended that he was present at the time. The Cavalier, however, says that he knew the Lutheran when in Leipzig, and adds, "I had the relation from his own mouth."

[59] *Memoirs*, p. 40; *Intelligencer*, I, 29. The Cavalier: "was advancing with his victorious troops"; the *Intelligencer*: "victoriously already advanc'd."

[60] *Memoirs*, p. 49.

[61] *Intelligencer*, I, 99.

[62] *Memoirs*, p. 41; *Intelligencer*, I, 46–47.

other course and comes into Tilly's army, "then at the siege of Magdeburg, May the 2nd." The famous account of the sacking of that city is indubitably founded upon the report in the *Intelligencer*, which has a large map showing the city, the position of the besiegers, and the Elbe, with the "sconce" over against it, from which the Cavalier pretends to have witnessed the butchery. It is true that Defoe adds some picturesque details not in the *Intelligencer*, but they are such as he was eminently capable of imagining; and on the whole his account is in agreement with that of the *Intelligencer*. The latter tells of the terms offered the city by Tilly, of the gathering to discuss them, the walls of the city left unwatched meanwhile, of the discovery of that fact by Tilly's men, and of the capture and sacking of the city.[63] Not infrequently there is borrowing of phraseology as well as of facts—as when the Cavalier says that the garrison "flew to the walls, twice beat the Imperialists off, but fresh men coming up, and the administrator of Magdeburg himself being wounded and taken, the enemy broke in." The *Intelligencer* had said: "Falkenburg now flying in upon them, beats them back to the very walls again: but a port being by this time opened and the enemy's horse let in . . . the Administrator [is] hurt both in the thigh and head, and so taken." [64]

The Cavalier reports that of 25,000 or 30,000 all were killed except 2,000 who found hiding places, and that these were finally protected. His source is the *Intelligencer*, which says: "Twenty thousand people, at least, were here killed, burned and smothered: six thousand . . . drowned in the Elbe . . . [Tilly] finding some hundreds of women and children in the church, he gives them their lives." [65] The Cavalier elaborates the phrase about the drowning and concludes that of the city nothing was "left but the great church and about a hundred houses." For this last bit he has warrant in the *Intelligencer*'s statement that "the whole town was . . . utterly turned to cinders, excepting 139 houses . . . [and that] the cathedral together with St. Mary's Church and cloister were . . . preserved."

The Cavalier next relates the effect upon the Protestant princes of the coming of Tilly's army. "If Tilly did but write a threatening letter to any city or prince of the union, they presently submitted . . . as the cities of Ulm and Memmingen, the Duchy of Wirtemburg . . . and almost all Suaben," leaving "only the Duke

[63] I, 117 ff.
[64] *Memoirs*, p. 43; *Intelligencer*, I, 118.
[65] *Memoirs*, pp. 43–44; *Intelligencer*, I, 119.

of Saxony and the Landgrave of Hesse [to uphold] the drooping courage of the Protestants." Every detail here is from the *Intelligencer*.[66]

Both accounts next proceed to the measures taken by Saxony in her defense. They relate that the Duke, attended by his field marshal Arnheim, mustered his forces at Leipzig. The Cavalier pretends to have witnessed this event on his way to meet the Swedes, and compares the raw Saxons with Tilly's "old weather-beaten soldiers." Both tell that Tilly sent four propositions to which he will have an immediate reply; both list the propositions and tell that the Duke, having refused them, marched to Torgau with his army and then, threatened by both Furstenburg and Tilly, who undertook a siege of Leipzig, hastened to join Gustavus Adolphus.[67] The Cavalier comes up with the Saxons at Torgau and meets the Swedes at Beltzig. The crossing of the Elbe by the Swedes at Wittenberg and their joining with the Saxons is related in every detail as in the *Intelligencer*. Both accounts give the date, 3 September, and mention Torgau, Beltzig, Coswig, and Wittenberg.[68]

Among the Swedes the Cavalier is again with friends, Lord Rheay, Colonel Lumsdell, and Sir John Hepburn (an old acquaintance of the Cavalier's father, we are told), being colonels of the three Scottish regiments in the Swedish army and extraordinarily esteemed by the King himself—as Defoe learned from the pages of the *Intelligencer*.[69] This work constantly refers to these men and their heroic actions; all three are mentioned together in the margin in the *Intelligencer*'s account of the battle of Leipzig.[70] Hepburn introduces the Cavalier to the King, who, upon hearing that he has just come from Tilly's camp, is anxious for news of Tilly's army. By degrees the Cavalier and his friend Captain Fielding engage themselves in the Swedish service.

---

[66] *Memoirs*, p. 47; *Intelligencer*, I, 33 f., 119 ff. The *Intelligencer* cites the defection of Duke Julius of Wirtemburg, of Ulm and Memmingen, and of other cities "both in the dukedom and through Swaben," and concludes that the "Landgrave of Hessen remains firm for all this: and Duke Bernard of Saxon-Weimar."

[67] *Memoirs*, pp. 47–51; *Intelligencer*, I, 34, 36–38, 110, 123, 124. In timing the Cavalier's movements from Magdeburg to Leipzig, Torgau, and Coswig, Defoe uses the dates given in the *Intelligencer*. Both works describe the distraction of the Leipzigers at the coming of Tilly, fresh from the sacking of Magdeburg, and relate tales of cruelty and ravishing on the part of Tilly's men. Elsewhere the Cavalier tells Gustavus Adolphus that Tilly has two armies, one of them made up of women camp followers.

[68] *Memoirs*, pp. 49, 54; *Intelligencer*, I, 38, 111–112.

[69] *Memoirs*, p. 62; *Intelligencer*, I, 53, 61, 87, 90, and *passim*. The *Intelligencer* (I, 123, 124) uses "Habron" instead of Hepburn, but it also uses "Hebron" and "Hepburne" (II, 46).

[70] I, 124.

Their first adventure was at the famous battle of Leipzig, and the whole account of that battle from the beginning, in which it is remarked that before dawn on 7 September the Swedish army marched from Dieben to the field about a mile from Leipzig where Tilly's army awaited them, until the end with the account of plundering the Imperial army, is taken from the section devoted to that battle in the *Intelligencer*.[71] Both stories inform us that Tilly had 44,000 men ("brave men," says the *Intelligencer;* "old soldiers," says the Cavalier), and the Saxons 22,000 and both explain similarly the disposition of the commands and the general course of the fight: how the Saxons early were routed but how Tilly allowed no premature pursuit.

Gustavus says: "Let them go, but let us beat the Swedes, or we do nothing."
. . . the Scottish brigades giving fire three ranks at a time over one another's heads, poured in their shot so thick, that the enemy were cut down like grass before a scythe. . . .
For had there been three hours more daylight ten thousand more lives had been lost. . . . The retreat was not sounded till seven o'clock.[72]

"Let them go, we shall overtake them time enough; but let us beat the Swede too, and then all Germany is our own". . . . The foremost rank falling on their knees; the second stooping forward; and the third rank standing right up, and all giving fire together they poured so much lead at one instant . . . that their ranks were much broken with it. . . . Had the King had but 3 hours more of daylight, scarcely had 1,000 enemies come off alive; but the darkness [came] . . . the joyful retreat is sounded, and the chase given over for that night.[73]

Defoe amuses the reader here with a lengthy account of the Cavalier's man who secures booty after the battle; but for the historical part he continues following the *Intelligencer*, which relates that after a day of "chase and slaughter" the King went on to Merseburg, Halle, Erfurt, and Köningshoven, and so into Franconia.[74] The

[71] *Memoirs*, p. 60; *Intelligencer*, I, 121 ff.
[72] *Memoirs*, pp. 62–66.
[73] *Intelligencer*, I, 123–125. Both accounts call attention to the gallant conduct of Baron Kronenburg. The only details given by Defoe's Cavalier which are not in the *Intelligencer* concern Gustavus Horn's commanding the main battle and the conduct of Colonels Hall and Cullembach and Baron Dyvel. The *Intelligencer* does not mention Horn or Dyvel (or Teuffel) in its account of Leipzig, and refers to Hall and Cullembach only as colonels who were slain. *Le Soldat suédois* (Geneva, 1633), pp. 68 ff., and *The History of Gustavus Adolphus*, tr. by F. Spence from Jean Le Royer de Prade (London, 1689), pp. 89 ff., both say Teuffel commanded the main battle for the Swedes and Horn the left wing. Defoe refers to Teuffel only as the colonel of the King's guards, who was killed. Horn he first assigns to the main battle and later to the left wing. Had Defoe another source, such as the history of Puffendorf? But such a source is important only for Hall and Horn and Cullembach.
[74] *Memoirs*, pp. 71, 73; *Intelligencer*, I, 127 ff., and II, 2, 3.

Cavalier, having been busy caring for his friend Captain Fielding, who was wounded at Leipzig, passes through Erfurt on 28 September and comes up with the King at Köningshoven; the *Intelligencer* mentions 28 September as the day on which the King continues his march to Köningshoven.[75]

The two accounts parallel each other continuously. Both mention that the King, now eager to master the Main River, takes the bishoprics of Bamberg and Würtzburg, the latter dominated by the castle of Marienberg. The capture of this castle the Cavalier describes in detail precisely as does the *Intelligencer*.[76] Both relate that the castle was on a high rock, that Sir James Ramsey led the Scottish soldiers, and that rich booty was secured. The Cavalier got into the action by joining a party of volunteers under Hepburn. Only the Cavalier quotes the King as "calling the soldiers his brave Scots," but the *Intelligencer* on a previous occasion cites him as remarking: "Now my brave Scots." A comparison of passages from the two works shows how Defoe recasts his material.

I cannot but give some short account of the glory of the morning. . . . There was first a magazine of very good arms . . . thirty-two brass field-pieces, and four mortars. . . . The . . . treasure . . . amounted to 400,-000 florins in money; and the burghers of the town in solemn procession, bareheaded, brought the king three tons of gold . . . to exempt the city from plunder. Here was also a stable of gallant horses which the king had the curiosity to go and see. When the ceremony of the burghers was over, the king came down into the castle court, walked on the parade . . . and round the walls, and gave order for repairing the bastion that was stormed by the Scots.[77]

[The castle was delivered to the soldiers for an hour's pillaging. They secured, among other valuable booty, thirty-four pieces of brass ordnance.] And thus was this goodly, rich, strong, and pleasant castle . . . taken . . . by eight o'clock on Saturday morning. . . . A palace it was . . . which having been something defaced by the cannon, the King caused to be forthwith repaired. . . . The town redeemed itself from pillaging by the payment of 4 tun of gold; or of 300,000 florins . . . so that the King and his soldiers never went so rich away from any place. Here was found a princely stable of goodly horses, with which the King was very much delighted.[78]

At this point in the story the Cavalier formally enters the Swedish service, and under Sir John Hepburn's tutelage joins the party of volunteers about the King's person. "The first piece of service he [the King] employed me upon," says the Cavalier, "had like to have

[75] *Intelligencer,* II, 6.
[76] *Memoirs,* pp. 74 ff.; *Intelligencer,* II, 11 ff.
[77] *Memoirs,* pp. 75–76.
[78] *Intelligencer,* II, 15, 16.

embroiled me with one of his favourite colonels." As all thought him headed for Heidelberg, the King suddenly drew up a force composed of members of his guard and five companies of Scots, and sent them by night to Oppenheim to take a post under the walls of the fort. "Ho, cavalier," said the King, "you shall command this party." "Grave Neels, the colonel of his guards, thought himself injured by this command, but . . . told me very familiarly afterwards, 'We have such a master,' says he, 'that no man can be affronted by.' " [79]

Here it must be admitted that Defoe brazenly ascribes to his hero the deeds of other men. For the *Intelligencer* describes the enterprise in agreement with the *Memoirs* at all points except one. Having related the King's determination to let Heidelberg wait until he had taken Oppenheim, it remarks: "Upon Sunday, Decemb. 4, Grave Neeles with the King's lifeguards sets down before it . . . being the next day relieved by Sir John Hebron." [80]

Curiously enough Defoe ignores some very interesting details of the sort he himself liked to use. The *Intelligencer* relates that before the attack upon the castle of Oppenheim, "one Hild, a poor fisherman . . . was the man . . . who not only brought two great boats down the stream with him . . . but showed the King also where the Spanish had sunk another very great Rhine-ship." With these the King and his men might have crossed safely but for an odd accident: "A certain soldier (a Sweden born) having gotten into a little boat by himself (which upon that river are only made of 3 boards) was skimming over himself at the same time also. But the stream carrying him . . . too low towards the town, he there chops upon some 500 Spanish horse. . . ." [81] Defoe only remarks that the King, being informed where some sunken boats lay, had them raised and crossed on three of them with his guards; but they were no sooner landed than they were charged by a body of Spanish horse. Defoe, however, adds some details of his own. The Cavalier, it is pretended, crossed in the boat with the King and observed his concern for his men.[82]

The relation of the capture of Oppenheim Defoe bases upon that in the *Intelligencer*'s statements that in the city was placed a garrison of 200 Scots, "all (or almost all) that were left of Sir James Ramsey's regiment: himself lay yet at Wurstburg to be cured of his wound which there . . . he received," and that, after the ad-

[79] *Memoirs*, p. 80.
[80] *Intelligencer*, II, 43. The Cavalier also has this detail (p. 81).
[81] *Intelligencer*, II, 43–44.
[82] *Memoirs*, p. 82.

vance of Hepburn's regiment, "those 200 Scots . . . fall immediately thereupon to storm the said castle" (II, 46). Here is a gap for
the Cavalier. Says he: "Sir James Ramsey being left wounded at
Würtzburg, the king gave me the command of those 200 men, which
were a regiment, that is to say, all that were left of a gallant regiment." He then describes the capture of the castle in which "my
reformado Scots" played a gallant part.[83] The Cavalier pretends to
be in charge of these men later at the taking of Creutznach, and
indeed thereafter until, upon leaving the Swedish service, he bestows
them upon his friend Captain Fielding. According to the *Intelligencer* Hepburn seems to have commanded them at Oppenheim,
and the *Intelligencer* (II, 77) tells us that Lieutenant Colonel Sir
George Douglas commanded them at the taking of Creutznach.
Another work [84] asserts that Douglas, having entered the Swedish
service in 1623, rose to be lieutenant colonel under Ramsey, and
commanded the regiment in his absence after he was wounded at
Würtzburg.[85]

Having followed the *Intelligencer* in recounting the taking of
Mainz and described the arrival of the King of Bohemia and Lord
Craven, Defoe next uses that work for his account of the siege of
Creutznach. That Sir George Douglas, and not the Cavalier, com-
manded Ramsey's regiment there has already been said. Though
Defoe may have known about the heroism of Lord Craven from
other sources, as Craven was a well-known Restoration figure, he
yet sticks closely to the *Intelligencer* in describing it.[86]

Being among the horse, the Cavalier has no share in taking
Donauwerth,[87] but he describes the action, briefly mentioning the
only facts given in the *Intelligencer;* namely, that Gustavus began
the siege on 26 March and carried it the next day, owing chiefly to
the bravery of Hepburn and the Scottish brigade and some English
volunteers, of whom the *Intelligencer* (but not Defoe) mentions Lord
Craven and Masters Nicholas Slanning [88] and Robert Masham.

[83] *Memoirs*, pp. 82–83.

[84] John Fowler, *The History of the Troubles of Suethland and Poland* (London, 1656), p. 216. The brief account of Sir George Douglas' adventures with the
Swedish forces seems to be the only portion of this book that could have contributed anything to the *Memoirs;* it seems uncertain whether Defoe knew the
book at all.

[85] *Intelligencer*, II, 79.

[86] *Memoirs*, pp. 87 ff.; *Intelligencer*, II, 81–82.

[87] *Memoirs*, pp. 90–91; *Intelligencer*, II, 135 ff. Compare also the two accounts
of Horn being beaten out of Bamberg by Tilly (*Memoirs*, p. 87; *Intelligencer*,
II, 89 ff.) and of Gustavus' advance into Bavaria (*Memoirs*, p. 90; *Intelligencer*,
II, 126 ff., 141, 147).

[88] *Memoirs*, p. 87; *Intelligencer*, II, 81 ff. The *Intelligencer* mentions "divers
English and French gentlemen volunteers" with Lord Craven, such as Lieutenant

The famous feat of Gustavus in leading his army on a hastily contrived plank bridge across the Lech in the face of Tilly's army is related at great length by the Cavalier, who, "having been an eyewitness to every part of it," can be "more particular in it than other accounts." And there are not wanting military men who have accepted as a fact the Cavalier's boast of being an eyewitness. It has been urged that Defoe was incapable of fabricating this great feat of military engineering, nor could he have found another equally detailed account. Defoe's source, nevertheless, is clearly the *Intelligencer,* which devotes eight pages to the action, and adds a large-sized chart showing in detail the terrain, the river, the trees, and the position of the bridge, of Tilly's cannon, and of Gustavus' army, with a key to explain it all.[89]

The only detail lacking in the *Intelligencer,* and a very interesting one it is, is Defoe's account of the steps taken by the King to discover the depth of the river at the point chosen for the bridge—an account which is an excellent example of Defoe's inventive fancy. His story represents the King as saying, "And he shall have fifty dollars, that shall bring me word how deep the water is." A sergeant of dragoons volunteering is chosen to make the venture. Disguised as a ploughman, the dragoon with a long pole "comes down boldly to the bank of the river, and calling to the sentinels which Tilly had placed on the other bank . . . pretended he wanted to come to them." Having reached the precise point where the bridge was intended,

he puts his long pole into the water, then finding it pretty shallow he pulls off his hose and goes in, still thrusting his pole in before him, till being gotten up to his middle, he could reach beyond him, where it was too deep, and so shaking his head, comes back again. The soldiers on the other side, laughing at him, asked him if he could swim? He said, "No." "Why, you fool you," says one of the sentinels, "the channel of the river is twenty feet deep." "How do you know that?" says the dragoon. "Why, our engineer," says he, "measured it yesterday."

Though this is precisely what he came to discover, the dragoon carried on the deceit until he knew also the breadth of the stream and the nature of the bottom and of the banks—to the delight of Gustavus, who "gave him a hundred dollars, and made him a quartermaster to a troop of cuirassiers." [90]

Colonel Talbot, Robert Masham, and Henry Wind; but none of them could have been the Cavalier. Nicholas Slanning later fought with the Cavalier for Charles I, but the Cavalier does not mention any earlier companionship in Germany.

[89] *Memoirs,* pp. 92 ff.; *Intelligencer,* II, 141 ff.

[90] *Memoirs,* pp. 93–94.

But this droll account, though more interesting than any which the *Intelligencer* relates of the event, is not wholly without parallel or suggestion in that work. We have seen that it sometimes relates homely details which Defoe for some reason ignores. One in particular concerning the siege of Creutznach is significant, for it appears to have been the basis for this anecdote about the Lech. The King, according to the *Intelligencer*, was inspecting the castle which overlooked the town, and his "sight being naturally none of the sharpest at a distance . . . spies a sergeant (whom he very well knew) to whom he immediately calls by his name; 'Come hither thou, such a one; thou shalt have 100 dollars to go up and see what the enemy doth in the next Traverse'. . . . The sergeant did so, came down safely, and had his money." Not fully satisfied, the King places himself "along the slope of the hill," and with the sergeant's help studies carefully the enemy's position.[91] In each case the King, desiring someone to spy out a dangerous enemy position, chooses a sergeant, and rewards him with a hundred dollars. As we cannot believe in the Cavalier's being an actual person or discover in authentic histories the anecdote about the dragoon-ploughman, it is easy to assume that Defoe invented it (or interpolated it from some other time and place), possibly from the passage I have designated in the siege of Creutznach.

More authentic (to return to the Lech) is the Cavalier's statement that the ground was ten or twelve feet higher "on this side" than on the other, and a hard gravel; the *Intelligencer* (II, 142) says: "a pike's length higher bank'd, and plainer withall, than that on Tilly's [side], which was both lower and woody." The Cavalier says that the bridge constructed "was only loose planks laid upon large tressels," whereas the *Intelligencer* describes the trestles and remarks: "the arches or tressels for the bridge, with the planks . . . [were] all brought and ready to be laid." On the night of 4 April (according to the Cavalier) the King sent 2,000 men to dig a trench along the river. By daylight the trench was finished and lined with musketeers and "all the utensils of the bridge lay ready to put together." Then "the Imperialists discovered the design." The account in the *Intelligencer* agrees in all details with that just given from the *Memoirs*.[92]

Another day is spent in which the spade plays a greater part than the sword. And yet, says the Cavalier, "the cannon and musket

[91] *Intelligencer*, II, 79.

[92] *Memoirs*, p. 95; *Intelligencer*, II, 142–143. *Le Soldat suédois*, p. 270, gives only a very brief account of this bridge.

bullets flew like hail." The *Intelligencer's* version is that "the small and great shot go off incessantly on both sides all this while." Both also record that Altringer is wounded and finally that Tilly himself is mortally wounded, and carried to Ingolstadt.[93]

With Tilly's departure the Imperial forces soon retreated. Upon hearing the good news from Captain Forbes the King cautiously sent parties to scout the forsaken quarters before venturing his army, and then, after taking Rains, he besieged Augsburg. In recounting these matters Defoe goes beyond the *Intelligencer* only in having his Cavalier command one of the parties to spy out the Imperial camp. When he had passed the bridge and come upon Tilly's fortifications, the Cavalier reflected upon the desperate battle which Tilly's death had prevented—and these sentiments are ascribed to Gustavus himself in the *Intelligencer*.[94]

Now that the Cavalier has attained experience, Defoe frequently ascribes to him the conduct of parties whose leaders are not otherwise indicated in the *Intelligencer*. So the King, at his coming before Augsburg, "sends me with my little troop [95] and three companies of dragoons to beat in these out-scouts." The *Intelligencer* says merely that the King "first of all beats in their outguards." But Defoe gives us a realistic account, two pages in length, of this minor action of which his Cavalier is the hero. Pursuing a party of the enemy, until in view of the city, the Cavalier comes upon another force which came near being too strong. In this crisis he acts as Defoe imagines a resolute and shrewd commander would (somewhat as Crusoe did in Siberia, Carleton at Arseele, and the Cavalier himself later in the Civil War), retreating when the odds were too great and drawing off his men in a manner that, to a layman at least, sounds plausible enough.[96]

For the account of the taking of Augsburg and, immediately thereafter, of Ingolstadt, Defoe continues using the *Intelligencer*, from which he gets such details as the date and the fact that just as Tilly was dying of his wound in Ingolstadt, Gustavus Adolphus had his horse shot from under him.[97] Both accounts next relate in complete agreement the plundering expedition of Gustavus Horn,

[93] *Memoirs*, pp. 96–97: ". . . the execution was so great . . . that Tilly was obliged to expose himself, and to come up to the very face of our line . . . and give his necessary orders." *Intelligencer*, II, 144: "The Bavarian captains found this so hot a service that Tilly himself was forced to come up to the point, and into the very face of the danger, to give directions."

[94] *Memoirs*, p. 97; *Intelligencer*, II, 147.

[95] Ramsey's?

[96] *Memoirs*, pp. 99–102; *Intelligencer*, II, 153.

[97] *Memoirs*, p. 102; *Intelligencer*, II, 161, 165.

the taking of Landshut by Horn and Hepburn, and the arrival of the King at Munich, where the wealth of the Duke of Bavaria fell into his hands, especially "the great chamber of the duke's rarities," of which the Cavalier was prevented from taking "a very exact account." [98] Again Defoe omits details of the King's action and passes on to condense the *Intelligencer*'s account of the relief of Biberach and of the King's marching to the defense of Nuremberg against Tilly's successor, Wallenstein.[99]

Here the *Intelligencer* takes up other threads of the story, and leaves the activities of the Swedish forces to part III, to which Defoe turned for his long account of the skirmishing about Nuremberg. As one may read in either account, the King lay under the walls of the city, his force too small to venture against Wallenstein's, while Wallenstein, threatening to make Nuremberg a second Magdeburg, lay opposite and ravaged the country round about. During the long lull, provisions were the chief concern of both armies, and the only fighting was between parties sent out to secure them. Having briefly described an attempt upon a convoy of ammunition, both the *Memoirs* and the *Intelligencer* begin in the next paragraph to relate the more important capture of Wallenstein's magazine of provisions at Freynstat—an action in which the Cavalier pretends to have had an important share.[100]

That Defoe here follows and slightly condenses the *Intelligencer*'s account is evident at the first glance. He omits some details related in his source, and thereby gains in directness and force. His is a model of vigorous narrative of military action. The chief invention is in the opening part. The *Intelligencer* related that Colonel Dubatell (Dubalt in the *Memoirs*) was the leader "that the King made choice of to do the feat," because he "knew the country thereabouts perfectly well," and that the party was "14 cornets of horse and some troops of dragooners." And from this Defoe conjures up the circumstances in detail:

> The king . . . sending for Colonel Dubalt . . . tells him his design . . . and ordered him to take what forces he thought convenient. The colonel, who knew the town very well, and the country about it, told his Majesty . . . he was afraid 'twould require some foot. . . . "But we can't stay for that," says the king; "you must then take some dragoons with you"; and immediately the king called for me. I was just coming up the stairs as the king's page was come out to inquire for me, so I went immediately in to the king. "Here is a piece of hot work for you," says the king, "Dubalt will tell it you. . . ."

[98] *Memoirs*, p. 103; *Intelligencer*, II, 163, 166, 168.
[99] *Memoirs*, p. 104; *Intelligencer*, II, 170–173.
[100] *Memoirs*, pp. 108 ff.; *Intelligencer*, III, 18 ff.

The two withdraw to concert their measures, but the King, impatient,

came into the room to us to know what we had resolved on, approved our measures . . . and, turning to me, "You shall command the dragoons," says the king, "but Dubalt must be general in this case, for he knows the country". . . . The king wished us good speed, and hurried us away the same afternoon. . . .[101]

Of the taking of Freynstat the Cavalier says only that "as soon as the ravelin was taken, they burst open the gate, at which I entered at the head of 200 dragoons, and seized the drawbridge."[102] He then recounts the union of all the King's forces on 21 August, and summarizes the fight at Altemberg—with passages slightly recast from the *Intelligencer*.[103]

Certain details of this fight are of accidental interest, and some parts of the two accounts are close. The Cavalier reports "the king leading the first party on with sword in hand"; and the *Intelligencer* says, "The King led on his men with his sword drawn in his hand."[104] A margin in the *Intelligencer* has an intriguing note saying: "this relation . . . received I from . . . Captain Fielding . . . then present in the action."[105] This, as Aitken has pointed out,[106] is no doubt the original of the Cavalier's friend Captain Fielding, who, we are told in the *Memoirs*, was wounded at Altemberg and there taken prisoner—later to be exchanged. Since Fielding was a known military name, identification of this particular captain is difficult.[107]

"Now," says the *Intelligencer*, "were the wars made altogether by commanded parties. . . ." Numerous brushes, not only between the Swedes and the Imperialists but also between the Swedes and the

[101] *Memoirs*, pp. 109 ff.; *Intelligencer*, III, 18 ff. Defoe's use of his source here seems evidence that his work was first written as a memoir and not as a history which he later converted to its present form.

[102] *Memoirs*, p. 110. The incident is not in the *Intelligencer*.

[103] *Memoirs*, pp. 112–113; *Intelligencer*, III, 36 ff.

[104] *Memoirs*, p. 113; *Intelligencer*, III, 41.

[105] III, 32.

[106] Introduction to the *Memoirs*.

[107] Aitken (introduction to the *Memoirs*) thinks that the Captain Fielding here noted was the Captain Fielding who in the Civil War was court-martialed for surrendering Reading to the Parliamentary forces. If so, his name was Richard, and he was a relation of the Earl of Denbigh. When he entered the Swedish service we do not know. There was a Captain Fielding who had sailed with the Earl of Denbigh to the Orient in 1631. He could hardly have returned in time to be with the Cavalier in Germany. If it was the Cavalier's friend who later surrendered Reading, Defoe either did not know it or at least failed to mention an acquaintance and friendship formed in the service of Gustavus Adolphus (see note 52 above).

Croats,[108] are reported. One of these, recounted in a few sentences, Defoe expands to three pages. Says the *Intelligencer:* "The King having now learned out that there were a many wagons of provision . . . in the Upper Palatinate . . . thitherward with all speed dispatches he a strong party of 3,000 horse for the cutting off of this convoy, which . . . was presently to come into the Imperial League. But the Swedish failed of their desire, Wallenstein having taken good order to have his convoy well assured." [109]

The Cavalier, having related that "the king had received advice of a convoy . . . from the Upper Palatinate" and that he (the Cavalier) was "commanded . . . to waylay them with 1200 horse, and 800 dragoons," gives us a very particular account of the adventure, in which his party was first routed by the forces with the convoy, then attacked by 200 Croats out for plunder, and finally soundly beaten by "3000 Imperial horse, who, on the expectation of the aforesaid convoy, were sent out to secure them."

In this misfortune the Cavalier was taken and held captive till after the battle of Lützen, in which Gustavus Adolphus lost his life. With the death of his hero, the Cavalier loses heart and resolves to quit the service. The Swedish part of the *Memoirs* practically ends here. For, as the Cavalier says, it was not his design to write of any more of these wars than he was actually concerned in; so he skims lightly over the remainder, summarizing Lützen in a few sentences and giving but a general account of what followed.[110]

But Defoe follows the *Intelligencer* to the end of its part III, as is shown by his account of the Cavalier's being a prisoner in Neustadt near Coburg,[111] of the taking of Leipzig by Wallenstein, of the approach of the Swedish army as Wallenstein went to besiege Torgau, of Wallenstein's sending for Pappenheim, of the battle of Lützen, and of the Diet of Heilbronn.[112]

---

[108] *Intelligencer,* III, 51. The Croats are called Crabats by both the *Intelligencer* and the *Memoirs.*

[109] *Intelligencer,* III, 50.

[110] *Memoirs,* pp. 114 ff.

[111] *Memoirs,* pp. 116–117; *Intelligencer,* III, 89: "Neustat and other dorps about Coburg." Colonel Spezuter, in whose charge the Cavalier was left, is not mentioned in the *Intelligencer.* He is very likely a fictitious character.

[112] *Memoirs,* pp. 117 ff.; *Intelligencer,* III, 103 ff., 109 ff., 114, 117 ff. There are serious differences between the *Intelligencer* and the *Memoirs* concerning the number of wounded and slain at Lützen. The Cavalier says 12,000 Imperialists were slain and 2,000 taken prisoner, whereas the *Intelligencer* reports but 3,500 slain and no prisoners of any number or quality. Gallobelgicus reports 9,000 slain but admits that "fame kills more than the sword ever" (*Intelligencer,* III, 153).

With Lützen part III of the *Intelligencer* concludes; and part IV, treating other matters, advances the story of military events no farther. Whether Defoe had later parts of the work we do not know. At any rate, he practically ends the Cavalier's Continental adventures with part III, whether because he wished to or because (as in *Carleton, Robinson Crusoe,* and elsewhere) his source had given out we do not know. The Cavalier, it is true, related that he traveled about Germany for two years thereafter, sometimes taking part in the councils of his former comrades, but describing only the battle of Nördlingen (17 August 1634). His source for this battle is certainly not a later part of the *Intelligencer,* for the two accounts have no recognizable similarity. *Le Soldat suédois* and Puffendorf's *Complete History of Sweden,* as part III of the *Intelligencer,* close with the battle of Lützen in 1632.

The Cavalier describes in detail the council of war before Nördlingen. Shall they fight or not?

Gustavus Horn was against it, and gave, as I thought, the most invincible arguments against a battle that reason could imagine.

But most of the generals were for fighting,

alleging the affront it would be to the Swedish reputation to see their friends in the town lost before their faces.

Gustavus Horn stood stiff to his cautious advice, and was against it, and I thought the Baron D'Offkirk treated him a little indecently; for, being very warm in the matter, he told them, that if Gustavus Adolphus had been governed by such cowardly counsel, he had never been conqueror of half Germany in two years. "No," replied old General Horn, very smartly, "but he had been now alive to have testified for me, that I was never taken by him for a coward; and yet," says he, "the king was never for a victory with a hazard, when he could have it without." [113]

The Cavalier, being pressed for his opinion, sided with General Horn, urging that at least they wait for the Rhinegrave to come up with reinforcements; but the other side carried their point and Horn submitted.

Other histories reported that Horn yielded only after the Baron had taunted him with cowardice, but Defoe depended upon Puffendorf's *Complete History of Sweden* (1702), which reported that Horn "was of the opinion that they should not put anything to risk . . . or at least, that they should wait the arrival of . . . the Rhinegrave. . . . Yet the other generals branded his prudence for cowardice, and Hofkirk particularly spoke of it in a very petulant

---

[113] *Memoirs,* pp. 122–123.

manner. This obliged Horn to comply . . . to show that it was not
. . . fear that influenced him." [114]

In his usual fashion Defoe puts into the Cavalier's story Puffendorf's account of the battle itself. One significant parallel may be
given:

We lost near 8000 men upon the spot, and above 3000 prisoners, all our
cannon and baggage, and 120 colours.[115]

6,000 of the Swedish foot fell upon the spot, a great many prisoners were
taken . . . and the enemy took 130 colours, with the ammunition and
baggage.[116]

The Cavalier further adds that being among the horse he had no
part in the fight, and that the Rhinegrave, coming "within three
miles" of the camp, checked the enemy's pursuit. Puffendorf had
said: "most of the Swedish horse escaped . . . the Rhinegrave being
but 3 miles off."

The Cavalier now sets out for England. On the way he travels in
Holland in 1635 and sees the Dutch army of Prince Maurice of
Nassau, who had been dead for a decade in 1635. This error is evi-
dence that Defoe, compiling his narrative from histories, confused
Prince Maurice with his brother Prince Frederick Henry, who in
1635 took a fort called Schenk or Schenkenschanz.

Royalists and Roundheads

For the later part of the *Memoirs* little has been done beyond
Aitken's suggestion that it contains nothing not to be found in
Clarendon, Ludlow, Whitelocke, and Rushworth.[117] Aitken remarks
further that the works of Ludlow, Whitelocke, Rapin, and Echard
were in Defoe's library. Dottin suggests Nalson as a source, and notes
that besides Clarendon, Ludlow, and Whitelocke, Defoe had in his
library Sprigg's *Anglia Rediviva* and Rapin's *History of England*.

It cannot be conclusively proved that Defoe did not consult all
of these works; but that he did seems extremely unlikely. As for
Rushworth's *Historical Collections,* I find only rare passages that
might have been of use to Defoe. Sprigg begins only after (or with)

[114] *Memoirs,* pp. 121 ff.; Puffendorf, *Complete History of Sweden . . . Translated out of the Original High Dutch . . .* (London, 1702), pp. 486 ff. (Such
quoted passages are modernized in spelling and typography throughout.) See
also David Jones, *A Compleat History of Europe . . . from . . . 1600,* II (London, 1705), 127. This work incorporates Puffendorf's account, and, of course,
Defoe may have taken his material from it rather than from Puffendorf directly.

[115] *Memoirs,* p. 126.

[116] Puffendorf, *Complete History of Sweden,* p. 487.

[117] Introduction to the *Memoirs,* pp. xvi–xvii. Aitken points out in particular
one phrase which was taken from Whitelocke.

1644, and the publication of Rapin's thirteen-volume *History* was begun only in 1724, and certainly the English translation which Defoe left in his library in 1731 could not have helped him in writing the *Memoirs* in 1719 and 1720. Nalson's *Impartial Collection* stops with January 1642, before the actual beginning of the war, and for the period he covers he parallels Rushworth too closely to be worth separate perusal. Both, furthermore, would have been difficult for Defoe to use, as their narratives are buried in endless petitions, lists, and other official documents, important but not adaptable to narrative. It can be shown, moreover, that except for fugitive passages, Defoe's entire account of the Civil War is based on the first three of the four works suggested by Aitken; namely, Clarendon, Whitelocke, and Ludlow.[118]

By 1720 the Swedish campaigns in Germany were at best of secondary interest to Englishmen, and Defoe could hazard wholesale dependence upon one less known source in recounting those wars. With the native materials concerning the English Civil War he proceeds more cautiously. His general knowledge of these later events naturally made a slavish dependence upon sources less necessary. His purpose was to give an air of genuineness and thus of authority to the *Memoirs*. Nalson had collected his materials to correct Rushworth, and Clarendon was in part an answer to Whitelocke and Hollis and Warwick and a host of other histories and memoirs, which in turn, as their prefaces show, intended to correct writers of an opposing faction.

For the opening part of the Civil War no definite source can be pointed out. The Cavalier recounts the events of the two "bishops' " wars, 1639 and 1640, when Charles marched with his English army to the Scottish border, only to compose the differences quietly, though much to his disadvantage. For these preliminaries Defoe seems to have relied partially at least upon his memory, as his account is untrustworthy in several important respects. In the closing pages of part I he says that the King, having camped his army at Berwick-on-Tweed, sent the Earl of Holland into Scotland to spy out the enemy, and that Holland, finding the Scots at Coldingham, retreated in a shameful manner. He refers here, of course, to a party in charge of Arundel (so says Gardiner) or of Holland alone (say Rushworth, Clarendon, and others), which went to Duns to read the King's proclamation to the Scots. They saw nothing of the Scottish

[118] Sir Edward Clarendon, *History of the Rebellion* (Oxford, 1702–04); Sir Bulstrode Whitelocke, *Memorials of the English Affairs* (London, 1682); Edmund Ludlow, *Memoirs* (Vevey, 1698–99).

army, paid a good price for simple refreshments, read the proclamation, and returned. These histories make no mention of Coldingham, which is as distant from Duns as from Berwick-on-Tweed.

Defoe's narrative, inaccurate in spots, is closer to that of Rushworth than to those of Clarendon, Nalson, or Baker. Rushworth, like the later historian Gardiner, says the Scottish forces were not seen at Duns. Whitelocke says only that the King marched to Berwick-on-Tweed "in the gaze of the enemy" (*Memoirs*, p. 140: "we stood at gaze with them"), but that no fighting occurred; Holland observed the enemy and retreated. Defoe is in general agreement with Clarendon and Echard for this first expedition, though he directs it to Coldingham and not to Duns.[119]

The second expedition of Holland (the Cavalier is not specific: he speaks of it merely as one of several) is described in more detail by Defoe than by any of these historians, but he is in general agreement with Echard, Rushworth, and Nalson.

The first real evidence as to Defoe's sources is seen in his account of the campaign of 1640. In describing the rout of Conway and Astley at Newburn he is closer to Whitelocke, whose very phrases he seems to echo,[120] than to other historians. Suspicion that he is following Whitelocke becomes certainty when he proceeds to discuss the Scottish demands: "But the eighth article of the Scots' demands expressly required, that an English Parliament might be called to remove all obstructions of commerce, and to settle peace, religion, and liberty" (p. 150). Now the Scottish demands are listed numerically in Rushworth and Nalson; but in them, the Cavalier's "eighth article" is joined with and is part of the seventh. Neither of them has an article numbered 8, though they have what one would expect to be 8, which contains what Whitelocke calls number 9. But Whitelocke gives as 8 this sentence quoted, which the other two join with 7: "That by advice of the Parliament of England . . . all impediments of free trade [may be removed] and peace settled for our religion and liberties." By citing this as the "eighth article" Defoe has definitely betrayed his source as Whitelocke, whom he continues to follow for some pages.

On Whitelocke is based also the account of the council of peers at York (24 September 1640) which led to an offer of peace. The Cavalier, it is pretended, bore the message of the offer to the Scots.

---

[119] Clarendon, I, 94–95; John Nalson, *Impartial Collection of the Great Affairs of State*, I (London, 1682), 239–241; Sir Richard Baker, *Chronicle of the Kings of England* (London, 1730), pp. 452–453; S. R. Gardiner, *History of England*, IX (London, 1884), 23; Laurence Echard, *History of England* (London, 1720), p. 472.

[120] Whitelocke, p. 34.

Their reply that they will not treat in York seems to the Cavalier an insult to the King unless they give their reasons. They admit finally that it is because Strafford, who had "declared them rebels in Ireland," had the chief command at York. The Cavalier returns with this message, and Ripon is substituted for York.

Whether Defoe actually knew that John Belasyse, son of Lord Fauconberg, bore this message (as both Rushworth and Nalson relate) we cannot tell.[121] One is inclined to think that he did not. For he is obviously following Whitelocke, the only historian of the group who discusses the reasons why the Scots preferred Ripon to York, and who simply says:

a messenger was sent . . . to the Scots army, to give notice to them that . . . sixteen of the English lords should meet with as many Scotch lords at York, to treat of the differences. But the Scots refused York to treat in . . . so long as the Lieutenant of Ireland commanded there in chief, who had proclaimed them traitors in Ireland before the King had done it in England. . . . This was the first public appearance of the Scots enmity against Strafford. . . . Another place of treaty was at Rippon.[122]

The results disappointed the Cavalier, who comments:

We were all amazed at the treaty, and I cannot but remember we used to wish much rather we had been suffered to fight [p. 152].

One sees here how Defoe adapts into his less formal "memoir" style an entry like Whitelocke's:

Many wondered, and some inveighed against this treaty, wishing the King would have put it rather to the issue of a battle than to have given such terms to his subjects in rebellion. . . .[123]

The Cavalier, following the concise entries of Whitelocke, next sketches the series of events which led to the outbreak of hostilities in 1642, first a Parliamentary action, then the King's reply or counteraction, and a vivid exposé of how the misunderstanding grew into civil war.[124]

Though Defoe does not proceed chronologically and repeats considerably, he continues to follow Whitelocke until the King goes to Shrewsbury. Some evidence of this indebtedness appears perhaps in the Cavalier's remark that "the king erected his standard

---

[121] John Rushworth, *Historical Collections of Private Passages of State,* II (London, 1680), 1276–77; Nalson, I, 443.

[122] Whitelocke, p. 35.

[123] Whitelocke, p. 35.

[124] *Memoirs,* pp. 147–155; Whitelocke, pp. 37–54. The Cavalier's phrase, "Sir John Hotham, the governor, upon the walls," in the account of the King's being refused entrance to Hull, may be an echo of either Whitelocke's "and from the walls appeared Sir John Hotham," or possibly Clarendon's "Sir John Hotham himself from the walls" (*Memoirs,* p. 155; Whitelocke, p. 55; Clarendon, I, 155).

at Nottingham, 22nd August 1642, and I confess, I had very melancholy apprehensions of the king's affairs, for the appearance to the royal standard was but small." Whitelocke's entry of 22 August (Clarendon gives the date as 25 August) reports succinctly that the King erected his standard at Nottingham, "to which not so many resorted as was expected." [125] Stronger evidence is the Cavalier's report (found also in Whitelocke) that Essex's rendezvous was at St. Albans, and that on 9 September Essex marched from thence to Northampton, Coventry, Warwick, and Worcester, to draw together his forces. Both Whitelocke and Clarendon recount that in Cornwall Sir Ralph Hopton, Sir Nicholas Slanning, and Sir Bevil Grenville held for the King, and that Sir John Byron's party of 500, upon the approach of Lord Say, left Oxford and captured Worcester.[126]

But Whitelocke's simple remark that the "King marched from Nottingham . . . to Wales; and at Shrewsbury his army increased to a considerable body" (p. 59) is hardly sufficient for the Cavalier's lengthy account of these activities. Shropshire is the Cavalier's native county, so we are told at the beginning of the *Memoirs,* and "he" naturally dwells at length upon this detail. He tells us that the King, having stayed overnight at the residence of the Cavalier's father, entered Shrewsbury the next day and found the people extraordinarily loyal. The "crowds which now came every day into his standard were incredible," so that in a six-week stay the King was supplied with money, ammunition, and men. The Cavalier's father "raised a regiment of horse at his own charge"; the Earl of Derby brought another from Lancashire; and "the Welshmen came in by droves" (pp. 158–159).

For these details Clarendon is the obvious source, since he has some details which Defoe could have got nowhere else.[127] Clarendon relates that the King at Derby "received clear information from the well-affected party in Shrewsbury that the town was at his devotion." He therefore started thitherward. Stopping at Wellington, "a day's march short of Shrewsbury," he delivered an address to his small force, and entered Shrewsbury on Tuesday, 20 September. He could not, therefore, have been the guest of the Cavalier's father on the night before, as the *Memoirs* says; but Clarendon's statement offers a lead for Defoe. Clarendon proceeds: "A more general and passionate expression of affections cannot be imagined, than he received by the people of . . . Shropshire as he passed; or a better reception

[125] *Memoirs,* p. 156; Whitelocke, p. 59; Clarendon, II, 1.
[126] *Memoirs,* pp. 161–163; Whitelocke, pp. 59–61; Clarendon, II, 14 ff.
[127] *Memoirs,* pp. 157 ff.; Clarendon, II, 12 ff.

than he found at Shrewsbury. . . ." [128] Presently "there was a very considerable conflux of the gentry . . . which . . . made great professions of duty to his Majesty: some of them undertook to make levies of horse and foot . . . at their own charge." [129] Clarendon relates the measures taken to provide funds and arms for the growing army. For as soon as "the king came to Shrewsbury he had dispatched his . . . agents into Wales, Cheshire, and Lancashire to quicken the levies of men which were making there." Like the Cavalier, Clarendon is impressed with the fact that within a few weeks the King was "able to get men, money, or arms." [130]

Further proof that Defoe was here using Clarendon is found in the Cavalier's description of the King's guards:

As for me, I rode a volunteer in the royal troop of guards, which may very well deserve the title of a royal troop, for it was composed of young gentlemen, sons of the nobility, and some of the prime gentry of the nation, and I think not a person of so mean a birth or fortune as myself. We reckoned in this troop two and thirty lords, or who came afterwards to be such, and eight and thirty of younger sons of the nobility, five French noblemen, and all the rest gentlemen of very good families and estates.

Clarendon's statement is less specific:

Most of the persons of quality . . . put themselves into the king's troop of guards, commanded by Lord Bernard Stewart; and made indeed so gallant a body that, upon very modest computation, the estate and revenue of that single troop, it was thought, might justly be valued at least equal to all theirs, who then voted in both Houses . . . which made and maintained that war.[131]

Both Clarendon and Defoe state that Essex and the King's general, Lindsey, had served together under Prince Maurice in the Low Countries.[132]

The Cavalier's paragraphs relating to the movements for and against the King are mainly from Whitelocke, with occasional suggestions from Clarendon and Ludlow. The skirmish between Prince Rupert and Colonel Sandys is related in Clarendon and Whitelocke; but Defoe, though he had already noted from Whitelocke that Sir John Byron with 500 horse had been forced to quit Oxford and retire to Worcester,[133] relies chiefly on Ludlow for this episode. It is true that traces of Clarendon appear in the opening part; but it is

---

[128] Clarendon, II, 14.

[129] Clarendon, II, 27.

[130] The Cavalier's phrase (p. 159) is "money, arms, ammunition, and a train of artillery."

[131] *Memoirs*, pp. 160–161; Clarendon, II, 31–32.

[132] *Memoirs*, p. 159; Clarendon, II, 33.

[133] *Memoirs*, p. 162; Whitelocke, p. 60.

from Ludlow that the Cavalier's story of the sharp encounter at the bridge is taken.[134] In comparing the account in the *Memoirs* with that of Ludlow, we must keep in mind that Ludlow, though not present in this action, was nearby in Essex's army: he tells the story from one side and the Cavalier from the other. Ludlow tells how "our men," seeing the enemy drawn up within musket shot of a bridge, "resolved to march and attack them" (I, 44), whereas the Cavalier tells how Prince Rupert posted his men within view of the bridge to await the Parliamentary party. Both accounts comment on the ground being disadvantageous to the Parliamentary troops and on Rupert's waiting until half the enemy had crossed the bridge and then charging and putting them into confusion. Both tell that many were drowned, and that Colonel Sandys was mortally wounded and taken prisoner.

Some of them [says the Cavalier] . . . were so frighted, that they never looked behind them till they came to Pershore, and, *as we were afterwards informed,* the life-guards of the general who had quartered in the town, left it in disorder enough, expecting us at the heels of their men.[135]

This passage, it is not difficult to see, is condensed from Ludlow's account:

The body of our routed party returned in great disorder to Parshot,[136] at which place our life-guard was appointed to quarter that night; where, as we were marching into the town, we discovered horsemen riding very hard towards us with drawn swords and . . . without hats, from whom we understood . . . that the enemy was hard by in pursuit of them: whereas it afterwards appeared, they came not within four miles of that place. . . . [Our men] not yet well understanding the difference between wheeling about, and shifting for themselves . . . retired to the army in a very dishonourable manner . . . where we received but cold welcome from the General, as we well deserved.[137]

It is Ludlow who misleads Defoe as to the time of this fight. Though it occurred on 22 September 1642, before the King had marched from Shrewsbury, the Cavalier places it after that event and just before the battle of Edgehill: "On the 10th of October the king's army was in full march . . . and the first action in the field

---

[134] Compare the statement from the *Memoirs,* pp. 164 ff.: "The king had notice that the Earl of Essex designed for Worcester, and Prince Rupert was ordered to advance with a body of horse and dragoons to face the enemy, and bring off Sir John Byron" with this from Clarendon, II, 19: "[The Earl of Essex] marched toward Worcester; of which his Majesty had no sooner intelligence than he sent Prince Rupert with the greatest part of the horse . . . to observe the motion of the enemy . . . but especially to join with Sir John Byron."

[135] *Memoirs,* p. 166. The italics are mine.

[136] The Cavalier's Pershore. Defoe mentions the place in *A Tour Through the Whole Island of Great Britain,* II (London, 1725), iii, 62.

[137] Ludlow, I, 45–46.

was by Prince Rupert and Sir John Byron [at Pershore]" (p. 163). Upon the approach of Essex, after the encounter, Prince Rupert "marched back to join the king's army, which lay then at Bridgnorth." The battle of Edgehill is related as following closely thereupon. Defoe is undoubtedly confused by Clarendon's statements that the King marched from Shrewsbury on 12 October and camped at Bridgnorth. But this was nearly three weeks after the skirmish at Pershore. Ludlow, however, passes directly from that skirmish to Edgehill (23 October), and Defoe does likewise.[138]

The famous fight at Edgehill Defoe must have known pretty well without consulting any particular history. The field of battle he had probably explored personally—at least he describes it in the *Tour,* and there gives a synopsis of the fighting.[139] Under the circumstances the strange thing is that we should be able to find any traces of his sources. Yet he certainly had Clarendon, Whitelocke, and Ludlow all before him at the time of writing. For though much of the account is invented or brought in from memory, there is distinct evidence of his borrowing from all three works.

As has been shown already, Defoe had utilized Clarendon's account of the King's affairs in Shropshire. He now follows him in recounting the King's march toward London. Thus he relates that the King, having left Shrewsbury on 10 October (Clarendon says 12 October; the others do not give the date), got "almost as far as Banbury" (Clarendon, II, 34: "within four miles of Banbury") when he heard that Essex had reached Kineton with his army. He thereupon called a council of war and decided to fight.

But Clarendon at times lacks appeal for one chiefly interested in action, and Defoe turned to the more succinct accounts of Whitelocke and Ludlow. From the former he drew his picture of the consternation in London at the prospect of the King's coming, and the general outline of the events of the battle itself. Defoe here intrudes a discussion of the expediency of the King's decision, and, urging that he should have marched on London, charges Prince Rupert with persuading him to do otherwise. Perhaps it was Whitelocke's entry of 24 October, in which he relates receiving the news of the battle fought the day before, that led Defoe to adopt that date. At any rate, Whitelocke remarks that "the king had the top of the hill, from whence he viewed the parliament's army, who saluted him with three pieces of cannon, which was answered with two shots of the king's" (p. 61); and the remark is incorporated in the Cavalier's

---

[138] *Memoirs*, pp. 163 ff.; Clarendon, II, 32; Ludlow, I, 46.
[139] *Tour*, II, iii, 44. The account there echoes the tone of the *Memoirs*.

statement that "when from the top of Edgehill the enemy's army was descried in the bottom . . . and that the enemy bid us defiance, by discharging three cannons, we accepted the challenge . . . answering with two shots from our army" (p. 168).

Defoe, as he could have learned from Clarendon, is in error in assigning the command of the right wing of the King's army to the Marquis of Hertford. Whitelocke says only that the "left wing of the king's horse . . . was broken and routed by the right wing of the parliament's horse commanded by Sir William Balfour." This detail Defoe also gives, and he tells us that Prince Rupert in the right wing of the Royalists routed Ramsey and pursued him "quite to the town of Kineton, where indeed he killed abundance of their men." Whitelocke says: "Pursued to Kineton down with great slaughter." More certainly from Whitelocke is the Cavalier's statement that "several of the officers rid clear . . . to London, where they reported that the Parliament army was entirely defeated—all lost, killed, or taken" (p. 176).

Consternation reigned until truer information came. The opinion of the Cavalier is: "Truly . . . the fight was a deliverance to them . . . but as to its being a victory, neither side had much to boast of" (p. 177). Whitelocke's version is: "Intelligence was brought . . . that divers of the officers . . . of the Parliament's army . . . rode hastily this morning . . . towards London, and reported that the Parliament's army was broken, and wholly discomfited, and many of the officers slain, and taken prisoners" (p. 61). Later messengers brought exaggerated accounts of the King's losses; and Whitelocke, much like the Cavalier, comments: "But the Parliament had a great deliverance and a small victory." [140]

Finally Defoe reports that Essex marched to Coventry [141] and that the King, after camping about Aynho, took Banbury and marched thence to Oxford.[142] From Whitelocke also he learns that immediately after Edgehill Essex received reinforcements, but Whitelocke does not mention the number except to say three regiments came after the battle. Defoe assuredly gets this detail from Ludlow; for, not to be partial, he makes use of all three of his principal sources for his account of Edgehill.

The enemy received a recruit of 4000 men the next morning.[143]

[140] *Memoirs*, p. 177; Whitelocke, p. 61.
[141] Whitelocke, p. 61, says Coventry; Ludlow, I, 52, says Warwick; the Cavalier says both.
[142] Although Ludlow tells of the King's taking Banbury and marching to Oxford, only Whitelocke comments upon the error of the Parliamentary army in not fortifying Oxford. He is therefore Defoe's source for a similar remark.
[143] *Memoirs*, p. 177.

Towards morning our army . . . received a reinforcement . . . to the number of about four thousand men.[144]

From Ludlow likewise is the Cavalier's statement that the enemy "quartered" that night upon the field of battle. A somewhat pathetic account of the night is added by Ludlow; being unable to find his servant who had his cloak and having "nothing to keep me warm but a suit of iron, I was obliged to walk about all night, which proved very cold." The Cavalier may have been echoing this complaint when he comments that the reason the Roundheads kept the field was that, "having lost their baggage and provisions, they had nowhere to go," whereas "we had good quarters at hand." [145] That Defoe is here using Ludlow will be more readily granted if it is recalled that from this very part of Ludlow Defoe inserts this footnote in the *Memoirs:* "General Ludlow in his Memoirs, p. 52, says their men returned from Warwick to London not like men who had obtained a victory, but like men that had been beaten" (p. 188). It is as though Defoe were saying, "See how my manuscript is corroborated by other accounts known to be authentic." His procedure here matches that of his preface, in which he mentions Clarendon's history as a document which his book will supplement and correct.

The *Memoirs,* having stated that Essex's army "made the best of their way to London, and were but in an ill condition" (p. 178), continues in Ludlow's very words to relate how the Parliament informed the King that they were desirous "to prevent the effusion of more blood, and to procure a right understanding between his Majesty and them." [146] Both the Cavalier and Ludlow remark that the King received the offer at Maidenhead, where he had advanced with his army, and that by Sir Peter Killigrew he signified his readiness for peace.[147]

Precisely at this point Defoe turns again to Whitelocke.[148] That

[144] Ludlow, I, 51.

[145] *Memoirs,* p. 176; Ludlow, I, 50. When the Cavalier reports that the Earl of Lindsey (who died shortly of his wounds), Sir Edward Stradling, and Colonel Lunsford were taken prisoners, Defoe is following Ludlow; for his account of Parliamentary losses (Colonel Essex, Colonel Ramsey, and Lord St. John) he is indebted to Whitelocke, p. 61.

[146] Ludlow, I, 52. This is the very page cited in Defoe's footnote: "The parliament . . . sent to the king . . . to assure him of their earnest desire to prevent the effusion of more blood, and to procure a right understanding. . . ."

[147] *Memoirs,* p. 180: ". . . that he desired nothing more, and would not be wanting on his part." Ludlow, I, 53: ". . . professed to desire nothing more, and that he would leave no means unattempted for the effecting thereof."

[148] Whitelocke, on the whole, is easier to borrow from than Clarendon or Ludlow, since he presents his material in a form more adaptable to Defoe's purpose.

he was not merely trusting to his memory (as he sometimes seems
to do with the bulkier work of Clarendon) but actually eyeing the
very sentences of Whitelocke is indisputable:

Upon this the Parliament name commissioners, and his Majesty excepting
against Sir John Evelyn, they left him out, and sent others; and desired
the king to appoint his residence near London, where the commissioners
might wait upon him. Accordingly the king appointed Windsor for the
place of treaty, and desired the treaty might be hastened.[149]

But he [the King] excepted against Sir John Evelyn. . . . But afterwards
the petition was sent to the King at Colnebrook, by the other commissioners without Sir John Evelyn, and was to desire him to appoint his
residence in some place near London, where the commissioners . . . might
attend him . . . and the King appointed his Castle of Windsor for that
purpose, and desired that the treaty might be speeded.[150]

The Cavalier introduces here an account covering several pages
of Rupert's plundering, which may or may not have more than a
general historical foundation; but when he returns to the King's
affairs, he returns to Ludlow at precisely the point where he left him
for Whitelocke. Occasionally using Ludlow's very words, he relates
that while the treaty was under consideration the "king ordered
the army to march, and, by favor of a thick mist, came within half
a mile of Brentford before he was discovered." [151] He further tells
us that two regiments of foot and a party of horse with great courage
barred the way, and that finally the place was taken and the de-
fenders cut in pieces or drowned in the river. Ludlow charges the
King with treachery for this action while a treaty was in progress,
and the Cavalier defends him, citing as a precedent the taking of
Prague by Carolus Gustavus while the treaty of Westphalia was
being negotiated—an action which, having not yet occurred in
1642, could not justly be cited as a precedent.[152]

From Whitelocke again come the details of the encounter at
Turnham Green, where the whole Parliamentary army of 24,000
faced the King and finally forced him to retreat. Both Whitelocke
and the Cavalier speak of the mingling of city troops and regulars in
the Parliamentary army, of Essex's sending a party to Acton to
attack the King's forces in the flank and then countermanding the

---

[149] *Memoirs,* p. 180.

[150] Whitelocke, p. 62.

[151] *Memoirs,* p. 186; Ludlow, I, 53: "But . . . the King taking advantage of a
very thick mist, marched his army within half a mile of Brentford before he was
discovered."

[152] *Memoirs,* p. 187: "The treaty of Westphalia, or peace of Munster, which
ended the bloody wars of Germany was a precedent for this."

order, of the want of ammunition being the real cause of the King's retreat, and of the onlookers (both men and women) who fled toward London whenever the Royalists advanced a little. Whitelocke's account, of course, was not the only one in which Defoe could have read these details, but his defense of the King's action against the censure of Whitelocke, like his earlier reply to the censure of Ludlow makes Whitelocke clearly his source:

the Parliament resent this attack, which they call treacherous, and vote no accommodation. . . . But . . . now they . . . petition him to desert his army, and return to the Parliament, and the like.[153]

This action of the King . . . was so ill resented by many men, that they spake very hardly of it; and the Parliament voted that they would have no accommodation. . . . [Yet] they again send a petition to him to desert his army, and to return to his Parliament.[154]

The Cavalier then expands into a paragraph some matters mentioned by Whitelocke (relating to affairs in the north where Goring came to the aid of the Earl of Newcastle with supplies from Holland) and passes on to relate an attack upon Cirencester, likewise from Whitelocke. The two agree in detail: they mention that Rupert had 3,000 men (Whitelocke says 4,000); that the Earl of Stamford's regiment was "cut in pieces" (Whitelocke says "put to the sword"); and that 1,200 prisoners (Whitelocke says 1,100), 3,000 arms, and "the county magazine" were taken. After Defoe's usual manner these details are expanded somewhat.[155]

There follows in the *Memoirs* a paragraph taken with but slight alteration from Whitelocke describing the Earl of Northampton's attack upon Lichfield and the King's march from Oxford to relieve Reading, which, however, surrendered before the King arrived. For this surrender, Colonel Fielding, commanding in the absence of Sir Arthur Ashton, who was wounded, was condemned to death by court-martial, but was pardoned by the King.[156] Continuing in Whitelocke, one finds an account of the Queen's joining the King at Edgehill with reinforcements: "3,000 foot, 30 companies of horse

[153] *Memoirs,* p. 190.

[154] Whitelocke, p. 63.

[155] *Memoirs,* pp. 191 ff.; Whitelocke, p. 64. The difference in the figures, far from indicating that Defoe is not using Whitelocke, simply shows Defoe's treatment of his sources. His figures suggest that he has (or pretends to have) more authentic information than his source. There seems here to be an echo from Clarendon, who records (II, 97) that it was February and that the roads were bad.

[156] *Memoirs,* p. 192; Whitelocke, p. 66. Had the Cavalier been a real person, he would almost certainly have mentioned Colonel Fielding as the Captain Fielding who had accompanied him on the Continent a decade earlier. See pp. 73, 93n, 107n above.

and dragoons, 6 pieces of cannon, &c." The "&c" Defoe expanded to "1500 barrels of powder, 12,000 small arms." [157]

Next the Cavalier records the battle of Roundway Down, following in general Whitelocke's narrative, with such details as that Waller had defeated the Royalists at Lansdown and driven them to Devizes, that the King sent out a party of horse from Oxford to assist them, that at Roundway Down Waller's horse fled at the outset and left his infantry at the mercy of the Royalists. Though some assert that Sir John Byron commanded the Royalist force sent from Oxford,[158] both Whitelocke and Clarendon name Lord Wilmot. That this was Defoe's opinion also appears from his other account of the event in the *Tour*. But in the *Memoirs* he does not scruple to assign the honor to his Cavalier.[159] The Cavalier's description of the capture of Bristol by Prince Rupert is likewise from Whitelocke, who mentions that the siege lasted three days and that Colonel Fiennes, though pardoned later, was sentenced to death for surrendering.[160]

The Cavalier's discussion of the King's council and the decision to besiege Gloucester offers an interesting example of the use of sources. Defoe is undoubtedly influenced by Clarendon in the arguments he advances for and against the siege. But he does not hesitate to pass judgment upon military problems like an expert, though of course he puts his criticism into the mouth of his hero. And to a layman his remarks sound plausible enough. Having decided to attack Gloucester, the King no doubt could not thereafter have united his forces and prevailed against the Parliamentary party. But as Gardiner reminds us,[161] Charles had no alternative. Royalist Yorkshiremen and Cornishmen would not join the King while Parliamentary garrisons held Hull and Plymouth; and similarly Welshmen refused to cross the Severn as long as Gloucester was

[157] *Memoirs*, pp. 192–193; Whitelocke, p. 66. Instead of "30 companies" Defoe gives "1500 horse and dragoons."

[158] As reported by Aitken in the introduction to the *Memoirs*, p. xvi.

[159] *Memoirs*, pp. 193–194; Whitelocke, p. 67; Clarendon, II, 223 ff. Some details of the battle of Roundway Down are not in Whitelocke, and Defoe seems to have been using Clarendon also. For instance, Clarendon says that Waller fled to Bristol; Whitelocke says to London; Defoe says both.

[160] *Memoirs*, p. 194; Whitelocke, p. 67. The Cavalier's remark (pp. 195–196) that at Exeter the Queen was "delivered of a daughter, the Princess Henrietta Maria, afterwards Duchess of Orleans, and mother of the Duchess-Dowager of Savoy" is a remarkable anachronism in a memoir that purports to have been written in the middle of the seventeenth century. The princess was actually named Henrietta Anne; her mother was Henrietta Maria. Whitelocke names the princess wrongly, and the Cavalier follows him.

[161] *History of the Great Civil War*, I (London, 1893), chap. 10

untaken. Further obstruction arose from discord among the King's officers, some of whom regarded the war as a simple military operation and some as a problem in statesmanship—to be won without engendering unnecessary hatred in the other party. Defoe, however, is never uncertain. The tone of his pamphlets and essays on public matters creates a strong impression that no problem baffles him; and it may be confessed that his judgment is often shrewd and wise. But he is equally positive when his knowledge is inadequate or when he merely echoes other men's opinions. When he censures the decision to besiege Gloucester he is merely repeating a popular, if mistaken, opinion. Later historians, Gardiner, for instance,[162] believe that the decision was not "the ruin of Charles's cause" since, when the siege was resolved upon, the time for successful action had already passed.

The Cavalier's account of the siege is based on Clarendon, with whom it is in general agreement. Occasionally there is a close similarity of phrase, as when Clarendon's statement that the enemy made "many bold and sharp sallies" reappears in the *Memoirs* as "frequent and desperate sallies." Clarendon's remark that sometimes the King's horse got between the attacking parties and the city Defoe expands into an episode wherein the Cavalier with a party of horse is made to cut off an enemy force issuing from the city. On the whole he agrees with Clarendon that the garrison gave more hurt to the Royalists than they received. Defoe evidently had Whitelocke's volume open too, for only Whitelocke reports that it was on 5 September that the approach of Essex forced the King to retire,[163] and that sending a party of six regiments into Gloucester, Essex himself followed the King with 3,000 horse.[164] The Cavalier's page-and-a-half story of his being sent to carry out a flanking movement against Essex seems to be entirely fictitious, suggested by the situation of the two armies. As usual the Cavalier is alert: when it is no longer safe to advance, he lines the hedges with his dragoons and pours a galling fire into the oncoming Roundheads. This maneuver is typical of the military episodes invented by Defoe in more than one novel.

[162] *History of the Great Civil War*, I, 197. The Earl of Worcester, who, according to Defoe, advises taking Gloucester, is not mentioned in Clarendon, Ludlow, Whitelocke, or even in Gardiner.

[163] To Berkeley Castle, says the Cavalier (p. 201); to Bristol, says Whitelocke (p. 69); to Sudley Castle, says Clarendon (II, 265). Whitelocke at this point mentions the fine of £20,000 imposed upon Judge Berkeley, and Defoe may have been confused by that detail.

[164] The Cavalier says "not above 4000" (p. 201); Whitelocke, p. 69.

At this point Defoe inserts a passage several pages in length taken from Ludlow (to be discussed presently); then, showing that he still has Ludlow and Whitelocke at least open before him, he returns to Whitelocke at the point where he left him for Ludlow, and comments for the third time on the mistake of besieging Gloucester. (This duplication in part arises from his jumping about among his sources.)

Had we marched to London, instead of besieging Gloucester, we had finished the war with a stroke. The Parliament's army was in a most despicable condition, and had never been recruited, had we not given them a month's time . . . at this fatal town of Gloucester.[165]

most men were of opinion, that when the King went to Gloucester, if he had marched up to London, he had done his work. For at that time the Parliament had no considerable body of an army . . . but by the time of the King's march, and stay at Gloucester, they had recruited their army. . . .[166]

At this point, as I have indicated, Defoe turned to Ludlow, for what is perhaps the last time. His Cavalier says: "About this time it was that we first began to hear of one Oliver Cromwell, who, like a little cloud, rose out of the east, and spread first into the north, till it shed down a flood that overwhelmed the three kingdoms." [167] Defoe now follows Ludlow closely for several pages: he introduces into the *Memoirs* Ludlow's brief report of the fight at Grantham where Cromwell with an inferior force defeated twenty-four regiments of the King's horse and dragoons; he tells of the relief of Gainsborough, where Lieutenant General Cavendish was killed, and of the skillful retreat to Lincoln and the defeat of Sir John Henderson at Winceby near Horncastle where were killed "the Lord Widdrington, Sir Ingram Hopton, and other persons of quality." [168]

Having returned to Whitelocke for the comment on the policy of besieging Gloucester, Defoe next expands into a page and a half the following sentence from Whitelocke: "At Cirencester, Essex beat up the King's quarters, drove Sir Nicholas Crispe and Colonel Spencer out of the town, with their two regiments of horse, and took thirty cart-loads of victuals, and about 400 horse." [169] The Cavalier tells us that he happened to be present in Cirencester "that night with Sir Nicholas Crisp, whose regiment of horse quartered there

[165] *Memoirs,* p. 204.
[166] Whitelocke, p. 69.
[167] *Memoirs,* p. 203.
[168] *Memoirs,* pp. 203 ff.; Ludlow, I, 68–70. Defoe really begins to use Ludlow when he begins his account of affairs in the north (p. 203).
[169] Whitelocke, p. 69.

with Colonel Spencer," when "a party of Essex's men beat up our quarters by surprise." [170] But Defoe is not content with Whitelocke's succinct account; he must present the whole episode in detail: "Sir Nicholas Crisp, hearing the alarm, gets up, and with some of his clothes on, and some off, comes into my chamber. 'We are all undone,' says he, 'the Roundheads are upon us.' " They consult, and, having wakened and collected their men in the yards of the inns, they bring off Colonel Spencer, who is engaged in a warm encounter with Essex's men, and retire badly shattered to Oxford.

Defoe (following Whitelocke) wrongly thought that Crisp was involved in this encounter; Crisp had been called away for trial because of a duel in which he had engaged.[171]

The Cavalier finds out when he reaches Oxford that the King has gone with his army to Newbury where he was that day engaged in battle with Essex. Actually five days (15–20 September) intervened between the affair at Cirencester and the engagement at Newbury, but Whitelocke does not clearly indicate the lapse of time, and Defoe seems to have been misled by that fact. At any rate the Cavalier gives only a summary of the fight at Newbury, based mainly on Whitelocke, as is shown by the declaration that the King's horse outdid the Parliament's horse; that the city trainbands fought as well as any of the Parliamentary troops; [172] and that Essex had the pillage of the dead. Clarendon, Ludlow, and Whitelocke all mention the Royalists' loss of the Earls of Carnavon and Sunderland and of Viscount Falkland; but only Ludlow anticipates the Cavalier in adding to the list "a French Marquis." [173]

Defoe next discusses the conduct of the Scots in coming to the help of the Parliamentary party. Some have thought the severe denunciation of the Scots here is evidence that Defoe did not write the book, since he had worked for the Union, and had vindicated the Scots in poetic and prose efforts. But there is similar ridicule of them in the *Memoirs of Captain Carleton* and the *Memoirs of*

[170] *Memoirs,* p. 204.

[171] See the account of Crisp in *DNB. Memoirs,* pp. 204–205. Whitelocke, p. 69, represents Crisp as in this fight.

[172] Clarendon, II, 268, says that the Royalists despised the city trainbands, who nevertheless saved the day for the Parliament.

[173] *Memoirs,* p. 207; Whitelocke, p. 70; Clarendon, II, 269–270; Ludlow, I, 66. The Cavalier reports that the King faced Essex the next day, but that Essex, in no mood to fight, marched away to London. A careful reading of Whitelocke would have told Defoe the truth: straitened for ammunition, the King retired into Newbury on the night of the battle (Gardiner, *History of the Great Civil War,* I, 216). From Whitelocke, p. 74, comes the Cavalier's account of the combats in Surrey between Waller and Sir Ralph Hopton.

Major Ramkins; and Dottin points out that in his private letters
Defoe revealed a dislike for the Scots which might not have been
expected.[174] Here, however, Defoe may be merely trying to reflect
the typical dislike of them by the Cavaliers. He is following Clarendon's discussion of the Irish cessation and of the Scottish demand
for money.[175]

Though Defoe follows Whitelocke in describing the entry of the
Scots with an army of 12,000 and the proclamation justifying their
action, he seems to have got from Ludlow the date of the event and
the account of their storming Newcastle. [176]

The Cavalier's account of Prince Rupert's mission to relieve
York, though more detailed than that in any of the histories, is
based mainly on Whitelocke. It has, to be sure, been partly patched
from Defoe's memory of what he had read, for it is replete with inaccuracies. According to it, Rupert first stormed Bolton and took
Liverpool,[177] relieved Lathom House, where the Countess of Derby
was being besieged by a Parliamentary force, and then hastened to
York. It is well known, however, that the relief of Lathom House
was simultaneous with the taking of Bolton and that the taking of
Liverpool came later.[178] But Defoe was following Whitelocke, who
describes the capture of Bolton after three repulses,[179] the taking of
Liverpool, and the relieving of the Countess of Derby, "who had
courageously defended Lathom House, besieged 18 weeks." Defoe
mentions all these details and gives them in the same incorrect
order.[180]

For his statement that Rupert recaptured Newcastle for the King,
Defoe seems to have had no authority; certainly, as Aitken remarks

[174] *Defoe et ses romans,* pp. 576–577.

[175] Clarendon, II, 291 ff.

[176] *Memoirs,* pp. 212–213; Ludlow, I, 83; Whitelocke, pp. 75 ff. Compare Whitelocke's "Colonel Grey, the Lord Greys brother, came in to them with a regiment of horse" with Defoe's "Colonel Grey, brother to the Lord Grey, joined
them with a regiment of horse." Compare also Clarendon's phrase (II, 295) "old
General Leslie" with Defoe's "old Leslie." So Defoe here seems to have all his
sources in mind or before his eyes. There is the difference of one day between
that given by Defoe and that named by Ludlow: Defoe says 15 January; Ludlow
says about 16 January. Furthermore, as Aitken points out in his introduction
to the *Memoirs,* p. xv, the statement attributed to the Cavalier by Defoe that
Newcastle was taken by the Scots in twelve days is erroneous, and has no warrant
in any of the histories.

[177] The Cavalier gives a two-page account of this event (pp. 214–216).

[178] Gardiner, *History of the Great Civil War,* I, 366.

[179] Defoe elaborates this episode. Compare his expression (p. 216) apropos of
the plundering "which the Parliament made a great noise about" with Whitelocke's "this was highly discoursed of the Parliament party."

[180] *Memoirs,* pp. 213 ff.; Whitelocke, pp. 85, 87, 89.

(citing Firth as his authority), it is untrue. Fictitious also is the statement that Rupert entered York before the battle of Marston Moor. Defoe here is misled by Whitelocke, "whose very words (fetching a great compass about) are copied." [181]

The Cavalier's account of Marston Moor, Aitken remarks, "is entirely at variance with all the authorities. . . . Newcastle had no command; Prince Rupert commanded the right and not the left wing, and was beaten altogether out of the field at once; Goring commanded the victorious left wing and not the main battle. The contest is apparently made to begin in the early morning, instead of five or six o'clock in the afternoon." [182] These charges against Defoe's accuracy are all true, but it is not true that all the authorities are against him. Whitelocke, obviously his source, records that Newcastle commanded the right wing, Prince Rupert the left, and Goring, Lucas, and Porter the main battle. He has the fight begin at seven in the morning, and credits Rupert with a victorious first charge and a too eager pursuit of the enemy. Similarly he reports that Goring and his supporters in the main battle routed their opponents, but that Cromwell routed Newcastle's wing and snatched victory from the Royalists. Defoe follows Whitelocke even in such details as naming Lucas and Porter as commanding the main battle with Goring, and in saying that the Parliamentary army captured all the Royalists' baggage, slew about 3,000 Royalists, besides those killed in the chase (Defoe says 4,000), and took 3,000 prisoners. The account of the battle itself Defoe expands to give the Cavalier a chance to conduct himself with gallantry, as a hero should, and to narrate events as if seen through his hero's eyes. Thus he gives the genuine air of a memoir to his compilation.[183]

But Whitelocke is not the only source for this account. For only Ludlow anticipates him in relating that Sir Charles Lucas and Major Generals Porter and Tilyard were among the prisoners. More interesting is the Cavalier's report of the efforts to prevent Rupert's hazarding the battle, in which the opinions of both Clarendon and Ludlow are echoed. Like the former, the Cavalier argues that disagreement between Leslie and the English generals was rife and that the Scots were on the point of deserting the Parliamentary army and that waiting was Rupert's cue. Like Ludlow he argues that Rupert had gained enough honor by relieving York in the face of a superior force and that those with him advised against attacking:

[181] *Memoirs,* p. xv.
[182] Introduction to the *Memoirs,* p. xv.
[183] *Memoirs,* p. 221; Whitelocke, p. 89.

I entreated him not to put it to the hazard; I told him that he ought to consider if he lost the day he lost the kingdom, and took the crown off from the king's head. I put him in mind that it was impossible those three generals should continue long together; and that if they did, they would not agree long in their counsels, which would be as well for us as their separating. . . . That he could subsist well enough, having York city and river at his back; but the Scots would eat up the country, make themselves odious, and dwindle away to nothing, if he would but hold them at bay a little. Other general officers were of the same mind; but all I could say . . . signified nothing. [184]

But that Rupert had what he considered positive orders from the King to fight, none of these works mentions.

After the defeat at Marston Moor the Cavalier escaped to join the King again in the west. He gives a long account of this episode, quite the most original and, to the student of fiction, the most interesting in the book. Covering sixteen pages, it relates the efforts of the Cavalier and a small detachment of Royalists to make their way through hostile territory to rejoin Rupert or to get to the King. They set out for Lancashire and came to the river Wharfe; there was a bridge at Wetherby, but the enemy held the town in wait for them; so they attempted fording the river. Several horses were drowned in this adventure, and they were replaced by others taken from the country people thereabouts. Coming to the edge of Bramham Moor they found an enemy force in pursuit of them. In this dilemma they crossed the moor and hid in a wood where they ambushed their pursuers, gave them a sound beating, and got fresh horses in the bargain. But now the country was up in arms against them, and they camped for two days in another wood three miles farther on. While there the Cavalier and two comrades plundered a farmhouse for clothing and went into Leeds for information and supplies. The Cavalier dressed himself

au paysan, with a white cap on my head, and a fork on my shoulder, and one of my comrades in the farmer's wife's russet gown and petticoat, like a woman, the other with an old crutch like a lame man, and all mounted on such horses as we had taken the day before from the country, away we go to Leeds by three several ways, and agreed to meet upon the bridge [pp. 226–227].

The information they secured was that the Roundheads had a greatly exaggerated notion of the party's strength and had sent off to York for a party of horse to assist the local garrisons against them. On the return from Leeds the Cavalier had a brush with three country fellows who met him some distance from his two comrades:

---

[184] *Memoirs*, p. 218. Cf. Ludlow, I, 123 ff.; Clarendon, II, 388.

I gave them the road very orderly . . . but one of them stopping short at me, and looking earnestly, calls out, "Hark thee, friend," says he, in broad north-country tone, "whar hast thou thilk horse?" I must confess I was in the utmost confusion . . . so I made as if I did not hear him, and went on. "Na, but ye's not gang soa," says the boor, and comes up to me, and takes hold of the horse's bridle . . . [pp. 228–229].

Vexed at not knowing what the fellow wanted or how to talk to him, the Cavalier "reached him a great knock on the pate" with his fork and hurried away. But the other two pursued him and forced him to face about again:

The first that came up with me was he that had no weapons, so I thought I might parley with him, and speaking as country-like as I could, I asked him what he wanted? "Thou'st knaw that soon," says Yorkshire, "and ise but come at thee." "Then keep awa', man," said I, "or ise brain thee." By this time the third man came up, and the parley ended; for he gave me no words, but laid at me with his long pole, and that with such fury, that I began to be doubtful of him. I was loth to shoot the fellow. . . . But at last, finding he would be too many for me with that long weapon, and a hardy strong fellow, I threw myself off my horse, and running in with him, stabbed my fork into his horse. The horse being wounded, staggered awhile, and then fell down, and the booby had not the sense to get down in time, but fell with him. Upon which, giving him a knock or two with my fork, I secured him. The other, by this time, had furnished himself with a great stick out of a hedge, and before I was disengaged from the last fellow, gave me two such blows, that if the last had not missed my head and hit me on the shoulder, I had ended the fight and my life together. 'Twas time to look about me now, for this was a madman. I defended myself with my fork, but 'twould not do. At last, in short, I was forced to pistol him and get on horseback again, and . . . get away to the wood to our men [pp. 229–230].

Presently the Cavalier's two partners came to the man who began the fray just as he regained consciousness, and the one who played the part of a cripple

gets off, and pretends to help him, and sets him up upon his breech, and being a very merry fellow, talked to him: "Well, and what's the matter now?" says he to him. "Ah, wae's me," says the fellow, "I is killed." "Not quite, mon," says the cripple. "Oh that's a fau thief," says he, and thus they parleyed. My cripple got him on's feet, and gave him a dram of his aqua-vitae bottle, and made much of him, in order to know what was the occasion of the quarrel [p. 230].

He discovers that the Cavalier was riding a horse that had been taken from the countryman's brother at Wetherby. Then, having aided likewise the second countryman and seen that the third was past help, the two Cavaliers rejoin their comrades in the wood.

The next morning the Cavaliers decamped, and coming to a village where the people were friendly, they tarried a day and a

night, during which time the Cavalier found himself being entertained in the house of the fellow whom he had struck down the
day before with his fork, and restored the horse to the brother.

The day following, the party set out for Blackstone Edge, the
ridge of mountains which separate Yorkshire and Lancashire, and
traveling through the night passed through Littlebrough, in Lancashire, and stopped at Rochedale, a little market town where they
felt themselves safe. Thwarted in their plan to go to Bolton, they
debated whether to try for Chester or go north to join Rupert and
Goring. Rumors of plans to capture them led finally to the latter
plan. Giving out that they are going back to Yorkshire, they set
out in the evening, but instead of retracing their road, as the enemy
expected them to do, they turned aside at the foot of the hills at
Blackstone Edge, and took "blind, untrodden paths, and with difficulty enough, by noon the next day had reached" a point near
Clitheroe. But the enemy was discovered to be in pursuit with 400
horse, and, with hostile forces ahead and behind, they broke up
into two parties, that of the Cavalier taking to the hills toward
Yorkshire. It was a difficult route, without villages or roads or
provisions. "At last, after a terrible fatigue, we began to see the
western parts of Yorkshire, some few villages, and the country at a
distance looked a little like England, for I thought before it looked
like old Brennus Hill, which the Grisons call the 'grandfather of
the Alps'" (p. 236).

Some food was got in the villages to relieve their distress and a
guide was impressed into service, who, like Singleton's Quaker
William, would not go of his own accord, but when forced to it,
went cheerfully enough. He led them slowly but surely along the
edges of vast mountains to the forest of Swale, where they rested
again. Going forward four days later they crossed the great York-
Lancaster road and entered still more mountainous regions, until
at last, nineteen days after Marston Moor, they reached Stanhope in
Durham, where some of Goring's horse had quarters. And the
Cavalier presently rejoined Rupert at Appleby.

Conclusions

Clearly there are in the *Memoirs of a Cavalier* passages of narrative vividness that owe much to Defoe's imagination and invention;
but in general the preceding pages have demonstrated that, like the
later Carleton story, the *Memoirs* is essentially a compilation based
on previously printed biographies, memoirs, and histories. Defoe
imitates autobiographies like that of Commines and the more or

less fictionized biographies like Du Fossé's *Memoirs of the Sieur de Pontis,* which resembles the *Memoirs of a Cavalier* more than any other earlier work. From them Defoe may have got a number of details, as also from Sandras. The Cavalier's account of the French campaign against Savoy in 1630 is based on Tom Brown's translation of Le Clerc's *Life of Richlieu,* a work not previously mentioned in connection with Defoe. The long account of the campaigns in Germany in 1631–32 is taken in like manner from the *Swedish Intelligencer,* an English newspaper (not quite a periodical) devoted to the Swedish campaigns against the Emperor.

So complete is Defoe's dependence upon the *Swedish Intelligencer* that we are under no necessity of supposing the use of other sources.

The English campaigns were closer to Defoe's own time and several histories of them were too well known to English readers for Defoe to have depended exclusively upon any one. That would have invited swift criticism. But it is surprising how bold Defoe was even here and how slow critics were to catch up with him, for he named two of his sources. Such acknowledgments slyly offer proofs of his own genuineness and superiority as a historian. In the preface he speaks of "that extraordinary history written by the Earl of Clarendon," the errors of which, among others, he sets out to confute. In a footnote in the text, which Aitken and Dottin regard as an anachronism, the *Memoirs* cites Ludlow's *Memoirs* in support of its account of the battle of Edgehill. This could be justified as an editorial insertion to call attention to the reliability of the *Memoirs* and not evidence that the whole was written after the publication of Ludlow's *Memoirs.*

Defoe, however, did not name his most important source, Whitelocke's *Memorials,* a sort of journal or diary with some dated entries of events. To Whitelocke Defoe returns again and again. But Whitelocke has gaps; and to fill them Defoe turns to Ludlow and Clarendon. One can usually tell just where the shift occurs and exactly where Defoe returns to Whitelocke—usually the place from which he departed. So detailed is his dependence upon these works that we can say positively that he had these books open before him as he wrote and that he used them by turns as one or the other suited his purpose. This is not to ignore Defoe's wide general knowledge of the war; he owned a copy of Sprigg and a collection of Civil War pamphlets, and he occasionally supplemented his sources with anecdotes and possibly authentic details which he got elsewhere. The surprising thing is that with all his knowledge he stuck so closely to these three works. There is no other work (unless possibly Rushworth or Sprigg and, for the Montrose episode, a Scottish account unidentified) which can be regarded as more than a *possible* source.

It need never again be asked whether the *Memoirs* is based upon a manuscript. It is not. The opinion of Aitken and Trent is proved correct. When one subtracts the portions based upon Le Clerc, the *Swedish Intelligencer*, Whitelocke, Clarendon, and Ludlow, there is left little more than the bare outlines of the story. The major portion is fabricated from published books of history and biography, one of which was not available until 1704—within sixteen years of the publication of the *Memoirs*. To suppose that Defoe, who for *Crusoe* and *Singleton* made similar use of Dampier, LeComte, and Ides, and in the *Journal of the Plague Year* borrowed from numerous printed accounts of the plague, did not himself do the compiling is highly improbable.

There still remains Dottin's theory that the *Memoirs* was first written as two works—one a history of the Scottish brigade in the service of Gustavus Adolphus, the other an account of the English Civil War—and that Defoe joined them and unified them as the memoirs of an imaginary Cavalier. In support of this, Dottin cites a passage from Defoe's *Scots Nation and Union Vindicated* (1714). To that work Defoe had added a list of Scottish "Officers" and another of Scottish colonels who had been in the service of Gustavus Adolphus. These lists Defoe says were taken from a manuscript which "I have had in my hands many years." [185] William Lee in 1869 advanced the view that the manuscript mentioned here is the manuscript of the *Memoirs* itself. Dottin thought that this manuscript, of which "nous n'avons pas le droit de nier l'existence," probably suggested to Defoe the idea of writing an account of the brave deeds of the Scottish brigade. These are interesting theories of Lee and Dottin, but they will not survive examination. In the first place Defoe does not claim to have a manuscript narrative but only a manuscript list of soldiers. He says:

And it shall remain as a record to the honour of the Scots nation, that we can show such a list as is hereto subjoined, of Scots gentlemen who raised themselves to the highest command in the Swedish armies. . . .

The manuscript I have had in my hand many years, neither is it to be contradicted, the histories of those times making frequent mention of their names.[186]

That the manuscript contains only lists of names is indicated in both sentences, but especially in the second one. Defoe does not say

[185] *Memoirs*, p. xvii.
[186] *The Scots Nation and Union Vindicated* (London, 1714), p. 24.

his narrative of Scottish exploits is corroborated by historians, but only that the names which appear in his manuscript appear frequently in the histories. In the second place, it is not true, as Dottin asserts, that all of the names of Scottish soldiers mentioned in the *Memoirs* are in the list of 1714. The Cavalier mentions but three, Lord Rheay, Colonel Lumsdell, and Sir John Hepburn. Sir John, the only one of the three who has any importance in the Cavalier's story, is not in the 1714 list. In the third place, Defoe found all three of these names in the *Swedish Intelligencer* along with the story of their actions as recounted by him.

When Dottin says that, stripping the *Memoirs* of some anecdotes meant for entertainment and of exploits invented to give the Cavalier an important role, we have "une véritable histoire de la brigade écossaise" in the campaigns of Gustavus Adolphus, he ignores the fact that Defoe treats only a small part of that history; that he tells only what the Scots do while the Cavalier is with them (and then not completely, since the Cavalier is the center of the story); and that the Cavalier hardly mentions the officers cited in Defoe's four-page list of 1714. Had Defoe's aim been to celebrate the bravery of the Scots in the service of the Swedes, he could hardly have omitted references to Hamilton's expedition, or Mackeye's, which Monro treats. Not even Leslie, later Earl of Leven, is mentioned until the Cavalier comes to the Civil War, and Leslie's Continental service is then alluded to in a brief phrase. The manuscript history of the Scottish brigade proves to be Dottin's creation out of Defoe's mention of a list of Scottish soldiers probably compiled when Defoe was in Scotland working for the Union with England. The *Memoirs* is not the only one of Defoe's long narratives to break into two parts. Such dual structure—*Singleton* is the most glaring example—was almost a habit with Defoe. He was perhaps sometimes interrupted in his writing, and when he returned to it, he had lost the thread or unconsciously changed the direction or emphasis of a story—as he seemed to do in the *Fortunate Mistress* and *Colonel Jacque*. But whenever the *Memoirs* was written, it was all of a piece. Defoe did not write it first as history and then convert it into fiction.

Scarron's *Roman comique*
and Its English Translators

The incidental consideration given *The Whole Comical Works of Scarron* (1700) in a recent study of Tom Brown emphasizes the need of further investigation of Scarron in England.[1] Professor Sturgis E. Leavitt made a beginning in a Harvard dissertation (1917). But only a small portion of it was published, and Leavitt had not seen the 1676 and 1700 translations of the *Roman comique,* which have since been acquired by the Harvard College Library.[2] The *Virgile travesti* influenced English burlesque, and the novels from the Spanish, translated by John Davies of Kidwelly and others, had a vogue in the seventeenth and eighteenth centuries. But the *Roman comique* (to be referred to hereafter as the *RC,* or, in English translation, as the *CR*) was ultimately to have a greater influence in England, especially on fiction, and is today the only part which may be said to live out of those ten-volume sets poured forth by De Luyne and David in Paris; Wolfgang (sometimes confused with the Elzevirs), Mortier, and the Wetsteins in Amsterdam; and by others in Lyons, Rouen, The Hague, and Rotterdam.[3] While the *RC*'s influence has yet to be treated, I intend here only a summary of the story of early English translations and editions.

The *RC* began its flourishing career in Paris, with part I in 1651 and part II in 1657; and by 1700 it had been printed over thirty times in France and Holland. A year or so before his death in 1660 Scarron wrote a third part; but, whether or not suppressed by his wife (later known as Madame de Maintenon, wife of Louis XIV),

---

[1] Benjamin Boyce, *Tom Brown of Facetious Memory* (Cambridge, Mass., 1939), pp. 82–83.

[2] *Scarron in England 1656–1800.* In 1919 Professor Leavitt published the section dealing with imitations of *Le Virgile travesti:* "Paul Scarron and English Travesty," *SP,* XVI, 108–120.

[3] Émile Magne's *Bibliographie générale des œuvres de Scarron* (Paris, 1924) is an admirably detailed description of editions, though it is better for individual works than for the early collections. The Elzevirs, Louis and Daniel, who were partners in Amsterdam during the years 1652–84, published some volumes of Scarron; but I am not certain they issued any sets. Magne, p. 185, revives an old error in confusing Wolfgang's press (mark: *Quaerendo*) with that of the Elzevirs.

it was not published.[4] Instead, in 1662 a part III, by Antoine Offray, a Lyons bookseller, but formerly ascribed to Jean Girault, Scarron's successor as canon at Le Mans, was published in Holland.[5] It is difficult to see how Dutch printers got hold of the text without a Lyons original which, Magne believes, must have been issued by Offray in 1662. But no such Lyons original is known. Part III was not, apparently, in Offray's edition of 1663 or any later one till 1678.[6] Presently, however, it was customary for all except the authorized Paris editions (and for them after the first quarter of the eighteenth century) to include Offray's part III.

Another continuation, *La Suite du Roman comique,* was written by Préchac and published separately at Paris in 1679. It was not, apparently, joined to the *RC* till the Lyons edition of 1695. But from early in the eighteenth century many editions included it with the other three parts as a second continuation. A third continuation, *Suite et Conclusion,* in two parts by M. D. L., was published in Paris in 1681.[7]

Until lately it has been held that the first parts of the *RC* to appear in English were the four intercalated novels; but John Davies published them in 1665, not in 1662 as Anthony à Wood said; and, though he added four new novels to the three published in French in 1659, only three of the four were from the *RC*. The second novel in *RC,* part I (*A Trompeur, trompeur et demi*), Scarron had borrowed from Castillo Solorzano, who had two versions of the story, one called *A un engaño otro mayor,* from which *A Trompeur* was taken, and another called *A lo que obliga el honor.* Davies seems to have omitted *A Trompeur* from his collection of Scarron's novels because he was publishing, also in 1665, Castillo Solorzano's *La Gardima,* containing *A lo que obliga.* At any rate, instead of *A Trompeur* he translated *Le Châtiment de l'avarice,* which he found with Scarron's letters published in 1663.

[4] Magne, p. 185n. In a letter of 8 May 1659, written to Marigny and subscribed "Lazarillo de Tormes," Scarron described "de quelle manière commence le troisième volume de mon *roman comique.*" Bastien's edition (1786) lacks "troisième," but Wetstein's edition of 1713 has it. See also Henri Chardon, *Scarron inconnu,* II (Paris, 1904), 331 ff. Chardon implies that Scarron's third part did not complete the story.

[5] Magne, no. 266 and p. 185. Chardon, *Scarron inconnu,* II, 277 ff., gives a full account of Girault, "le successeur de Scarron dans sa prébende, le chanoine du Mans." For a refutation of Chardon's attribution, see *Le Roman comique,* ed. by Henri Bénac (Paris, 1951), pp. 82–85.

[6] See Magne, nos. 266, 267, 269, 276.

[7] Magne, nos. 282, 346, 347. Chardon, II, 392 ff., reports an unsuccessful verse dramatization by La Fontaine and Champmeslé (1684) and a verse narrative by Le Tellier d'Orvilliers (1733).

Davies' translations of the three novels from the *RC* did not appear until 1665; and they may not have antedated the 1665 translation of the *RC* itself. An investigation of this little-known first English translation of the *RC* will throw light upon three later and better-known "versions" and present a minor seventeenth-century hack as the best, or more accurately, the only independent English translator of Scarron's two parts of the *RC*.

The First English Translation of the Roman comique

John Davies was, in 1665, "informed that some years since, a person of quality" translated "not onely the work [*RC*], but also the scene out of France into England." But "that person being highly engag'd in the transactions happening upon his Majesty's happy restauration," the translation "hath remain'd imperfect ever since." Davies concluded that it must have so far transcended ordinary translation that "no other hand durst attempt it." [8] Since Katherine Philips was so interested in Scarron's novels as to urge Davies to translate them, someone in her circle may have been the "person of quality" who undertook the *RC*.[9] Her Poliarchus, Sir Charles Cotterell, is an obvious possibility. He was a skilled translator, and a firm Royalist, busy at the Restoration as master of ceremonies at the court of Charles II.

Confirmation of Davies' assertion is given by an entry for Henry Herringman in the *Stationers' Register,* 1 December 1656: ". . . *The Romance of Players,* written in French by the great Witt of these tymes Monsr Scarron, under ye name of the *Romance Comique.* Translated into English & the scene altered by a person of quality." [10] As part II was not issued in France till 1657, this book could have included only part I. Davies implies that it was not published, and no other references to it are known. I shall, therefore, assume the 1665 translation of the *RC* to be the first. It included the authentic parts, I and II, and followed the chapter divisions of the French, with new pagination and chapter numbers for part II.

This 1665 translation was unknown to the Scarron bibliographer, Émile Magne, as well as to the British Museum cataloguer, to Esdaile, and to Chandler, Baker, Charlotte Morgan, and, so far as I can discover, all other literary historians, though in 1904 a copy appeared in the auction rooms, and other copies have appeared in

[8] *Scarron's Novels* (London, 1665), preface.
[9] Ernest Baker, *History of the English Novel,* III (New York, 1950), 30, 40.
[10] *A Transcript . . . 1640–1708,* II (London, 1913), 99.

more recent auctions.[11] The book is an octavo printed on cheap paper. What must be a very rare copy has been in the Harvard College Library since 1900; it lacks dedication and preface. The title page reads as follows: "The Comical Romance: or, a facetious history of a company of stage-players. Interwoven with divers choice novels, rare adventures, and amorous intrigues. Written originally in French by the renowned Scarron; and now turned into English by J. B. London, Printed for John Playfere, at the White Lion in the Upper-walk of the New Exchaunge: and William Crooke, at the Three Bibles on Fleet-Bridge, 1665." [12]

Professor Leavitt and others have suspected that "J. B." was a misprint for "J. D." and that John Davies translated the *RC* as well as the Scarron novels.[13] The fact that Davies translated Castillo Solorzano's *A lo que obliga el honor* as *The Trepanner Trepann'd,* a title which differs only in spelling from that given the parallel story, *A un engaño otro mayor,* in the 1665 translation of the *RC,* Leavitt adduces in support of this conjecture. He cites, from Gerard Langbaine, Davies' regret that Scarron did not live to finish his romance; and he might have pointed out that Davies was later to translate Scarron's letters. Under the circumstances, who was more likely than Davies to have translated the *RC?* Presumably not John Bunyan; and no other J. B. has hitherto been identified.

Though the 1665 *CR* is superior to much of Davies' work, his importance as a translator would compel serious consideration of his claim were there not insuperable objections. In the first place, the publishers would have put his name clearly on the title page instead of misprinting his initials and then dropping them altogether in a later edition. Secondly, Davies' version of the intercalated novels is too unlike that of the *CR* to allow a single translator. And, finally, Davies twice implies that he had not translated the *RC:* once in the 1665 preface to *Scarron's Novels,* when he

[11] Magne's otherwise excellent bibliography is inadequate for the English translations of Scarron, for which he apparently listed only what he found in the British Museum catalogue without checking the books themselves. Davies' translation, *The Unexpected Choice* (1670), the first English translation of the novels listed by Magne, is not identified with its original, *Plus d'effets.* The *Whole Comical Works* (1700) is listed under "Œuvres," though it contains only the *RC,* the novels, and the letters. Jusserand's reprint of this (omitting the letters) is listed under *RC.* Magne is, of course, following title pages; but cross references, like those to the French editions, are needed.
[12] The Harvard copy is bound with the translation of Furetière's *Roman bourgeois* falsely called *Scarron's City Romance.*
[13] Leavitt, *Scarron in England,* pp. 60 ff.; *Book-Prices Current,* XXXIII (1919), 606, attributes the translation to John Davis (*sic*).

alludes to the adaptation by "a person of quality," and again in 1677 in the epistle dedicatory [14] to *Monsieur Scarron's Letters,* where he speaks of the "former productions of this . . . author, of my publishing in English," that is to say, his novels. Thereby he excludes the *RC*.[15]

John Bulteel

That the initials J. B. are correct and that they stand for a writer almost unknown to literary history, John Bulteel, I was convinced long before coming upon the following entry for John Playfere and William Crooke in the *Stationers' Register,* 18 April 1665: *"Le Romant Comique, or, the Comicall Romance in two parts . . . by Mr. Scarron and translated . . . by John Bulteele Gentleman."* [16] Additional support for the identification is provided by an entry in the *Stationers' Register,* 8 April 1667, in which John Playfere assigns to William Crooke, cosponsor of the 1665 edition, his rights in *"Le Romant Comique . . . translated by John Bolteele gent."* [17] We must then accept John Bulteel as the English translator of the *RC* in 1665. Though in the seventeenth century the *RC* had in England nothing like the vogue it had on the Continent, that cannot have been the fault of Bulteel, who usually, though not always, caught the spirit of the *RC* and, without getting far from the original text, put it into good idiomatic English.

Davies' and Bulteel's translations of the intercalated novels, though different, are not wholly independent. In the novels, as later in the letters, Davies is free with the text; his title page says "rendered into English with some additions." In *The Hypocrites* he expands Scarron's conclusion by a page to arouse interest in a promised continuation. In the final sentence of *The Innocent Adultery* he introduces a slight deviation. In regard to novels within the *RC,* in *The Rival Brothers* (chap. 41) he inserts sixteen lines of his own about Don Sancho's reflections, and a little later expands by half a page a speech by Feliciana.[18] In *The Invisible Mistress* he has an interpolated reference, reminiscent of the translations of Sorel, to "so many *Extravagant Shepherds* and *Don Quixote.*" [19]

[14] To William Hammond, uncle of Thomas Stanley.
[15] In the "Advertisement to the Reader" he mentioned the publication in 1670 of *The Unexpected Choice (Plus d'effets),* "the last novel I could meet withal of Monsieur Scarron's." He still avoided mentioning *A Trompeur.*
[16] *A Transcript . . . 1640–1708,* II, 355.
[17] *A Transcript . . . 1640–1708,* II, 375.
[18] Davies, pp. 253–256.
[19] Davies, p. 284.

In places he breaks up Scarron's text into paragraphs—a thing no other English translator before 1775 was to do.

Bulteel, unlike Davies, was faithful to the French, and that is why, lacking conclusive evidence of which translation appeared first in 1665, I suspect the borrowings may be Davies'. A passage in the *RC* reads:

le *Cyrus,* qui est sans doute aussi bien que les autres que j'ai nommez, le livre du monde le mieux meublé.[20]

Bulteel and Davies translate this passage as follows:

the *Grand Cyrus,* which not to disparage those others I mentioned, is, without doubt, one of the most magnificently furnished Books in the World.[21]

the *Grand Cyrus,* which not to disparage those others I named, is one of the most magnificently furnished books of any in the world.[22]

There is no compelling reason for "disparage" or "magnificently"; the former is, in fact, an unlikely if not a wholly inaccurate rendering.

A few lines below the passage just quoted from the *RC* comes the statement, "Mais nostre Espagnol ne s'en esmeut non plus, que s'il eust esté en son hostellerie, ou hauberge." [23] Davies translates these words, "But our *grave* Spaniard was no more troubled at it, than if he had been in some inne, or country-house"; [24] and Bulteel translates them, "But our grave *Spaniard* was no more moved with all this, then if he had onely been in some common Inn, or Country Cottage." [25]

One more obvious borrowing must suffice. In the *RC* occurs the following sentence:

A quelque temps de là, des officiers masquez, & fort bien vestus, vinrent mettre le couvert, et l'on servit ensuitte le souper.[26]

Bulteel and Davies translate this sentence as follows:

certain Officers belonging to the House, with Vizards and Rich Cloaths on, came in to lay the cloath; which done, Supper was brought up. . . .[27]

certain officers belonging to the house all in vizards, but very richly clad, came in to lay the cloth; which done, supper was brought up. . . .[28]

[20] Bénac, I (chap. 9), 128. Quotations from the *RC* are given from the two-volume edition of Henri Bénac (Paris, 1951).
[21] Bulteel, 1665, I (chap. 9), 46; 1676, p. 25.
[22] Davies, p. 290.
[23] Bénac, I, 128.
[24] Davies, p. 290.
[25] Bulteel, 1665, I (chap. 9), 47; 1676, p. 25.
[26] Bénac, I, 128–129.
[27] Bulteel, 1665, I (chap. 9), 47–48; 1676, p. 25.
[28] Davies, p. 292.

Whichever was the borrower, he did not borrow extensively so far as I can discover from a comparison of numerous passages, and he constantly checked with the French original, though Bulteel is the more faithful.

The *1676 Edition of the* Comical Romance

I come now to the 1676 edition of the *CR,* issued by William Crooke and sometimes regarded as the first in English. Whereas the volume Playfere and Crooke issued in 1665 was a drab octavo with crowded margins, that of 1676 was a folio,[29] with a frontispiece engraving by W[illiam] F[aithorne] showing the actors' entrance into Le Mans, against a background of buildings that is described in the Harvard catalogue and in the auction-room records as Old Smithfield.[30]

The 1676 title page bears no indication of the translator or the history of the text. *Book-Prices Current* occasionally refers to it as by John Phillips, possibly because Phillips translated Scarron's *Typhon;* once it attributes the 1665 translation to John Davis (*sic*) and this of 1676 to Phillips.[31] Charlotte Morgan attributes it to P. Porter, and Professor George Kitchin suggests Dryden.[32]

But the 1676 edition is, except for a few slight modifications, a word-for-word reprint of Bulteel's translation of 1665. That explains why the *Stationers' Register* does not record the 1676 edition, though it does record (8 April 1667) John Playfere's assignment to William Crooke, cosponsor of the 1665 edition, of his rights in "*Le Romant Comique* . . . translated by John Bolteele gent." [33] When in 1676 Crooke reissued the *CR* in folio, he revised the title but little, inserting "strolling" before "stage-players" and altering "the renowned Scarron" to "the famous and witty poet Scarron."

[29] The publisher advertised it as a folio; the chain lines are vertical, and one discernible watermark is in the middle of the leaf. It is gathered in fours.

[30] Louis Fagan, *A Descriptive Catalogue of the Engraved Works of William Faithorne* (London, 1888), p. 78, accepts it as Faithorne's. Bartholomew Fair was held in Smithfield, and it included theatrical extravaganzas.

[31] *Book-Prices Current,* XXXIII, 606. *Book-Prices Current,* XVII (1903), 435 (no. 4166), calls the 1676 the first edition, attributes it with a question mark to John Phillips, and mentions its engraved frontispiece "by W. Faithorne, supposed to represent the old Smithfield, with strolling players. . . ." See also vols. III (1888–89), pt. 1, p. 125 (no. 1934); XX (1906), 459 (no. 5031); XXVIII (1914), 676; XXXIV (1920), 581 (lists the sale of the copy, which went to Harvard in 1926); and XL (1926), 792.

[32] *Rise of the Novel of Manners* (New York, 1911), p. 186; *L'Estrange* (London, 1913), p. 381n. Kitchin here gives the date as 1692; but his reference is to Jusserand's discussion of the 1676 edition.

[33] *A Transcript . . . 1640–1708,* II, 375.

He departed from the 1665 edition by having continuous pagination and chapter numbering throughout the two parts.

Jusserand, who had not heard of the 1665 edition, gave the impression that this one of 1676 is an adaptation like that by "a person of quality" entered in the *Stationers' Register* in 1656, an adaptation which transfers the scene to England and substitutes English characters.[34] It does add Shakespeare, Ben Jonson, Fletcher, Davenant, Shirley, Denham, and Cowley to Roquebrune's list of his literary familiars, which in the original included only Frenchmen. The "Duke of Epernon's" is changed to the "Duke of Orleans's" (p. 3); "Pont-Neuf" is changed to "London Bridge" (p. 9); "les barbiers du royaume" to "finical barbers and taylors in London" (p. 33); "Mairet's *Soliman*" to "Denham's *Sophy*" (p. 39); "Astrea" to "Cassandra" (p. 48); and there are some details added to the 1665 text: a title, "the *French Valet*" (for Scarron's *Jodelet ou le Maître valet?*), replaces an unnamed play; after *"Candy"* is added the phrase "against the Turks" (p. 85); and another unnamed play is given the name of Bulteel's *Amorous Gallant, or Love in Fashion.* Among other English touches one finds a reference to Hobbes: "Seneca, Homer, &c. (which last is excellently translated into English by the famous Mr. Hobbes)" (p. 48), the insertion of "English Spring-gardens" along with "French Tuileries" (p. 49), and the addition of "which are as proper to those places as Ap to Wales and Mac to Ireland" (p. 147).

Besides these changes there are some slight thrusts at Nonconformists at the end of chapter 2 (p. 10 of part II in the 1665 text), where as an "Itinerant Priest" Ragotin declaims "like one inspired," but more obvious ones in the 1676 text (p. 123), where he declaims "like one of the zealous Brothers inspired"—"like an Itinerant Nonconformist Parson." Similarly, "like the English infatuated fanaticks" is inserted (p. 196).

A minute search would doubtless uncover other changes of the sort. They are more irritating than significant, and the story is not altered in incident or setting, except for a twenty-six-page continuation (pp. 225–251), which concludes the 1676 text.

Scarron had ended the second part with an adventure in which Ragotin, having been gored by a ram, was intercepted in his flight from the inn by the host demanding the reckoning. Offray resumed the story without saying how the reckoning was settled. Préchac, whose continuation did not appear till 1679, began with a long quarrel in which Ragotin not only complained of the bill but found

<hr />

[34] Introduction to *The Comical Romance* (1892).

fault with the wine. The English edition of 1676 provides a continuation without even a break in the paragraphing at the end of part II. Here Ragotin, as surety for the reckoning, offers the manuscript of "a little history, or novel . . . after the newest mode," written by a gentleman acquaintance. Ragotin then reads "The Novel of Millamant, or the Rampant Lady," given as chapter 43.

A short preface is inserted before the "novel" itself: it praises "naturalness" as the highest eloquence and recommends Lucian, Petronius, Apuleius, Boccaccio, and Quevedo as the only ones who have attempted it; it thrusts at French preoccupation with "romantique ideas" and the pomp of tragical poetry; and it recommends the *Millamant* as coming nearer the ancients than any story except one by Bussy-Rabutin.

The story, coarser and much inferior to the *RC,* begins in Putania where women are given to pleasure. Millamant, to have greater freedom, marries Schelicon, who discovers her in Cleander's embrace. She pretends a rape and persuades Schelicon to take her to Viconia to recover her tarnished reputation. There for a lover she has Anthonine, an ex-monk, and then a bashful lord named Nicasius, who agrees to pay Schelicon a round sum in exchange for a share in Millamant, as though she were a stock company.

As Ragotin struts about after finishing this story of Millamant, a dog seizes the manuscript, bites Ragotin in his attempt to rescue it, and rumples his clothes. Onlookers persuade the innkeeper to let Ragotin go in search of the author to repair the tattered manuscript, and thus concludes the 1676 volume.

So far as I can discover, the only early printed mention of this additional matter is by Langbaine, who cited the story of Millamant as the source of a scene in Otway's *Soldier's Fortune,* and remarked that it was not in the French original of the *RC* but was probably a translation from *Les Amours des dames illustres de notre siècle.*[35] He seems to have got this idea from the prefatory allusion to Bussy-Rabutin, who wrote parts of *Les Amours* in imitation of the *Satyricon* of Petronius. I have not found the story of Millamant either in the French originals or in the English translations of *Les Amours.* Langbaine did not indicate that the story of Millamant is an appendage to the *CR,* and he so provided authority for the misconception held by Leavitt and Jusserand that the 1676 edition was an adaptation in which other stories were substituted for those of Scarron.

The mention of Bulteel's play, *The Amorous Gallant* (p. 201),

[35] *An Account of the English Dramatick Poets* (Oxford, 1691), p. 399.

suggests that Bulteel himself was the reviser of the continuation. If he was, he did not perceive clearly wherein his virtues lay. The edition must have had but modest success. Crooke advertised it in 1681,[36] but seems not to have reprinted it.

The Whole Comical Works of Scarron (*1700*)

With the 1700 translations of Scarron's prose by Brown, Savage, and others, the *RC* became truly popular in England. Seven editions were issued in less than sixty years, and though there was a later English version of the *RC* attributed to Goldsmith, the Brown-Savage text, reprinted by Lawrence and Bullen in 1892, has been the only one generally available. It included more than the *RC*, though not, as Baker says,[37] all of Scarron or even all of his prose. A considerable delay in publication is probable from the fact that the work, first announced in the *Term Catalogue*, June 1700, was reannounced the following February. The printing was obviously hurried, and copies vary slightly in their arrangement. Gaps and other features in pagination and signatures indicate that compositors were at work simultaneously on the several parts.[38] Obviously the pages of part II of the *CR* were being made up before all of part I was ready to print, and the compositor was twenty-four pages off on his estimate. Pagination and signatures begin anew with the novels and again with the letters. The letters specifically credited to Brown were set up hurriedly; they were crowded to fit into their sixty-four pages, with some headings to individual letters abbreviated or omitted or misnumbered.[39]

[36] At the end of Lancelot Addison's *The Moores Baffled*.

[37] *History of the English Novel*, III, 41.

[38] The Whole Comical Works of Monsr· Scarron. Containing I. His Comical Romance of a Company of Stage-Players. In Three Parts, Compleat. II. All his Novels and Histories. III. His Select Letters, Characters, &c. A great part of which never before in English. Translated by Mr. Tho. Brown, Mr. Savage, and others. [Latin quotations from Horace and Martial.] London, Printed for S. and J. Sprint . . . J. Nicholson . . . R. Parker . . . and Benj. Tooke . . . MDCC.

8vo. A^4 II1(= ^{2}L8) B–H^8 I^4 ^{1}L^8 M–Z^8 2A^4 *B–*K^8 ^{2}L^8(–^{2}L8) 2*A–2*D^8.

4 engraved plates, inserted before A1, C1, L1, *B1. F4 missigned E4; P3 unsigned. Errors in paging: 121–144 omitted from first series; 49–64 in second series misnumbered 59–74.

Contents (omitting plates): A1, title; A1^v, blank; A2–A2^v, A Character of Monsieur Scarron's Works; A3–A4^v, To the Courteous Reader; X1–X1^v, The Booksellers to the Readers; B1–I4^v, Scarron's Comical Romance, part I; L1–S3^v, part II; S4–S4^v, A Table of the Chapters in the Second Part; S5–Aa3, part III; Aa3^v–Aa4, A Table of the Chapters of the Third Part; Aa4^v, blank; *B1–L7^v, Scarron's Novels; *Aa1–*DdS^v, Select Letters of M. Scarron.

[39] *Term Catalogues*, III (1906), 199, 229. The second edition (1703) is called a revised and corrected edition. Other editions of *The Whole Comical Works* are dated 1712, 1727, 1741, 1752, and 1759. Volume I of 1759 is called the seventh

Tom Brown's name came first on the title page and is better known than that of John Savage, who in 1701 became a Hertfordshire rector. Naturally critics have assumed that the virtues of the edition are owing chiefly to Brown. But in spite of the publishers' note,[40] three-fourths of the matter in *The Whole Comical Works* had already appeared in English; and one cannot be sure how large a part Brown had in the new reworking.

Offray's part III of the *RC* had not previously appeared in English; the 1700 translation of it must, therefore, be a genuinely new one. Part I and much of part II, however, are a revision of Bulteel's translation as it stood in the second edition of 1676. Chapter headings and text show likenesses which cannot be explained by common reliance upon the French original. The 1700 translators usually retranslate verse, but they reproduce one stanza with only a minor transposition.[41]

The problem in the earlier chapters of part I is complicated. Scarron's transparent French makes identical phrases and almost identical sentences unavoidable in translations. The two English texts do not always agree even when English idiom parallels French; and when it does not, they sometimes differ a good deal. Yet Bulteel's influence is apparent from the first. In the second sentence of the romance, "la pente du chemin" is translated by Bulteel "sloapiness of the way"; it is given in the Brown-Savage text as "slopingness of their way." A few lines or so later in the *RC* comes the sentence:

La charette estoit pleine de coffres, de malles, et de gros pacquets de toilles peintes, qui faisoient comme une Pyramide. . . .[42]

It appears in Bulteel and the Brown-Savage text as follows:

The cart was full of Trunks, Portmanteaux, and huge bundles of Painted Cloth, which made a kinde of Pyramid. . . .[43]

The Cart was loaden with Trunks, Portmantles, and great Packs of painted Clothes, that made a sort of Pyramid. . . .[44]

Most of this is predetermined by the original, but not "trunks" and "portmanteaux." So "assassiné" need not have become "murthered" in Bulteel and "murder'd" in the Brown-Savage text. When the 1700

edition, and volume II, the ninth edition. From 1727 the work was in two volumes (Boyce, p. 197, and British Museum catalogue). Magne, no. 437, is mistaken in reporting two volumes in the edition of 1703.

[40] "The Booksellers to the Readers." This may, of course, be by one of the translators.

[41] Bulteel, 1665, II, 172; 1676, p. 211; 1700, p. 246.

[42] Bénac, I, 93.

[43] Bulteel, 1665, I, 2.

[44] 1700, p. 1.

translator gives "without doubt a kind of turban," he shows the influence of Bulteel's "No doubt a turban" and also of the French "un manière de turban." It is impossible that two independent translators should stay so close together as Bulteel and the 1700 translator do, in many long sentences, like the following, near the opening of the second chapter: [45]

This answer made every one prick up his ears: *La Rappiniere* profer'd an old Gown of his Wives to *Cave*, and the Tennis Court woman two or three sutes of Cloaths she had in pawn to *Destiny*, and *Rancour*.[46]

The Player's Answer made every Body prick up their Ears: *La Rappiniere* offer'd an old Gown of his Wife's to *Cave*: and the Tennis-Woman two or three Suits of Clothes, which were left in pawn, to *Destiny* and *Rancour*.[47]

Of the several legitimate opportunities to differ, for example, "fit ouvrir les oreilles," the Brown-Savage text passes up all except "players," and departs from Bulteel in the phrase "which were left" ("in pawn") when it ought to have followed him. "Caleçons" almost inevitably becomes "drawers," but "méchante" (in "jupe méchante") is not necessarily "tattered" as both English translations give it.

The debt of the Brown-Savage text to Bulteel is much less disguised toward the conclusion of both parts I and II. In part I more slavish copying begins in chapter 14, the long opening sentence of which is clearly out of Bulteel. A few lines below this sentence "il partit" becomes in Bulteel "This good pastour, I say, went"; and in the Brown-Savage text it is "This good priest, I say, set out." Both translate "écuré" as "newly scowered"; "par le cul" as "with [1700: "by"] his shoulders"; "je le tue" as "I'll pistol him"; and "double carogne" as "double whore and carrion." [48]

Beginning with chapter 15 the debt is full and obvious. Chapter headings are borrowed with the text. Long passages from Bulteel reappear with slight alteration. From the last line on page 119 (1700) to the close of part I on page 120,[49] there are no variations more extensive than the changes from "resolutions you had taken" to "resolutions you were in," "wont" to "us'd," "monies" to "money," "hath furnished" to "has sent," "geldings" to "horses," and "son and heir" (for "fils") to "son." Although the 1700 compiler

---

[45] The French reads: "La response du Comedien fit ouvrir les oreilles à tout le monde; la Rappiniere offrit une vieille robe de sa femme à la Caverne, et la Tripotiere deux ou trois paires d'habits, qu'elle avoit en gage, à Destin, et à la Rancune" (Bénac, I, 96).

[46] Bulteel, 1665, I, 5.

[47] 1700, p. 3.

[48] Bulteel, 1665, I (chap. 14), 107–108; 1676, pp. 57–58.

[49] Bulteel, 1676, p. 117.

consults the French text and is often closer than Bulteel to it, it is obvious that he has in general merely revised Bulteel. In the last sentence of part I the 1700 edition accidentally omits "not," so that "Roquebrune, who could not" becomes "Roquebrune, who could." [50] The whole chapter (the last of part I) is almost identical in the two versions, though Bulteel's "Star perused the note, which contained the following lines" is less accurate for "l'Étoile lut ce que vous allez lire, si vous en voulez prendre la peine" than "Star perused the following note, which you may read if you think fit"— a passage which shows simultaneously influence of Bulteel and of the French.[51]

It is significant of the way in which the translators worked that the translation of part II, also, begins by obscuring its debt to Bulteel, and then toward the end suddenly begins copying him closely. It must be confessed that the earlier chapters of part II seem not very much indebted to Bulteel. Though there is much similarity, it can usually be explained as faithfulness to the original. Only occasional phrases like "jugea à propos" (last sentence, part II, chap. 1) and "pied du lict" (last sentence, part II, chap. 4), which Bulteel and Brown-Savage render "thought fit" and "beds feet," suggest borrowing. The 1700 translator, by rendering "comme un forcené" (last sentence, part II, chap. 2) as "with the emphasis of an enthusiast," echoes the thrusts at Nonconformists inserted in that place in the 1676 edition of Bulteel's *CR*. The 1700 title of chapter 9 echoes that of Bulteel; both differ from the French.[52]

Further debt shows in the 1700 captions of chapters 15 and 16; and in chapter 16 the text also begins to reflect copious borrowings. The following sentence in both translations could not be accidental:

Leave we this man running away with his spoil, it being the same distracted Fellow that had before affrighted *Destiny* so terribly. . . .[53]

Leave we this Man to run away with his Spoil, he being the same that had 'formerly so terribly frighted *Destiny*. . . .[54]

Both render "si yvre" as "damnably drunk," and "tombe dans la boue" as "like David's sow in the mire." From chapter 17 to the end of part II (chap. 20) the 1700 translator transcribed shamelessly from Bulteel.

[50] This misprint was not corrected; see the edition of 1892, I, 176.

[51] Bulteel, 1676, p. 117; 1700, p. 119. Later editions, including that of Jusserand (1892), have at the very end of the chapter an awkward phrase not in the editions of 1665, 1676, and 1700, or in the French: "therefore he must be contented."

[52] The French title is simply *Autre disgrâce de Ragotin*.

[53] Bulteel, 1665, II (chap. 14), 142; 1676, p. 195.

[54] 1700, p. 228.

An interesting passage in part II, chapter 20, identifies the edition of Bulteel's translation used by the 1700 compilers, who follow Bulteel word for word in the opening sentence of the chapter. A few lines later the overstuffed Ragotin nods, "comme on fait plus souvent qu'ailleurs au sermon, quand on s'y ennuye." Bulteel originally translated this "as drowsie people do but too often at church it self"; his edition of 1676 changed that to "as drowsie people do at city-conventicles, and too often at church it self"; and the 1700 edition gives "as drowsy sinners are wont to do at conventicles." The word "conventicles" proves the 1676 edition to have been the one used.

The title page in 1700 echoes both the title pages of 1665 and 1676 in describing the *CR* as of "a company of stage-players." More significantly, it reproduces without credit the Faithorne engraving of the actors entering Le Mans, which was the frontispiece to the 1676 edition. Finally, the remark of "The Booksellers to the Readers" that the earlier translations of Scarron had been "part in folio, and partly in octavo, and so could not be bound together" shows they knew the 1676 edition, the only one that was a folio. Whether they or the translator-compilers knew the 1665 edition, they cannot have meant it as the part in octavo; no one would wish to bind together differing formats of the same work. Hence they must have been referring to Davies' translation of Scarron's novels and letters, which were in octavo. Perhaps it was the 1676 continuation and other modifications of the *CR* which led them to boast of the superior accuracy of the texts from which their translation was made.

The usual procedure of the 1700 translators was to delete unnecessary words in Bulteel's translation and to make it more brisk and faithful. But they sometimes are less literal than Bulteel, who translated "[I]l falloit combattre ou se rendre" as "He must now have fought it out or surrendered"; they say that "these lovers were thus pleasing each other." "Whilst these people were digesting or voiding their wine" is nearer the French ("cuvent leur vin") than "Whilst matters passed thus." [55]

The Novels and Letters

Davies' translation of Scarron's five separate novels had appeared in four or five editions before 1700. Davies translated freely, and his style lacked the economy and directness which the Augustans admired. Perhaps the 1700 translators of the novels were more conscientious or more competent than their partners who were en-

[55] Bulteel, 1665, II (chaps. 9, 13), 69, 83; 1676, pp. 155, 162; 1700, pp. 185, 194.

gaged in translating the *RC*. Whatever their reason, they took little from Davies.[56] Occasionally identical phrases crop up, but they can usually be explained from the French text.[57] On the whole the 1700 translation of the novels is new and, unlike Davies', accurate.

The Select Letters and Characters, attributed specifically to Brown in the headnote on the first page of the section, is also a genuinely new translation.[58] Davies had published his translation of *Monsieur Scarron's Letters to Persons of the Greatest Eminency and Quality* in 1677. Brown here and there reflects its diction but was not much indebted to it. Not counting the Balzac-Costar letter prefixed to Davies' edition of the letters and to the 1700 volume, Davies has fifty-nine letters and Brown fifty-eight, approximately two-thirds of those then available in editions of *Les Dernières œuvres*. Brown's fifty-eight include three which, unnumbered at the end of the 1700 edition, are numbered 56–58 in later editions, epistles dedicatory respectively to Ménage and Sarrazin (*La Relation véritable,* 1648), to Morreau (*sic*) (*Le Précaution inutile,* 1655), and to "the Lady Guillemette, my sister's little greyhound bitch" (*Recueil des œuvres burlesque,* 1648).[59] "A Character" (numbered 42 in the 1700 edition but unnumbered in later editions) inadequately justifies the plural, "Characters," in the title of the volume.[60]

Of Brown's fifty-eight letters, forty-seven are in Davies; that is, Davies has twelve and Brown eight that are not in both translations. Davies, as his title indicates, placed first letters to eminent persons, beginning with the letter to the Queen of Sweden, misnumbered 13, and following it with letters (not in Brown) to the Queen Regent and the Prince of Condé respectively, and two to the Countess of Brienne (Brown, nos. [15] and [16]). Davies' sixth is to Sarrazin (Brown, no. 4), and from that point, as Brown was to do from the start, Davies followed the French order.

Scarron's French is so simple and clear that doubtless Brown

[56] I assume this to be also true of *The Generous Lover* (*Plus d'effets*). I have not seen Davies' version of it, called *The Unexpected Choice* (1670).

[57] As significant as any is the phrase "so excellent a page" for "un si bon page" in both translations, near the opening of *The Chastisement of Avarice.*

[58] Boyce, pp. 94–95, gives a brief paragraph to the letters, fifty of which he says Brown translated "with understanding and discrimination." He mentions "some inaccuracies and tawdriness of diction."

[59] Magne, nos. 9, 10, 75, 356.

[60] "A Character," in the same relative position as in the French text, comes in the edition of 1700 between letters 42 (misnumbered 41) and 45 (unnumbered). Inserted also among the letters in the French text was *Le Châtiment de l'avarice,* which in the 1700 English edition is placed with the other novels. The Don Juan and Mantigny fragments, which have never been translated, were omitted in the edition of 1700.

found it easier to translate directly without consulting Davies' version, though an occasional phrase suggests that he knew it. Davies, as usual, is not only very free with the text but sometimes ignorant or careless of its meaning.[61] Usually he omits verse or renders it in prose, and occasionally he omits wanton passages. In number 20 he wanders off into a comparison of Scarron with Prometheus and Job, and omits the last third of the letter. In the important letter that followed, subscribed "Lazarillo de Tormes," he omits seven lines telling how the new part III of the *RC* begins, and eleven lines opening the next (and final) paragraph.

Brown, too, sometimes omits sentences,[62] and in his number 28 he telescopes two letters by prefixing the opening sentence of one to what in the French was the letter following.[63] Scarron, informal as he is, often approaches the clarity and directness that Boileau and Pope so greatly admired. Brown was well suited to translate him. His comment upon writers who learn judgment from the standard of the ancients and delicacy of expression from the variety and turns of the moderns, as well as some witty passages in his *Amusements*,[64] show that he understood the principles of good writing. His observational method, his vivacity, and his style made him what he still remains, a mirror of his age.

The French Text Used in the Translation of 1700

In "The Booksellers to the Readers" we learn that the translation is made from "this last Paris edition." What that means is not clear. The edition could hardly be that issued in ten volumes in 1700 by Michel David, the authorized Paris publisher of Scarron's works; for though volume I was printed in January 1700, volume V was not printed till April, and volume IX (containing the letters) not till 31 December.[65] The English edition, though it may not have appeared before February 1701, was announced as early as

---

[61] In his no. 6, Davies misconstrues the statement about Guyonet; in no. 13 he omits some verses ("While you all naked") which Brown makes more audacious; in no. 10 Davies omits the final sentence; in no. 18 he condenses a page of verse into prose; in no. 19 he omits the verses of Bois-Robert and adds a sentence after later verses; in nos. 38 and 39 he expands the openings; and in no. 38 he inserts a closing remark.

[62] Brown, in his no. 22, omits two sentences at the end and also the postscript. In the prefatory Balzac-Costar extract, he omits eight lines or so before the comment on Seneca.

[63] These are nos. 29–30 in Davies.

[64] *Amusements Serious and Comical* (London, 1702), p. 6.

[65] See Magne, no. 396: *Les Œuvres de Monsieur Scarron. Reveuës, corrigées et augmentées de nouveau.* Vols. III–IV contained the *RC;* VII–VIII, the novels; and IX, the letters, *Le Châtiment,* and "A Character."

June 1700.[66] The Paris edition of 1700, however, was practically identical with that of 1695, to which the English publishers could have referred.

But no Paris edition for another quarter of a century contained Offray's part III of the *RC;* and the translators must have gone for it either to a Lyons or to a Low Country edition. David's edition lacked also the four engravings reproduced in the English volume. The Faithorne engraving might have been found in the English edition of 1676. The other three were available only in Low Country editions. One used as frontispiece to *The Whole Comical Works* was copied, in reverse, by Vander Gucht from Stephano della Bella's famous scene showing Scarron in his chair writing as the muses, satyrs, and Pegasus look on.[67] Another engraving, from J. Van Vianen, represents a scene from a play, and, though designated in *The Whole Comical Works* as accompanying part II of the *CR* to which it is prefixed, a note describes it correctly as referring to page 82 (in part I).[68] The last engraving prefixed to the novels is a copy of another well-known illustration—Daret's bust of Scarron, reversed like the della Bella sketch. Except for the Faithorne engraving from the 1676 English *RC,* all the plates in the English edition of 1700 had appeared in the 1695, 1697, and 1700 printings of Scarron's works by Mortier of Amsterdam. They were not in the Paris editions.[69]

It is possible that Brown consulted a Paris edition of *Les Dernières œuvres* for the letters. I have not seen Mortier's; but the comparable Wetstein *Les Dernières œuvres* (1713) sometimes omits Scarron's "Je suis" in the complimentary close of a letter, as in the

[66] *Term Catalogues,* III, 199, 229.

[67] Della Bella's sketch had appeared as early as 1659 in a Rouen printing of *Les Œuvres* (Magne, no. 120), and twice in the Wolfgang *Œuvres* (Amsterdam, 1668), as the frontispiece and (p. 253) before *La Relation véritable,* where it is called "Le Portrait de Monsieur Scarron." A Harvard copy lacks the Balzac-Costar extract which Magne describes as part of his own copy. It differs further in having among the preliminary matter fourteen (not sixteen) unnumbered leaves. The first leaf with the frontispiece (Daret's Scarron, unsigned) is conjugate with the twelfth, which concludes the "privilège du Roy." There follow two conjugate leaves with the three sonnets to the King.

[68] Magne, no. 266. The engraving is not to be confused with the unsigned frontispiece of the original Paris edition of part I (see Magne, nos. 256–260), though that too was a theatrical scene. Magne reproduces it opposite p. 142. What was the part I frontispiece, signed I. Veenhieysen, and used by Wolfgang from 1662 to 1693? (See Magne, nos. 265 ff.)

[69] See Magne, nos. 393–397. The Harvard copy of David's *RC* (Paris, 1706), which is really two volumes in the *Œuvres,* has no engravings. Wetstein, *Les Dernières œuvres* (1713), has Daret's Scarron reversed. Magne uses it in its original form as his frontispiece.

letter to Segrais, misspelled "Segruis" in the English translation. The Paris editions must have had the "Je suis"; at least it occurs in Bastien's edition of 1786, and in Brown's translation.[70] But it may have been in the Mortier editions also. From them Brown got a passage in the letter to Marigny [71] telling how the volume of the *RC* begins, but only editions printed outside Paris specify the volume as the "troisième." Since "The Booksellers to the Readers" mentions Amsterdam printings, it seems certain that, in spite of the assertion about Paris texts, the English translation was made from one of Mortier's editions of Amsterdam (1695, 1697, 1700).[72]

The Translators of 1700

The most difficult problem concerning this translation is the identification of the parts translated by each translator. They can hardly be determined; but if the problem is at least stated clearly, others may see in the facts implications that escape the present writer. The title page and typography indicate that various persons were working simultaneously and independently for the publisher. Practically all of the work had already appeared in English. Only part III of the *RC*, eleven letters, and the brief "Character" were making their first appearance in English—less than one-fourth of the whole.[73] More than a third, that is, *RC,* parts I and II, was principally a dressing-up of Bulteel's translation. The translations of the novels and the letters were new, yet with an awareness of Davies' versions.

Because Brown was specifically credited with translating the letters, whereas no indication was given of the translators of the other parts, Boyce has warned against the old assumption that the whole work owed its excellence to Brown, especially the *RC*. My

[70] Bastien, I, 261; Brown, no. 46 (misnumbered). Magne, nos. 403–404, says that Bastien's edition of Scarron is a reproduction in different format of the Wetstein edition of Amsterdam (1752), the errors of which Bastien boasts of rectifying. Many errors, however, remain; for example, the letter given by Bastien, I, 216, as to Surintendant Foucquet was in reality to Chancelier Séguier. Davies, who used the Paris edition of 1663, credits the letter to Segrais, and Brown does likewise. In spite of some errors remaining, Magne calls Bastien's the most accurate and best edition of Scarron's works.

[71] Brown, no. 21.

[72] It may be significant of an Amsterdam text of the *RC*, part III, that the 1700 translator follows the practice of Low Country printers in rendering the words to the chimes (chap. 14), giving "Boisgenci," "Cleri," and "Vendosme" where the earliest of the French editions I have seen (David, 1727) have "Bugency," "Clery," and "Vendôme."

[73] The prefatory Balzac-Costar extract and "To the courteous reader that never saw me" Davies had prefixed to the letters (1677) and to *Scarron's Novels* (1665 and later), respectively.

discovery of the indebtedness to Bulteel for parts I and II of the *RC* has in part confirmed Boyce, at the same time questioning his comment upon the uniformity of style in the novels. But Brown's name was removed from the letters after the first edition, where it probably never would have appeared except for the haste with which the edition was prepared. The ascription of the letters to Brown is no indication that his share was limited to them. Boyce finds traces of his pen in "To the courteous reader" and, more significantly, in one of the novels, *The Useless Precaution*. I should be surprised to discover that his share was less than Savage's.

The inadequate and doubtless faulty biographical sketches of John Savage do not make it improbable that he worked on the translation. We are told that for eight years in his youth Savage traveled on the Continent with the young Earl of Salisbury, who presented him with the living at Bygrave (Hertfordshire) in 1701.[74] The *DNB* places this traveling just after Savage's departure from Cambridge, where he became B.A. in 1694 and M.A. in 1698. Salisbury, however, was not born till 1690, and he was hardly mature enough for extensive traveling before the turn of the century. Meanwhile, from 1694 till well past 1700, Savage was steadily publishing in London.[75] He is said to have assisted Brown in translating St. Evremond (1694). What he described as his maiden dedication is in a work dated 1695.[76] Other pieces prior to 1700 are: *Brutes Turned Critics* (1695), a translation of *Memoirs of the Transactions in Savoy* (1697), *History of Poland* (1698), and a revision of the Knolles-Rycaut *Turkish History* (1698). In 1702 Abel Boyer acknowledged assistance from his friend Mr. Savage in his English and French dictionary.[77] The travels with Lord Salisbury, whatever they were, did not seriously interfere with Savage's literary activity, and they constitute no bar to his participation with Brown in translating Scarron. They probably came later than the account in *DNB* indicates.

Quite unknown are the collaborators with Brown and Savage, the unnamed "others." But the implication of the title page that

---

[74] John Nichols, *Literary Anecdotes*, II (London, 1812), 141 ff., 703, and IX (1815), 492; *Illustrations*, IV (London, 1822), 351; Robert Clutterbuck, *History . . . of the County of Hertford*, III (London, 1827), 505 ff.; Joseph Welch, *List of the Queen's Scholars . . . Westminster* (London, 1852), pp. 209 ff.; Bishop Thomas Newton, *Works*, I (London, 1782), 44.

[75] *Term Catalogues*, II (1905), 560. Boyce, p. 51, says Savage was of the Inner Temple.

[76] *DNB*. Savage published various works later than 1700. He brought out two volumes of sermons in 1704 and *Horace to Scaeva* in 1730. From 1701 until his death in 1747 he was a Hertfordshire rector.

[77] *Dictionnaire royal, français et anglais* (The Hague, 1702).

there were at least two of them is supported by other evidence. Toward the end of part I and also of part II of the *CR* the hack translators cease translating and begin to copy Bulteel's translation. Since one who had been copying in part I would hardly have reformed suddenly at the beginning of part II, a natural assumption is that there were two "copiers" working independently but similarly. They began honestly to translate, but found the process of copying Bulteel an easy way to hurry the work.

It seems likely that the three sections showing hasty work (the conclusions of parts I and II of the *CR* and the letters) were all produced under pressure from the printer, and were being completed simultaneously by three different translators. If this was the case, Brown, who is credited with the letters, could hardly have translated the *RC*. There are, however, two reasons for ascribing the novels to him: the definite echo of his style in one of the novels, which Boyce has pointed out,[78] and the fact that like the letters, the novels are competently translated. My tentative suggestion is that Savage took charge of the *CR* and Brown of the novels and letters; that two assistants helped with the *CR,* and that Savage or a third assistant may have helped with the novels.

The "Goldsmith" Translation (*1775*)

In the year after Goldsmith's death, the publisher of *The Good Natured Man* (1768) and *The Deserted Village* (1769) issued Goldsmith's *Select Poems* and "The Comic Romance of Monsieur Scarron, translated by Oliver Goldsmith. In two volumes . . . London: Printed for W. Griffin, in Catharine Street, Strand. 1775." [79] An "Address to the Public" prefacing the second volume says that all but a few sheets were "executed by the late Doctor Goldsmith," who was peculiarly fitted for the undertaking:

Mr. Savage and some others gave a translation of the same author some years ago, but whether owing to want of attention, or from adhering too implicitly to the French idiom, it is but a meagre substitute for the original. It will be necessary to acquaint the reader, that the third part of the Comic Romance was not written by Scarron. Before he could enter upon it, death snatched the pen from his hand, and it was unfortunately resumed by one without a spark of his taste or spirit. Great liberties have therefore been taken by the translator with this part. As far as his discernment assisted him, he has curtailed its redundancies, and expunged the impotent efforts of false wit, which frequently gleam through it. Indeed he has retained very little more than sufficient to maintain the thread of the nar-

---

[78] Pp. 82–83.

[79] See Iolo Williams, *Seven XVIIIth Century Bibliographies* (London, 1924); **Arthur Lytton Sells**; *Les Sources françaises de Goldsmith* (Paris, 1924), pp. 170 ff.

rative, supposing that the plainest food dressed after the English fashion, would be more agreeable . . . than a miserable French ragout, composed of nothing but garlick and sallad.

So much for the publisher's blurb. The text is carelessly printed. The chapters of volume I are numbered consecutively (1–29). In standard texts chapter 23 ends part I, and chapter 24, with the silly and irrelevant title "And that's all," which ordinarily begins part II, follows in the "Goldsmith" text without any indication of the break between parts I and II. Volume II starts with a new numbering of chapters, its chapter 1 corresponding to part II, chapter 7, of the standard texts; it misnumbers its chapters 7 and 8 as 6 and 7; and with the next chapter, called 15, it returns to the chapter numbering of the standard texts.

Part III is altered less than the blurb indicated. Seventeen chapters are reduced to thirteen. Chapter 6 (the death of Saldagne) is telescoped with 4, parts of which, with nearly all of 5, are omitted, as are two intercalated novels (usually chaps. 15–16). The famous chapter 14, here called 12, in which Ragotin attacks the bell ringer at Notre Dame (Alençon) for mocking him, as he thinks, with the bells, is slightly condensed, but is in some ways more accurately translated than in the 1700 edition. The bowdlerizing omissions in chapters 4 and 5 describe comic adventures of the players on the way to Alençon. This low comedy (mix-ups in inns, adventures with chamber pots, and the like) is apparently what the blurb meant by "a miserable French ragout, composed of nothing but garlick and sallad."

What else may be said of the translation apart from its being bowdlerized? Professor Arthur Lytton Sells decided purely on stylistic grounds that Goldsmith had translated only the first nine chapters of part I and perhaps chapter 14 of part II, and that after his death, his publisher set several translators to finish the work. When in chapter 10 Sells finds crude phrases and sentences, to be discussed presently, he was certain Goldsmith's hand had not passed there. Similar blemishes appear in later chapters. Sells's reason for supposing several hands at work in completing the translation is that numerous inconsistencies occur in the text. "Caverne" is variously "Miss," "Mrs.," "Madam," and "Madame Cave." "L'Étoile" is first "Stella" or "Mrs. Stella," later "Star," and then "Stella" again.

This hypothesis is a good one; but it would have been more accurate if Sells had compared "Goldsmith" with earlier translations of the *RC*. He would have understood the lapse from "Stella" to "Star," the misprint of "critics" for "crickets" ("grillons"), and the bad English.[80] Till well past the middle of part II, the 1775 edition is basically the Brown-Savage translation from the "revised and corrected" editions. The first seven or eight chapters (not nine as Sells supposed) have been superficially revised, the most noticeable change being that of "Star" to "Stella." In an illustrative passage (I, 4) the English names "Pit, Fox, Legge, Pott, or Hill" are substituted for "Mountain, Valley, Rose, or Thorn."

"Goldsmith" condensed (as in the opening sentence) and expanded (as in I, 18: "The reader whose curiosity," etc.) at will; but he gives little indication of having consulted the French original. In such a passage as "Rancour went into the inn [with a hearty meal on his stomach and] something more than half drunk," [81] the bracketed phrase is not in the original, but the sentence is otherwise identical with the 1700 English text. In the preceding chapter (p. 29) "Goldsmith" had begun with a two-page expansion and rearrangement of the earlier translation which he follows in giving "Phyllis" for "Chloris."

Chapter 6 has even less revision of the 1700 English text; and chapter 8 becomes almost a word-for-word reprinting of it,[82] much more slavish than the 1700 translation was in its use of Bulteel. Verses and usually chapter headings are identical in the 1700 and the 1775 editions. Volume I, chapter 23, concludes with the awkward appendage, "therefore he must be contented." These words are not in the French and only in the revised editions of the 1700 translation, and in that of 1892. Hence "Goldsmith" must have used one of the revised editions.

This opinion is supported by tracing the stylistic defects which Sells points out. For instance: "To compleat his defeat, his antagonist . . . gave him a sound kick on the head, which, after a very sudden retrogradation, made him fall at his feet" appears verbatim in all editions I have seen of the Brown-Savage text. But "his whole head was enchased into his hat" is in only the revised editions; [83] the 1700 edition read "in his hat." Also from the revised editions comes: "The rest of the impertinents left likewise the players at liberty." [84]

We have seen that toward the ends of parts I and II of the Brown-

---

[80] Sells, *Les Sources françaises de Goldsmith*, pp. 170 ff. "Critics" (at the opening of part II) may have been used intentionally in the "revised" Brown-Savage text. The 1665, 1676, and 1700 editions of the *CR* all say "crickets."

[81] I, 33.

[82] Through a strange error, probably due to the printer, "Twelfth Day ("Jour des Rois") becomes (I, 30) "the twelfth day of."

[83] For example, I (1759), 40.

[84] In the Brown-Savage text the passage reads: "all other impertinents left also [revised editions: "likewise"] the players at liberty."

Savage *CR* the translators begin wholesale copying from Bulteel. The 1775 *CR* reverses the procedure by abruptly ceasing to copy about two-thirds of the way through part II. In the midst of *The Judge in Her Own Cause,* this sentence, taken punctuation and all from the Brown-Savage text, concludes the borrowing: "This wonderful action of hers, did not go without its reward." [85] Thereafter the 1775 *CR* became a new translation and, except for alterations in part III already described and for occasional echoes of the Brown-Savage *CR,* as in Ragotin's epitaph [86] and the "drowsy sinner" passage (part II, chap. 20), continues so to the end of the story.

Bolton Corney is said to have claimed for Goldsmith the translation of some verses in part II, chapter 19; they read:

> Thus, when soft love subdues the heart
> With smiling, hopes, and chilling fears,
> The soul rejects the aid of art,
> And speaks in moments more than years.

Sells suggests that Goldsmith may have translated the whole chapter, which contains *The Two Rival Brothers,* a novel Scarron had taken from Castillo Solorzano.

It will not help Goldsmith's reputation to credit the 1775 text to him. In spite of the publisher's assertion that Goldsmith left it nearly complete, he could have had, as Sells surmised, but small part in it; he could have done no more than begin revision of the Brown-Savage text. The inconsistencies in style and form, which Sells pointed out as evidence of more than one hand in the work, are significant. The fact that the copying from the Brown-Savage *CR* ends at a definite place is conclusive proof that a new workman began there. Probably neither he nor the publisher knew that his predecessors had been cheats. Otherwise the copying would have been continued, since there is no point in putting a good patch on a shoddy garment.

Goldsmith may have started to recast the Brown-Savage text, and have got into chapter 6 at the time of his death. Then, as Sells thought, his literary executor, perhaps Griffiths himself, looking about for a way to use the fragment, turned it over to two or more hacks. Of the dishonesty of any such hacks Griffiths was, as I have

---

[85] II, 96–97. Additional proof that the translators returned to the French version is provided by the fact that they return at this point to the chapter numbers of the French texts.

[86] End of part III: "Lequel fut amoureux d'une très belle Étoile." The Brown-Savage text translates: "Who liv'd a Slave to fair Star's Eyes." "Goldsmith" reads: "For years a slave to Stella's bright eyes."

pointed out, possibly unaware. But he was aware of and perhaps responsible for the bowdlerizing in part III, since it is mentioned in the "Address to the Public."

Two-thirds of the volume is either paraphrased or copied from Brown-Savage, and has, therefore, a good deal of Bulteel in it.[87]

Jusserand and the 1892 Reprint

In 1892 English readers were again offered the *RC* and Scarron's novels in two fine volumes with the famous Oudry illustrations and Jusserand's critical essay on Scarron, which later appeared in his *English Essays*. This latest English edition, *The Comical Romance . . . Done into English by Tom Brown of Shifnal, John Savage, and Others,* omits the letters but is otherwise a reprint of the Brown-Savage text from one of the "revised" editions after 1700.[88]

A Resurvey of the English Translations

Three English texts of the *RC* exist. The earliest and the only one that can be called an independent translation of the two parts by Scarron is John Bulteel's, published in 1665 and, with slight alterations and a continuation, in 1676. The best-known version is the second, published with Scarron's novels and letters in *The Whole Comical Works of Scarron* (1700 and "revised and corrected," 1703, 1712, 1727, 1741, 1752, 1759, and 1892). Only the Offray part III, which had not earlier appeared in English, was a genuinely new translation; the major portion of parts I and II is only a revision, sometimes almost a reprint, of Bulteel's text. The third and last text, that of 1775 (reprinted in Dublin *ca.* 1780), was possibly begun by Goldsmith as a recasting of the Brown-Savage text. It was continued from the sixth or seventh chapter by anonymous hacks, who copied the "revised" Brown-Savage text almost verbatim to the middle of part II, chapter 16. At that point it suddenly became and

[87] There are some indications that "Goldsmith" consulted Bulteel directly in the 1676 edition: (1) The continuous numbering of chapters in vol. I; (2) "sun" and "course" in the opening sentence, where the Brown-Savage text says "Phoebus" and "career"; (3) the first chapter's description of Destiny's coat as a "brown frize" (Bulteel, 1665: "freez-coat"; 1676: "gray freez"; 1700: "griset-coat"; Bénac: "casaque de grisette"); "Mariamne" for "Mariane" (vol. I, chap. 2); "drowsy sermon" (vol. II, chap. 15 [20]). But the 1775 translation nowhere copies extensively from Bulteel.

[88] I judge the infelicities of diction in the "Goldsmith" *CR* discussed previously, the awkward and unauthorized phrase at the end of part I, "therefore he must be contented," which was not in the 1700 text, and the phrases cited by Sells to be evidence that Goldsmith did not make the translation of 1775. They are in the 1712 and 1759 editions, and one may suppose them present in other editions appearing after 1700.

continued to the end a new translation, though in part III condensed and bowdlerized.

Bulteel's text, then, is in Scarron's two parts of the *RC* the basis of the other English texts. Bulteel is not uniformly felicitous in his language. The Brown-Savage *CR* is on the whole more brisk, more economical, and more faithful to the French. But it should be pointed out that the crudities which shocked Sells in the *CR* of 1775 are none of them in Bulteel, and, on the other hand, many of the virtues of the Brown-Savage *CR* were absorbed from Bulteel. Guided by him, they have given us the most readable text we have of Scarron's prose.

The text published as Goldsmith's is neither Goldsmith nor a translation. Even the small portion which possibly is Goldsmith's was done in haste, and its virtues, as Sells inadvertently points out, were borrowed. The major portion is no better (though sometimes worse) than the Brown-Savage *CR* from which it was taken. The last third (part II, chaps. 16–20, and part III), though an independent translation, is bowdlerized and, were it not, is too small a portion to give the whole a claim to serious consideration.

In France, three early eighteenth-century artists made elaborate illustrations,[89] and the *RC* showed no abating of popularity in the nineteenth century. Besides several popular editions, there were scholarly ones, like that of Victor Fournel in 1857, and others by men of letters like Paul Bourget and Anatole France. Théophile Gautier based the plot of his *Capitaine Fracasse* on the romance of "Star" in Scarron's work. But in England the Brown-Savage *CR* was, apparently, not reprinted between 1759 and 1892. The Goldsmith *CR* of 1775 was reprinted in Dublin about 1780.[90] English novelists like Fielding, Smollett, Sterne, and Goldsmith, not to mention Thackeray and Dickens (who may have been unconscious of his debt), have taken a good deal of the *RC* into their novels and perhaps satisfied their readers' appetite for the *RC* itself.

APPENDIX

Because of the importance of John Bulteel's translation and the scarcity of other data, I give this account of Bulteel and his other works. According to Anthony à Wood, John Bulteel, son of John (or Jean?) Bulteel, a Frenchman living at Dover, was an Oxford M.A. and a secretary to the

---

[89] Coulon, whose pictures are said to be in the museum at Le Mans, J.-B Oudry, whose plates were reprinted in the edition of 1892, and J.-B. Pater, assisted by J. Dumont, whose plates were reprinted in Montaiglon's edition of the *RC* (1883). See J. J. Jusserand, *English Essays* (London, 1895), pp. 154–155; Magne, nos. 340, 348, 349.

[90] Magne, no. 428.

Earl of Clarendon in 1661. "One Joh. Bulteel gent. translated . . . A general . . . History of France . . . 1683. . . . [W]hether he be the same with the former who was created M. of A. [and who, Wood reports, died in 1669], I know not." [91] The *DNB* identifies John Bulteel, translator and miscellaneous writer, as son of a French Protestant minister who lived near Dover at the beginning of the seventeenth century; but, since he was writing after 1669, believes he was not the Oxford M.A. who was secretary to Clarendon and an M.P. His last known work is dated 1683.[92]

The following publications are among those which may, with more or less probability, be attributed to Bulteel:

1. *A Triumphant Arch Erected . . . to the Glory of the Feminine Sexe: by Monsieur* [i.e., Mdlle.] *de Scudery: Englished by I. B., Gent., London, Printed for William Hope, and Henry Herringman . . . 1656.* This work was entered by William Hope in the *Stationers' Register* (II, 1), 6 July 1655, as "Englished by John Leetlub" (i.e., Bulteel). Though "Leetlub" reappears in the *Stationers' Register* (II, 55) in 1656, when Herringman bought a share in the book, Bulteel seems to have published nothing else with that anagram. The Harvard copy bears the names of both Hope and Herringman, showing that the transfer was made before the book was published; but it lacks the Faithorne engraving. See Louis Fagan, *A Descriptive Catalogue of . . . William Faithorne,* p. 78.

2. *London's Triumph or the . . . Reception of R. Tichburn, Lord Mayor,* London, 1656. Subscribed J. B., and attributed to Bulteel by the British Museum catalogue, *DNB,* and Halkett and Laing, *Dictionary,* VI (1932), 390.

3. G. F. Loredano, *Academicall Discourses,* London, 1664. "Englished by J. B. Gent." Entered by Playfere in the *Stationers' Register,* 31 October 1663, with John Bulteel named as translator. William Hope had entered, 4 August 1656, "all the works of Loredano . . . translated out of Italian by J. B. Gent." No copy of this last has, so far as I know, been reported. A remark in "To the Reader" in *Academicall Discourses* says that some of Loredano's other works were ready for the press.

4. *Relation of the State of the Court of Rome . . . Translated . . . by J. B., Gent.,* London, 1664. Entered by Playfere in the *Stationers' Register,* 31 October 1663, as "translated out of Italian by John Bulteel." Halkett and Laing, *Dictionary,* V, 57, and VI, 432, describe this work as the second part of *Rome Exactly Described.* Part I was "Englished by Gio Torriano."

5. *Birinthea, a Romance,* London, 1664. Attributed to J. B. on the title page and in the entry for Playfere in the *Stationers' Register,* 31 October

---

[91] *Fasti Oxonienses (Athenae Oxonienses,* vol. V), pt. II (London, 1820), p. 252. *Biographia Dramatica,* I (1812), 77, accepts Wood's identification of Bulteel, but mentions only *The Amorous Orontus.* There may be two Bulteels whose works are being confused.

[92] Of Jean or John Bulteel, senior, there are these possible traces. Wood, *Fasti,* pt. I (1815), says John Bulteel, a minister, translated into English (1617) Dr. Primrose's French text of *Jacob's Vow.* The British Museum catalogue and Samuel Halkett and John Laing, *Dictionary of Anonymous and Pseudonymous English Literature,* V (Edinburgh and London, 1929), 57, attribute to John or Jean Bulteel *A Relation of the Troubles of the Three Foreign Churches in Kent . . . 1634 . . . Written by J. B., Minister of the Word of God,* London, 1645

1663. Halkett and Laing, *Dictionary*, I (1926), 192, report a copy with Bulteel's name on the title page. He called it a youthful piece which his friends urged him to publish.

6. *The Amorous Orontus*, London, 1665. Identified by Langbaine, *Dramatick Poets*, p. 526, as a translation of Thomas Corneille's *L'Amour à la mode*. It was acted and published in 1675 as *The Amorous Gallant; or, Love in Fashion. A Comedy in Heroick Verse. By J. B., Gent.* It was entered for Playfere in the *Stationers' Register*, 1 July 1665, as "translated out of Italian . . . by John Bolteele," and, 8 April 1667, transferred, along with the *CR*, to William Crooke as sole proprietor. Crooke advertised it at the end of the 1676 edition of the *CR*. R. Genest, *Some Account of the English Stage from 1660 to 1830*, X (Bath, 1832), 140, classifies it among plays not acted; the plot he thought tolerably good but the language frequently very bad. The *DNB* reports that it is "not altogether deserving of the verdict 'miserable poetry.'"

7. *The Characters or Portraicts of the Present Court of France . . . Made English by J. B., Gent.*, n.p., 1668. The British Museum catalogue suggests this may possibly be by Bulteel.

8. A translation of François Eudes de Mézeray, *General Chronological History of France*, London, 1683, is attributed to Bulteel in the *DNB*.

9. *Apophthegmes of the Ancients*, London, 1683. Attributed to Bulteel in the *DNB* and Halkett and Laing, *Dictionary*, I, 124.

10. Three booksellers entered in the *Stationers' Register*, 27 November 1661, *The History of King Henry the Great*, translated from French "by John Bulteel." But they and two others entered the same work, 15 September 1662, as translated by John Dancer. The contradiction may be a simple error, or possibly an indication that the book was entered before the booksellers had closed the agreement with the translator. *The Amorous Traveller; or, Night Adventures*, translated from Spanish into French, was translated into English by J. B., who may be Bulteel.[93] The dedication of the *Apophthegmes*, says the *DNB*, alludes to other works to which he did not put his name.

[93] *Stationers' Register*, 12 August 1671; *Term Catalogue*, 20 November 1671.